Emerging Technologies for Digital Infrastructure Development

Edited by

Muhammad Ehsan Rana
School of Computing
Asia Pacific University of Technology & Innovation
Kuala Lumpur
Malaysia

&

Manoj Jayabalan
School of Computer Science & Mathematics
Liverpool John Moores University
Liverpool
UK

Emerging Technologies for Digital Infrastructure Development

Editors: Muhammad Ehsan Rana & Manoj Jayabalan

ISBN (Online): 978-981-5080-95-7

ISBN (Print): 978-981-5080-96-4

ISBN (Paperback): 978-981-5080-97-1

need for a court order if at any point you breach any terms of this License Agreement. In no event will any delay or failure by Bentham Science Publishers in enforcing your compliance with this License Agreement constitute a waiver of any of its rights.

3. You acknowledge that you have read this License Agreement, and agree to be bound by its terms and conditions. To the extent that any other terms and conditions presented on any website of Bentham Science Publishers conflict with, or are inconsistent with, the terms and conditions set out in this License Agreement, you acknowledge that the terms and conditions set out in this License Agreement shall prevail.

Bentham Science Publishers Pte. Ltd.
80 Robinson Road #02-00
Singapore 068898
Singapore
Email: subscriptions@benthamscience.net

**BENTHAM
SCIENCE**

CONTENTS

FOREWORD

This book contains a collection of chapters related to emerging technologies for socio-economic and secure infrastructure development in computer science and systems perspectives. This book is intended for those seeking advanced knowledge to conduct research and/or development.

There were 16 informative and scientifically proven chapters in this book, covering both areas of socio-economic and secure infrastructure development. Each article holds specific knowledge, with empirical analysis and scientifically proven for readers' better understanding and replication. These articles focused on areas such as system performance, tracking and monitoring, analytics, internet of things (IoT) environment, and web applications for the emerging technologies scope, while areas focused on system security are such as sentiment analysis, cyber security, intrusion detection, privacy and fake/deepfake handling.

Hopefully, this book will be the source of reference to recent emerging technologies implementation and advancement in catering to socio-economic and software security horizons.

Thank you.

Rodziah Atan, Ph.D., P.Tech. (IT)
Head, Lab of Halal Policy and Management
Halal Products Research Institute (HPRI) & Dept. of Software Engineering and Information Systems
Faculty of Computer Science and Information Technology Universiti Putra Malaysia
43400 Serdang
Selangor, Malaysia

PREFACE

Social and economic factors have a growing impact on our lifestyle. These factors provide the basis for our decisions in choosing healthcare, education, shopping, and other key choices of our life. The advancement in various technologies like the Internet of Things (IoT), Artificial intelligence, Data Analytics and Machine Learning has made it possible to measure and positively impact these socio-economic factors. In this competitive world, companies must identify trends and make projections to estimate the future direction of their business. In addition, businesses need to incorporate various technologies to gauge their customer buying behaviour and overall opinions on the products and services. Customer buying behaviour is determined by capturing the customer's involvement in purchase decisions before buying a product or service through various technological platforms, including search engines, social media posts, and a variety of other tools.

Similarly, sentiment analysis is among the critical approaches that businesses must employ to detect and quantify attitudes, opinions and emotions among various customer segments. However, the significant influence of technology on these socio-economic factors has escalated several serious concerns. Among those concerns, the digital divide and the security issues are the biggest challenges to overcome. The digital divide is primarily caused by insufficient technological access, lack of digital skills and cost of the underlying infrastructure. Moreover, knowledge and comprehension of the underpinning security technologies and their application to safeguard these systems are critical. Furthermore, understanding the key issues pertinent to using security technologies and the legal framework within which the security technologies are used is of utmost importance. Investigating the use of emerging technologies for socio-economic and secure infrastructure development will not only support technological sustainability but will also significantly affect the future development trends.

Muhammad Ehsan Rana
School of Computing
Asia Pacific University of Technology & Innovation
Kuala Lumpur
Malaysia

Manoj Jayabalan
School of Computer Science & Mathematics
Liverpool John Moores University
Liverpool
UK

List of Contributors

Ali Ahmed Mohammed Ali Alwashali	School of Technology, Asia Pacific University of Technology and Innovation, Kuala Lumpur, Malaysia
Ameer A. N. Alasaad	School of Technolog, Asia Pacific University of Technology and Innovation, Kuala Lumpur, Malaysia
Chan Yu Hang	School of Computing, Asia Pacific University of Technology and Innovation, Kuala Lumpur, Malaysia
Daniel Mago Vistro	Forensic and Cyber Security Research Centre, Asia Pacific University of Technology and Innovation, Kuala Lumpur, Malaysia
Faridzuan Bin Barakath Rahman	School of Computing, Asia Pacific University of Technology and Innovation, Kuala Lumpur, Malaysia
Hen Kian Jun	School of Computing, Asia Pacific University of Technology and Innovation, Kuala Lumpur, Malaysia
Henry Khoo Shien Chen	School of Computing, Asia Pacific University of Technology and Innovation, Kuala Lumpur, Malaysia
Intan Farahana Binti Kamsin	Asia Pacific University of Technology and Innovation, Kuala Lumpur, Malaysia
Kamalanathan Shanmugam	School of Computing, Asia Pacific University of Technology and Innovation, Kuala Lumpur, Malaysia
Kelvin Tan	School of Technology, Asia Pacific University of Technology and Innovation, Kuala Lumpur, Malaysia
Loo Jun Hao	School of Computing, Asia Pacific University of Technology and Innovation, Kuala Lumpur, Malaysia
Matthew Tan Xian Long	Asia Pacific University of Technology and Innovation, Kuala Lumpur, Malaysia
Mien May Chong	School of Computing, Asia Pacific University of Technology and Innovation, Kuala Lumpur, Malaysia
Mohammed Adnan Islam	School of Computing, Asia Pacific University of Technology and Innovation, Kuala Lumpur, Malaysia
Muhammad Ehsan Rana	School of Computing, Asia Pacific University of Technology & Innovation, Kuala Lumpur, Malaysia
Mohammad Haziq Roszlan	Forensic and Cyber Security Research Centre, Asia Pacific University of Technology and Innovation, Kuala Lumpur, Malaysia
Nik Nurul Ain Nik Suki	School of Computing, Asia Pacific University of Technology and Innovation, Kuala Lumpur, Malaysia
Nik Sakinah Nik Ab Aziz	School of Computing, Asia Pacific University of Technology and Innovation, Kuala Lumpur, Malaysia
Nor Azlina Abd Rahman	School of Technology, Asia Pacific University of Technology and Innovation, Kuala Lumpur, Malaysia
Nurul Husna Binti Mohd Saad	School of Computing, Asia Pacific University of Technology and Innovation, Kuala Lumpur, Malaysia

Pit Khien Leong   School of Computing, Asia Pacific University of Technology and Innovation, Kuala Lumpur, Malaysia

Prabu Setyaji   School of Computing, Asia Pacific University of Technology and Innovation, Kuala Lumpur, Malaysia

Rajasvaran Logeswaran   School of Computing, Asia Pacific University of Technology and Innovation, Kuala Lumpur, Malaysia

Raja Rajeswari Ponnusamy   School of Computing, Asia Pacific University of Technology and Innovation, Kuala Lumpur, Malaysia

Shubashini Rathina Velu   School of Computing, Asia Pacific University of Technology and Innovation, Kuala Lumpur, Malaysia

Siti Azreena Binti Mubin   School of Computing, Asia Pacific University of Technology and Innovation, Kuala Lumpur, Malaysia

Sivaguru A/L Subarmaniyan School of Computing, Asia Pacific University of Technology and Innovation, Kuala Lumpur, Malaysia

Tanveer Khaleel Shaikh   School of Computing, Asia Pacific University of Technology and Innovation, Kuala Lumpur, Malaysia

Soon Qi Huan   School of Computing, Asia Pacific University of Technology and Innovation, Kuala Lumpur, Malaysia

Veerakumar Soundrapandian School of Computing, Asia Pacific University of Technology and Innovation, Kuala Lumpur, Malaysia

Vinesha Selvarajah   School of Computing, Asia Pacific University of Technology and Innovation, Kuala Lumpur, Malaysia

Wong Wan Jing   School of Computing & Technology, Asia Pacific University of Technology and Innovation, Kuala Lumpur, Malaysia

Wong Xin Yi   School of Computing, Asia Pacific University of Technology and Innovation, Kuala Lumpur, Malaysia

Yusnita Yusof   School of Technology, Asia Pacific University of Technology and Innovation, Kuala Lumpur, Malaysia

CHAPTER 1

Determinants of Impulse Purchase Behaviours on e-Commerce Websites

Mohammed Adnan Islam[1] and **Rajasvaran Logeswaran**[1,*]

[1] *School of Computing, Asia Pacific University of Technology and Innovation, Kuala Lumpur, Malaysia*

Abstract: This work investigates the various types and aspects of the determinants that cause impulse purchase behaviour within the context of e-commerce websites. It delves into finding the factors that trigger impulse purchase behaviour for consumers of both male and female gender within the age brackets of earning potential. The findings of this review highlight the factors that need to be in place before a purchase behaviour from a consumer can be observed. These determinants above of impulse purchase behaviour can generally be categorised into internal and external components, which are analysed in this work.

Keywords: Consumer, e-Commerce, e-Retailer, Purchase behaviour, Triggers of online purchase.

INTRODUCTION

Just as outdated products are removed from the shelves to make place for the latest ones, the cohort of the latest generation to enter the consumer market are those who fall under the umbrella of Generation Z [1]. To be more specific, these are individuals born between the years of 1995 and early 2010s. They are often considered "digital natives" as they are the first generation to have grown up surrounded by such an extensive degree of digital communication [2]. As pointed out in a study [3], Generation Z constitutes about 32% of the global population at the time of this writing and is deemed to impact consumer sales in global proportions significantly.

Studies have found that Generation Z is among the cohort of generations who spend at least 11 hours a day liking and sharing digital content across all their devices. As a result, the chances of being exposed to digital advertisements while

* **Corresponding author Rajasvaran Logeswaran:** School of Computing, Asia Pacific University of Technology and Innovation, Kuala Lumpur, Malaysia; E-mail: Loges@ieee.org

Muhammad Ehsan Rana and Manoj Jayabalan (Eds.)

checking various social media platforms of their choice at least five times a day are very high [4]. This is why Generation Z consumers are referred to as being more aware and informed than previous youth generations. Consequently, traditional marketing messages struggle with consumer avoidance [5], as this population segment knows how to pick up brands that blatantly advertise just for sales.

Since traditional advertisement messaging is disregarded by Generation Z consumers, who represent 32% of the global population, it becomes essential to find out more about the determinants of impulse purchase behaviours in e-commerce websites for this consumer group. Although Generation Z consumers have been in the limelight of this chapter so far, a recent development in the global arena in 2019 has necessitated identifying the determinants of online impulse purchase behaviours for other generation cohorts like the Millennials, Gen-X, and Gen-Y. This global development that has shaken the way entire business processes work and disrupted supply chains of various industries is none other than the global pandemic caused by the novel coronavirus.

Just as its predecessors had done in the past, this pandemic has essentially brought the world to a complete standstill to curb the spread of the deadly virus. In other words, regardless of age, sex, or location, most consumers have been confined within the vicinity of their own homes. As customers cannot visit physical sites, businesses in all industries have had to shift their focus and rely heavily on the online retail wing of their existing businesses. This had the effect of consumers meeting most, if not all, of their shopping needs online.

As Fig. (1) illustrates, the purchase amount among consumers doubled in 2020 compared to only a year ago. This increase can only be thought to remain at this level or even increase in the near future. Although the world is on its way to a recovery phase due to the invention of vaccines, most consumers have been shopping online almost exclusively for the past year. It is only natural to expect them to become accustomed enough to continue to shop online whenever possible in the foreseeable future. As a result, there has never been a better time to identify the factors influencing consumers to show impulse purchase behaviour online.

INTERNAL DETERMINANTS OF A PURCHASE DECISION

Although the effects of the global pandemic combined with the disregard of marketing messages by Generation Z pose a unique set of challenges for selling online, attempts to sell goods and services to consumers are nothing new. One form of consumer behaviour that has existed since the dawn of commerce and is of particular interest for dealing with consumers who have become desensitised to marketing efforts is that of impulse purchase. The reasons for a consumer to purchase out of impulse are described below.

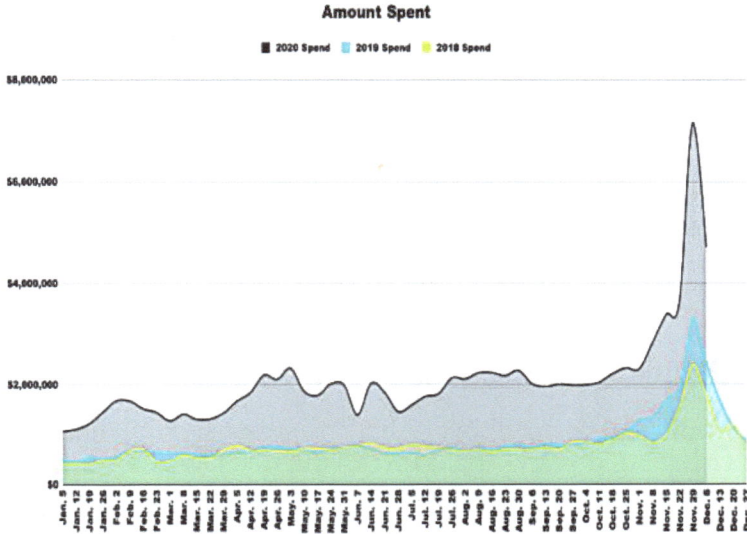

Fig. (1). Drastic 2020 increase in online spending [6].

Trait and Related Determinants

According to [7], several individual traits and self-identification may act as internal sources of impulse buying. Unsurprisingly, psychological impulses strongly influenced impulse buying [8]. Research has shown that people who achieve high scores on tests that measure impulsivity traits are more likely to participate in impulse purchases [9].

Three specific sub-traits within impulsivity stand out when dealing with impulse purchases. First is the sub-trait of *sensation-seeking* behaviour, which directly impacts impulse buying. Sensation-seeking, variety-seeking, novelty-seeking, and similar traits are reported as contributing to impulse buying [5].

Secondly, a tendency to buy things impulsively reflects a deeply rooted longing to act *spontaneously* within the context of consumption. This is what turns into an urge or motivation for actual impulse buying [5]. Impulse purchase tendencies seem easier to observe and detect than other traits.

Finally, *buyer-specific beliefs* are about own perceptions, and the lack tends to cause impulse purchase decisions [10]. Impulse generally occurs when a product is seen as offering high identity-expressive potential. This is intended to compensate for the lack of the consumer's perception of themselves [11]. As elaborated below, the said contextual factors might play a role in the impacts of such a lack of perception of one's identity [10].

Even though a casual observer may not be able to appreciate it completely, consumers have two main motives when they are on an online e-commerce website. These motives are known as hedonic and utilitarian [12]. A place of seeking pleasure inspires hedonic motives. Should the product reflect their belief systems, consumers may be browsing their favourite e-commerce website simply out of boredom and purchasing something on impulse. A utilitarian motive, on the other hand, gains inspiration from a practical standpoint and looks into solving a problem. It was thought in earlier literature that utilitarian motives would prevent consumers with a hedonic motive from making an impulse purchase, but that was consequently disproven.

The belief systems indicated above are considered crucial internal sources of impulse purchases, highlighting goal-directed tendencies and leading to specific beliefs about purchasing behaviour. For example, some consumers believe purchasing will bring emotional gratification, internal rewards, or the possibility of alleviating their negative feelings. As discussed in more detail in the following sections, these belief systems can serve as opportunities for retailers. When retailers align these consumer belief systems with their product image, consumers tend to make the purchase immediately and get relief from their pain [13].

Self-Control

Unlike the traits described, self-control prevents a consumer from indulging in an impulse purchase. However, as pointed out in [14], self-control requires attempts by individuals to control their desires, abide by rules, and change the general thought process of how one feels or acts. It has also been raised that self-control failure can occur because of conflicting goals, lack of self-monitoring, or depletion of mental resources [15]. Also known as "ego depletion," the depletion of cognitive resources is said to be temporal. In other words, it is at its weakest at the end of the day [11], and a consumer is likely to take part in an impulse purchase when mental resources have depleted. This is likely a valuable tactic for marketers to attract attention to their products.

Emotions

Consumers who purchase on impulse tend to have a strong need for arousal and go through an uplifting of emotions from continuous purchasing behaviours over extended periods [16]. The study [15] adds that consumers who engage in impulse purchases tend to be uplifted with emotions at any point, before, during, or after the point of purchase.

In some cases, these arousals are said to be a more substantial reason for impulse purchase than owning the product itself [17]. On the other hand [6], points out that negative mood states like sadness can also contribute to an impulse purchase. Multiple studies highlight how self-gifting is a form of retail therapy that helps consumers manage their moods [3].

As a result, whether it is positive or negative, emotional states likely affect impulse buying. However, there is little consensus on whether or how different moods play a part in impulse buying.

EXTERNAL DETERMINANTS OF A PURCHASE DECISION

There are several determinants for a purchase decision, especially for impulse purchases. The main determinants identified in the literature are described below.

Resources

While it may seem obvious, consumers who are rich in resources tend to make more impulse purchases than those who are poor in resources [14]. On a similar note drawing from prior research [15], points out that younger shoppers, particularly those who may belong to Generation Z, tend to be more likely to buy impulsively. Unsurprisingly, older adults are expected to regulate their emotions better and control themselves.

Research, such as that of [18], has pointed out gender differences in the context of consumer behaviour. Men and women have different considerations while shopping, so they impulsively purchase different variations of products. Interestingly, it has been found that men are less likely to experience regret after purchasing than women [2].

Marketing Stimuli

Within the marketing context, several advancements have been made in applying tactics that gain attention from target impulse-purchase consumers. The empirical study in [8] discovered that specific platform attributes make them particularly popular among Generation Z females to purchase fashion-related goods. These Generation Z female consumers follow micro-influencers and willingly purchase on impulse as a form of self-therapy when they like the style of the products they see. Men prove to have no such effect on impulse purchases, so marketers should focus on female consumers. That said, marketers ought to invest with these micro-influencers to appeal to Generations Z female consumers, as they are known to avoid branded promotional content actively.

One of the most recent and popular marketing tactics among the e-commerce giants, such as Alibaba, Taobao, and Tmall, is the tactic of gamification. Zhang *et al.* in [19] find that reward-giving and badge upgrade gamification systems are positively associated with perceived enjoyment and social interaction. This social interaction has been found to promote impulse purchases among consumers. As consumers enjoy the company of their online friends through points and upgrades, they can participate in various forms of gaming activities that involve spending impulsively. As a result, e-commerce websites should attempt to recognise the crucial nature of gamification mechanisms, such as giving rewards and upgrading badges, in stimulating impulse buying. Moreover, gamification seems to trigger men to purchase on impulse. Contrary to the abovementioned case, female consumers need to be more impressed to engage in these gamification mechanisms. Since female consumers are more interested in tangible rewards, they would use discounts and sales when shopping on e-commerce websites [20]. As such, they are more likely to indulge in gamification for rewards rather than for the game itself.

Another tactic marketers have been employing is the one-step payment process. Although this may not seem much at face value in terms of an impulse purchase, according to [19], security, convenience, and popularity among other consumers are the most important factors when making transactions purchases on impulse. If something falls short and the payment is not smoothly processed, the sale may be gone forever. Ensuring consumers do not worry about payment security is a hidden step to making it conducive for impulse purchases.

Contextual

Regarding impulse purchases, factors such as price levels vary depending on the context. For example, product price can be crucial for an impulse purchase. This is because financial constraints suppress impulse purchases [12]. Additionally, impulse purchases become less evident in product categories at higher price ranges. Another example of a contextual trait is only focusing on the advertising volume in hopes of an impulse purchase from consumers. Instead, paying attention to the advertisement distribution intensity within the industry context is also essential to optimise impulse purchase conditions. Advertising for firms in industries that invest heavily in advertisement practices is said to be less effective. This is because consumers are not expected to recognise or consider these triggers, just as Generation Z consumers ignore them.

In addition, distribution intensity in any product tends to influence impulse buying since the urge to make a purchase increases when products are rare or possess qualities of exclusivity [21]. Some products tend to be purchased on impulse more than others, mainly when the product displays qualities of self-belief held by the consumer. As a result, it would be logical to identify such products and try to emulate their qualities in other products [16].

Fig. (2) summarises the factors involved in an impulse purchase and illustrates how they can lead to consumers buying on impulse. The moderators for impulse buying behaviour are also indicated.

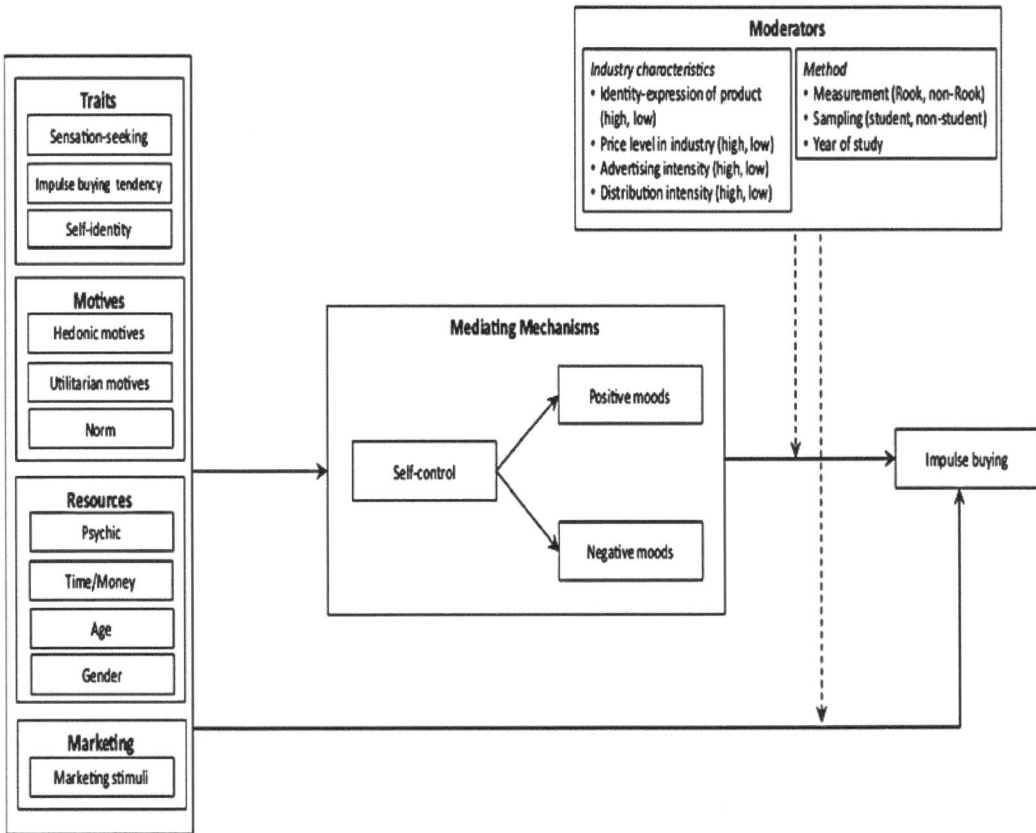

Fig. (2). Impulse purchase process [16].

CONCLUSION

This chapter explored various avenues in impulse purchasing, especially concerning the latest generation entering the consumer market. Generation Z is primarily averse to the marketing efforts carried out by branded promotional content. In addition to not having the full attention of Generation Z's 32% of the global consumer market stake, the global pandemic and lockdowns have necessitated a more effective way of selling goods to consumers.

As impulse purchase tends to be caused by deep internal longings, marketers and e-commerce websites require trigger desires among their consumers. This can be done with industry-specific insights that companies should gear up towards accordingly. Such as how micro-influencers drive the fashion industry sales.

On the other hand, it has also been found that tactics such as gamification tend to work more on male consumers than female ones. E-retailers could use the findings to understand these triggers for impulse purchases and turn them into an untapped source of business income.

CONSENT FOR PUBLICATION

Not applicable.

CONFLICT OF INTEREST

The authors declare no conflict of interest, financial or otherwise.

ACKNOWLEDGEMENTS

The authors wish to express their sincere appreciation to the Asia Pacific University of Technology and Innovation (APU) for the opportunity to conduct the research.

REFERENCES

[1]   O. Adeola, R.E. Hinson, and O. Evans, "Social media in marketing communications: a synthesis of successful strategies for the digital generation", *Digital Transformation in Business and Society,* vol. 4, pp. 61-81, 2020.
[http://dx.doi.org/10.1007/978-3-030-08277-2_4]

[2]   M. Blut, C. Teller, and A. Floh, "Testing retail marketing-mix effects on patronage: A meta-analysis", *J. Retailing,* vol. 94, no. 2, pp. 113-135, 2018.
[http://dx.doi.org/10.1016/j.jretai.2018.03.001]

[3]   J.K. Mullins, and R. Sabherwal, "Gamification: A cognitive-emotional view", *J. Bus. Res.,* vol. 106, pp. 304-314, 2020.
[http://dx.doi.org/10.1016/j.jbusres.2018.09.023]

[4]   A. Vitelar, "Like me: generation Z and the use of social media for personal branding", *Manag. Dyn. Knowl. Econ.,* vol. 7, no. 2, pp. 257-268, 2019.

[5]   N.J. Evans, B.W. Wojdynski, and M. Grubbs Hoy, "How sponsorship transparency mitigates negative effects of advertising recognition", *Int. J. Advert.,* vol. 38, no. 3, pp. 364-382, 2019.
[http://dx.doi.org/10.1080/02650487.2018.1474998]

[6]   J. Hwang, and L. Choi, "Having fun while receiving rewards?: Exploration of gamification in loyalty programs for consumer loyalty", *J. Bus. Res.,* vol. 106, pp. 365-376, 2020.

[http://dx.doi.org/10.1016/j.jbusres.2019.01.031]

[7]   L.V. Casalo, C. Flavia, and S. Ibáñez-Sánchez, "Be creative, my friend! Engaging users on Instagram bypromoting positive emotions", *J. Bus. Res.,* vol. 130, pp. 416-425, 2021. [http://dx.doi.org/10.1016/j.jbusres.2020.02.014]

[8]   Y. Chen, Y. Lu, B. Wang, and Z. Pan, "How do product recommendations affect impulse buying? An empirical study on WeChat social commerce", *Inf. Manage.,* vol. 56, no. 2, pp. 236-248, 2019. [http://dx.doi.org/10.1016/j.im.2018.09.002]

[9]   Y. Chen, Y. Lu, S. Gupta, and Z. Pan, "Understanding "window" shopping and browsing experience on social shopping website", *Inf. Technol. People,* vol. 33, no. 4, pp. 1124-1148, 2019. [http://dx.doi.org/10.1108/ITP-12-2017-0424]

[10]   J. Fromm, and A. Read, *Marketing to Gen Z: the Rules for Reaching This Vast and Very Different Generation of Influencers.* AMACOM: New York, 2018.

[11]   S. Fernandes, and R. Panda, "Influence of social reference groups on consumer buying behaviour: a review", *J. Manag. Res.,* vol. 19, no. 2, pp. 131-142, 2019.

[12]   R.C. Handayani, B. Purwandari, L. Solichah, and P. Prima, "The impact of Instagram "Call-to-Action" buttons oncustomers' impulse buying", *Proc.2nd Intl. Conf. Business and Info. Mgmt.,* pp. 50-45, 2018. [http://dx.doi.org/10.1145/3278252.3278276]

[13]   K. Sokolova, and H. Kefi, "Instagram and YouTube bloggers promote it, why should I buy? How credibility and parasocial interaction influence purchase intentions", *J. Retailing Consum. Serv.,* vol. 53, 2020.101742 [http://dx.doi.org/10.1016/j.jretconser.2019.01.011]

[14]   M. Stachowiak-Krzyżan, "M. Stachowiak-Krzyz an, "The use of social media by young consumers in purchasing processes"", *Marketing of Scientific and Research Organizations,* vol. 31, no. 1, pp. 84-108, 2019. [http://dx.doi.org/10.2478/minib-2019-0014]

[15]   M. Sundström, S. Hjelm-Lidholm, and A. Radon, "Clicking the boredom away – Exploring impulse fashion buying behavior online", *J. Retailing Consum. Serv.,* vol. 47, pp. 150-156, 2019. [http://dx.doi.org/10.1016/j.jretconser.2018.11.006]

[16]   R.W. Palmatier, M.B. Houston, and J. Hulland, "Review articles: purpose, process, and structure", *J. Acad. Mark. Sci.,* vol. 46, no. 1, pp. 1-5, 2018. [http://dx.doi.org/10.1007/s11747-017-0563-4]

[17]   L. Hassan, A. Dias, and J. Hamari, "How motivational feedback increases user's benefits and continued use: A study on gamification, quantified-self and social networking", *Int. J. Inf. Manage.,* vol. 46, pp. 151-162, 2019. [http://dx.doi.org/10.1016/j.ijinfomgt.2018.12.004]

[18]   E. Tsichla, L. Hatzithomas, and C. Boutsouki, "Gender differences in the interpretation of web atmospherics: A selectivity hypothesis approach", *J. Mark. Commun.,* vol. 22, no. 6, pp. 563-586, 2016. [http://dx.doi.org/10.1080/13527266.2014.903507]

[19]   Y. Zhang, K.P. Winterich, and V. Mittal, "Power distance belief and impulsive buying", *J. Mark. Res.,* vol. 47, no. 5, pp. 945-954, 2010. [http://dx.doi.org/10.1509/jmkr.47.5.945]

[20]   M. Sailer, J.U. Hense, S.K. Mayr, and H. Mandl, "How gamification motivates: An experimental study of the effects of specific game design elements on psychological need satisfaction", *Comput. Human Behav.,* vol. 69, pp. 371-380, 2017. [http://dx.doi.org/10.1016/j.chb.2016.12.033]

[21]   S. O'Brien, "Consumers Cough Up $5,400 a Year on Impulse Purchases", *CNBC,* Feb 23, 2018. https://www.cnbc.com/2018/02/23/consumers-cough-up-5400-a-year-on-impulse-purchases.html

CHAPTER 2

Issuer Credit Rating Performance Report Using Sentiment Analysis

Prabu Setyaji[1] and **Raja Rajeswari Ponnusamy**[1,*]

[1] *School of Computing, Asia Pacific University of Technology and Innovation, Kuala Lumpur, Malaysia*

Abstract: Indonesian Credit Rating Agency (CRA) is currently on its way to becoming the early mover of digital transformation. CRA controls macroeconomics and has a significant impact on many industries across the world. However, there are always those that can exploit it through asymmetric information and human interaction. A solution to reduce human interaction and enhancement is to build Natural Language Processing (NLP) sentiment analysis models and then display the results using an interactive dashboard story. Objectives are created for the aim of the project to be able to conduct a feasibility study, develop a model based on a press release dataset, conduct model evaluation, and display the results on an interactive dashboard. The research aims to utilise press release documents with NLP sentiment analysis to produce prescriptive analysis with interactive visualisation as the final output. Press release files are processed by using several Machine Learning (ML) algorithms such as Support Vector Machine (SVM), Multinomial Naive Bayes (MultinomialNB), Logistic Regression (LR), and Multi-Layer Perceptron Artificial Neural Network (MLP-Ann). This research will be carried out under Dynamic Systems Development (DSDM) and Knowledge Discovery Database (KDD). This will allow the researchers to achieve all objectives, permit models to perform very well, and let the output get displayed on a dashboard as a storyboard.

Keywords: Credit Rating Agency (CRA), Natural Language Processing (NLP), Press Release, Sentiment Analysis.

INTRODUCTION

Credit Rating Agencies (CRA) are institutions or organisations responsible for investigating companies' business activities, economic conditions and sectors. The analysis and demonstration from the company regarding the credit rating institution can justify deciding whether the company shares integrity and soundness from its activity. This was based on what [1] stated on the CRA

* **Corresponding author Raja Rajeswari Ponnusamy**: School of Computing, Asia Pacific University of Technology and Innovation, Kuala Lumpur, Malaysia; E-mail: raja.rajeswari@apu.edu.my

Muhammad Ehsan Rana and Manoj Jayabalan (Eds.)

assessment on securities, and what [2] mentioned about the rating agency being affected by the financial and leverage ratio of the company to determine the rating score.

CRA has significant control over the financial market as it involves many parts of the world in determining the rating. On the other hand [3], has not only determined the impact of credit rating on the capital structure of a particular company but has also divided the factors impacting the decision as Internal and External factors. Additionally, the assumption in [4] states that CRA negatively influences the economic sector as it picks a side on the issuer rating. CRA could favour the new issuer with a higher rating; downgrades or upgrades of the issuer occur more often when it has many rivals. This situation has resulted in the asymmetric information exploitation theory by [2], also known as the 'lemon effect'. Subsequently, this led to a statement by [5] regarding the need for performance enhancement to avoid misclassification and invalid information from being generated.

One lead CRA from Indonesia is being concealed as company 'ABC' and is currently struggling to digitalise the infrastructure. In addition to that, the CRA did not even have a prescription and interactive visualisation to support data-driven decision-making. Therefore, this research aims to provide CRA ABC from Indonesia with an interactive performance analysis dashboard visualisation generated from the model that utilises the NLP sentiment analysis technique to calculate a value based on the CRA press release indicating each of the company ABC's issuer. A reusable press release is being proposed to bring a new perspective in establishing a future rating based on past events of the client.

Technology inclusion in the business must be carried out as [6] mentions that digitalisation can help increase productivity, lower overall costs, and reduce human interaction, possibly resulting in the lemon effect or disjunction in the rating process. The whole research sequence will start from data collection until an evaluation using Software Development Life Cycle (SDLC) along with data mining methodology is done. Furthermore, classification modelling combined with the sentiment analysis technique will be carried out to predict the score of each issuer's press release.

MATERIALS AND METHODS

This research focuses on prescriptive analysis based on content from client press releases. The data is primary (in a PDF format) from the company, indicating that content selection must be made. Fig. (1) shows what a press release looks like. 408 press releases from 57 bank issuers will be based on the last five years' performance. The primary function will rely on the sentiment analysis technique to calculate the score of the content, based on a range from -1 to 1, indicating the negative or positive meaning behind the sentiment.

Fig. (1). Press Release Sample.

The data will be in CSV format when transformed manually in Excel from a PDF file. The features in the data include the bank name, date, and sentiment. Raw data will be processed and scored in the NLP model using the TextBlob library (Python-based) after the visualisation is generated using Tableau software. The other four classification algorithms will utilise different libraries of Scikit Learn and Natural Language Toolkit (NLTK) as the base library to conduct the analysis modelling.

Python has emerged as the pioneer of NLP-related modelling, thanks to its vast active community and a massive variety of libraries catering to specific issues, as stated in [7]. It has been mentioned that even though Python is the most powerful and dynamic, it has simple implementations supported by widely popular libraries such as NLTK, pandas, and Sklearn [8]. The procedure will be executed based on a modified Dynamic Systems Development Methodology (DSDM) combined with Knowledge Discovery Database (KDD) to assess the data mining.

LITERATURE REVIEW

NLP is widely used and is currently the most desirable system in some digital-based companies. This is because the companies need extra resources/information from a third-party perspective, also referred to as soft information [9]. The term soft information originates from financially based companies that use nonfinancial related information as supporting material used for identifying the creditworthiness of a company's credit score. It has never been used before as input for performance analysis in the case of a press release. It is only done once by [10] that utilizes a press release on a firm earning statement based to conduct pessimist optimist sentiment analysis using textual-analysis software different from the NLP approach. A press release has been viewed as an underwhelmed resource. On the other hand, it has been vowed that press release has never caused a negative impact but still focuses on brainstorming ways to re-strategize the plan for future execution, which is why it is called support for unprecedented solution material [11].

Raw text documents can be processed with an NLP technique that utilises a Machine Learning (ML) algorithm as the background of the process, which is the based term for Artificial Intelligence (AI) in advance that works best for predicting events in the future and it has been mentioned that all big four firms have started using the kind of technologies to improve performance by reducing work timeline and assessing complex data structure [12]. AI technology and the NLP technique have been applied to conduct speech recognition and risk management assessment on a big company [7]. Four other big firms are examples of related industries working with such practices. However, the industry has generally started focusing on AI development, including changing the company's structure to fit in with digitalisation adaptation.

NLP modelling has different purposes and measurements from the classification model, even though it still uses a similar process to standard modelling from data collection to evaluation. It utilises sentiment as input and calculates the polarity score to identify the true meaning of positive and negative values. Identifying polarity cannot be done by accessing raw unstructured data. There were several processes introduced in 2011 to make sentiment readable by systems such as Part of Speech (POS) tag, Named Entity Recognition (NER), chunking, etc., which became a necessary procedure as the pre-processing method [6]. This pre-processing method removes stop words, URLs, abbreviations, and unnecessary space, as mentioned [13]. Each chunk or lexicon will be combined with the n-gram technique to produce a higher model accuracy. The model's accuracy can be modified to fit business needs by creating rule-based pre-processing. This ensures there are no misclassified or misleading removals from the sentiment, and the rules are kept simple for better interpretation [14].

The most desirable models in NLP are the Support Vector Machine (SVM) and Naive Bayes (NB) due to their use in solving NLP-related issues. They both have their capabilities. SVM works best with the bigram technique for data with high volumes and small features that work on the text of the mining technique review for sentiment analysis [15]. On the other hand, NB is used for handling small tasks with small non-complex data. Moreover, NB is being re-invented with more capabilities to remove its naive characteristics by allowing the algorithm to remove duplicated words to quicken the analysis process compared to other algorithms [16].

Despite the status SVM and NB have in NLP modelling, there are attempts to use other algorithms or even create custom models to solve the issues. One of the major algorithms in classification, Multilayer Perceptron Artificial Neural Network (MLP-ANN), is being used to handle various problems. This is because an experiment conducted by [17] on ML model evaluation among black box algorithms has proved that MLP-ANN can surpass Random Forest (RF), SVM, and Extreme Gradient Boosting (XGBoost) in predicting survey consumer finance data on a rating-based system classification with the maximum Area Under the Curve score being 87.5%. Moreover, MLP conducted sentiment analysis on an Amazon Product Review Dataset and achieved a total accuracy of 93.3% in identifying the sentiment score based on reviewing the customers' comments [17].

METHODOLOGY

Credit rating assessment follows a modified DSDM methodology and the KDD procedure to handle the data processing. SDLC is being adopted to complete the backbone framework of the project, as mentioned by [18]. The same source also stated that when the project is more flexible and requires multiple revisiting of the same step, agile will be better suited with more customer/client interaction, and sudden change could even be done without breaking the whole plan. Fig. (**2**) below shows the overall architecture of the modified methodology.

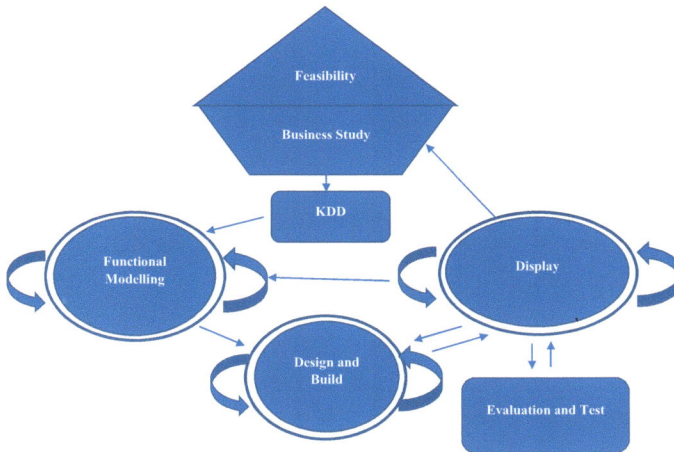

Fig. (2). Proposed Methodology [5].

DSDM methodology was introduced in 1998 and is considered the successor of the Rapid Application Development (RAD) methodology [5]. The methodology focuses on having high-quality features of the product and documentation clarity when deployed. The proposed methodology works based on a timebox schedule for feedback and revision. The credit modelling is shown to fit with the actual scenario. Using the primary data received, DSDM utilises available resources rather than seeking external materials, so it only works when fewer people contribute to the project, making it the most suitable [1]. KDD is included to be the framework for processing the data as it is the oldest framework for data mining and has five tasks in total, as shown in Fig. (**3**) [19].

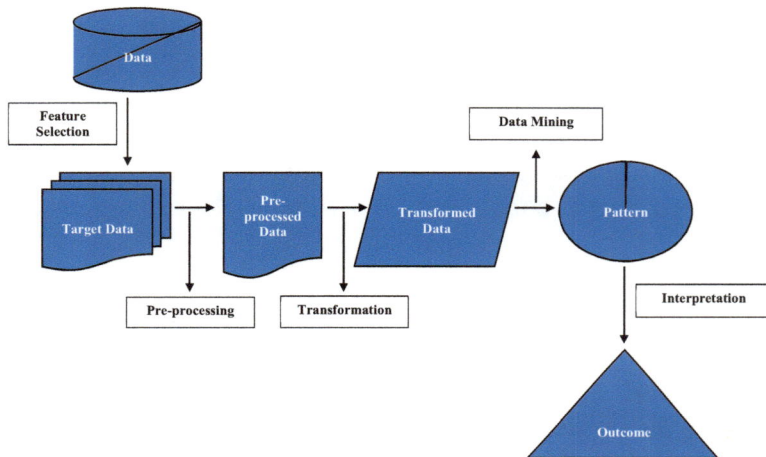

Fig. (3). KDD [9].

This process comes right after the feasibility and business study stage, reviewing past projects, CRA business, and scoring method infrastructure. The project discussion starts from the KDD process on data acquisition, transformation, and cleaning with additional feature selections from the unstructured (PDF) data.

The data processing and mining phase will follow. This phase is step three after the studies have been conducted. 409 press release data will be processed, the first action being conversion and feature selection from PDF files to CSV format. This process will be done manually because the data is received as non-processed data from the company authority. Most of the pre-processing procedure will be conducted in Excel. In contrast, the furnishing words assignment and case sensitivity will be done on Python codes using the hyperparameter for vectorisation. The original data's form will be similar to Fig. (**1**), and the amount of information will be taken from its content into the CSV table format with three features: company/bank name, date, and text/sentiment (Fig. **4**).

Fig. (4). Converted Data.

This is the data for TextBlob NLP modelling that is only specified to produce a sentiment polarity score as the outcome. The alternative solution to Company ABC will be the datasets generated as a train and test set for sentiment classification models. This data will differ slightly, only focusing on the label assigned based on the issuer rating mark.

The classes will be divided into six different ratings [20]. This is because the head analytics of Standard & Poor (S&P) 500 mentions that the rating assignment is based on the issuer's capability; AAA means it is superior, D means it is the default, and R means it is under supervision. In the first data, all these marks are converted back to their meaning for the system to read the value behind its score and generate scores based on its content. Out of the 409 PDF files, several press releases contain DUD or unrated content that is automatically excluded since it does not affect the issuer's performance. The decision to carry out pre-processing and data splitting on Excel is because there is some unequal distribution of class 0 and 1, implying that the ADEQUATE and MORE THAN ADEQUATE rating mark is the actual data needing to be processed to meet the real scenario of what the company is currently facing. Therefore, it is better to avoid unnecessary changes or modifications to the data with any kind of over/under sampling since the system has to adapt to the data and not the other way around. Moreover, random sampling cannot be done to avoid bias because of uneven classes. The implementation phase has a slightly pre-processed component on the vectorisation and hyperparameter assignment to cope with the rules of the company's rating system (rule-based).

IMPLEMENTATION

The TextBlob model has a more simplified implementation and syntax than other models utilising the Sklearn library package. Textblob library is a complete set of text manipulation functions consisting of POS tagging, sentiment analysis, and translation per [21] explanation in Textblob documentation. To support Textblob, which can only read through data in a data frame format, the most efficient data manipulators library, Pandas, has been included as it can convert raw/spreadsheet data files into the data frame format [22]. Pandas' library is assisted with the itertools library for faster-reading processes. The model's purpose is to calculate the sentiment score based on the Text column, as Fig. (4) shows, and then convert it back to a CSV file to be used for visualization, as shown in Fig. (5).

A	B	C	D	E	F
Bank	Date	Press Release	Sentiment	Polarity	Subjectivity
Bank Pemba	24/01/2011	PEFINDO assigned strong rating for PT Bank Pembangunan Daerah Aceh . Outlook for the	Sentiment(polarity=0.3899999	0.39	0.62
Bank Pemba	18/10/2011	PEFINDO assigned its corporate rating of PT Bank Aceh to strong. The outlook is stable. T	Sentiment(polarity=0.1892857	0.189	0.504
Bank Pemba	02/04/2020	PEFINDO has rated PT Bank Aceh Syariah at strong. The outlook for the corporate rating i	Sentiment(polarity=0.2596428	0.26	0.515
Bank BNP	10/03/2016	PEFINDO has assigned its superior rating to PT Bank BNP Paribas Indonesia. The outlook	Sentiment(polarity=0.4566666	0.457	0.702
Bank BNP	26/04/2017	PEFINDO has assigned its superior rating to PT Bank BNP Paribas Indonesia. The outlook	Sentiment(polarity=0.3446296	0.345	0.554
Bank BNP	30/11/2018	BNP Paribas Indonesia is a joint venture bank that focuses on corporate banking, targetin	Sentiment(polarity=0.0535714	0.054	0.107
Bank BNP	08/10/2019	An obligor rated superior has the highest rating assigned by PEFINDO. The obligor capaci	Sentiment(polarity=0.3430952	0.343	0.583
Bank BRI Sya	07/11/2017	PEFINDO has assigned its very strong rating to PT Bank BRI Syariah. The outlook for the r	Sentiment(polarity=0.1316665	0.132	0.571
Bank Bukopir	02/12/2014	PEFINDO has affirmed its more strong rating for PT Bank Bukopin Tbk. At the same time	Sentiment(polarity=0.2148148	0.215	0.484
Bank Bukopir	15/04/2015	PEFINDO has reaffirmed its more strong rating for PT Bank Bukopin Tbk and strong ratin	Sentiment(polarity=0.2703703	0.27	0.568
Bank Bukopir	01/06/2015	PEFINDO has reaffirmed its more strong rating for PT Bank Bukopin Tbk and strong ratin	Sentiment(polarity=0.1847222	0.185	0.474
Bank Bukopir	05/04/2016	PEFINDO has affirmed its more strong rating for PT Bank Bukopin Tbk along with its stro	Sentiment(polarity=0.3592592	0.359	0.623
Bank Bukopir	18/06/2016	PEFINDO has affirmed its more strong rating for PT Bank Bukopin Tbk along with its stro	Sentiment(polarity=0.3513227	0.351	0.639
Bank Bukopir	31/08/2016	PEFINDO has affirmed its more strong rating for PT Bank Bukopin Tbk along with its stro	Sentiment(polarity=0.2206349	0.221	0.435
Bank Bukopir	12/06/2017	PEFINDO has affirmed its more strong ratings for PT Bank Bukopin Tbk and its medium t	Sentiment(polarity=0.2055555	0.206	0.432

Fig. (5). TextBlob Output.

There are three extra columns on the right of the table: sentiment, polarity, and subjectivity. They show how much positive or negative information each text contains. However, since the data is factual and not based on opinion, only polarity is used, as subjectivity is not efficient enough. Additionally, TextBlob has approximate accuracy of 70% [23], as the library package runs on Naïve Bayes and does not have any accuracy features.

The model type used here is Support Vector Classification (SVC) which uses the Sklearn library with the support of NLTK and Pandas. NLTK's role is to provide English stop words dictionary for vectorisation, and SVC has to read the vector instead of the data frame. SVM also has to focus on classification instead of calculating the sentiment score and utilising the divided train and test dataset. The alternative solution is to provide a model that can predict the classes of score marks from 0 to 6 (representative of AAA until C). SVM has several components to tune up within its vectorisation by using Sklearn's own Tfidvectorizer, such as min_df to indicate minimum appearance and max_df to indicate the maximum appearance, lowercase, n-gram and whether it is unigram or bigram or trigram and many more. SVM has been categorised as a black box algorithm, thanks to its elaborate metaphors within its modelling and how each fine-tuning gives different accuracy.

Two additional attributes from Sklearn have to be added as [24] mentions that sublinear_tf does the tf scaling and use_idf is to reinvent the weighting as it is known as the default attribute for vectorisation. At the same time, the significant point is lowercase, and the n-gram attribute greatly improves the model by looking at the first-row and second-row differences. At the same time, the use of

Kernel Linear is suitable to find a pattern on matching class with its dependent variables in NLP cases, as mentioned [24]. It was proven to be the best, with 77.5% accuracy during the testing.

MultinomialNB is the advanced version of Naive Bayes with its ability to ignore duplication in textual processing and has faster processing time than any standard modelling [25]. MultinomialNB has a similar implementation process to SVM, using the same library package. However, some hyperparameter attributes do not give any effect, such as stop words, sublinear_tf, and use_idf. Therefore, only ngram, max_df, min_df, and lowercase are utilised.

Unlike the previous model, MultinomialNB works better when a trigram is implemented, while the other attribute assigns the same value for the tuning. It strengthens the fact that ngram and lowercase play a big part in deciding the effectiveness of a model, improving it slightly by 1-3%, referring to the last two models. Regarding the minimum number of thresholds to be declined, changing the value from 10 to ignore the 2% improves the overall modelling with an accuracy of 73.5%.

Among other classifiers, Logistic Regression (LR) is always marked as a straightforward algorithm. The most beneficial feature of LR is an easily interpretable output [26], and despite its simplicity, LR is still reliable and can compete with black box algorithms, as proven in [21]. LR can produce 86% AUC, comparable to ANN and RF. Sophisticated and simple, LR is one of the most widely used algorithms in handling sentiment analysis tasks [25]. The LR has an iteration hyperparameter to make sure the model converges with the needs of 1650 max_iter to fulfill the convergence.

2 solvers are used as the default parameter. Saga is being used as the solver to handle massive data and can scale down the model to meet the convergence [24]. Moreover, the solver must match with its penalty as there is a lasso, ridge, and elastic net. Elastic net has proposed the regulator be the successor of the earlier L1 and L2 introduced in 1996, proven with an accuracy of 78.75%, with a difference of only 0.25% [26].

MLP-ANN will be used in this research as it is marked as the top-tier NLP modelling algorithm to be chosen. This is all credit to its capability as a feedforward model designed to fit in with the given cases and the fact that ANN has a very high dependency on its hidden layer and neurons combined with proper iteration being assigned to meet its convergence [17]. To handle the credit rating in this particular modelling dataset, appointing a minimum of 250 max iterations, 25 hidden layers, and 100 batch sizes are required. This is all done while activation remains ReLu, and those numbers assigned were based on the requirement from the model itself to converge and gain an accuracy of 77.5%.

RESULTS AND DISCUSSION

The Press Release Prescription result is based on the TextBlob modelling sentiment analysis result. It is an obvious observation that the company lost 14 of its clients from January 2019 to April 2020, which implies that the company has lost a quarter of the total overall clients from 2005 to 2020. Regarding the polarity score, there were 12 Bank clients marked with negative highlights across the year, and two of the clients' rates were withdrawn due to them being unsatisfied [22]. The primary expectation from CRA is for the issuer to get higher marks. Most of the clients' performance is superior, totalling 147 out of 408 press releases. Since the company has nine companies still attached to Company ABC's issuer list, those Banks must constantly be on the lookout to prevent spreading asymmetric information to the CRA competitor.

Five models have been created and implemented to handle press release documents for polarity scoring and classification to predict each content rating. However, TextBlob models do not have any measurement because their only purpose is to conduct simplified sentiment analysis as the model is considered a package to use, and there is no tuning of hyperparameters to improve the model [18]. The model will be excluded from the comparison, although it can produce reliable results to be used as the actual output Company ABC desires. Four models were compared to each other, all conducting sentiment classification, as shown in Table **1**.

Table 1. Model Summary.

Model	Runtime	Complexity	Final Accuracy
SVM	0.1 seconds	Intermediate	77.5%
MultinomialNB	0.2 seconds	Low	73.5%
LR	3 seconds	Low	78.75%
MLP-ANN	3 seconds	High	77.5%

Despite LR having the highest accuracy, SVM has a lower runtime and needs much tuning to implement. This is due to the LR iteration, which must be executed 1650 times to converge. LR is still proven to be the best model in the case of handling the kind of press release dataset as the data size is relatively small but has complicated content within the text data to be processed. Suppose the case is different, and the data has more features and instances. In that case, SVM might be more suitable because it can handle things faster because of its tuning options that can be used with a lesser accuracy but a higher prediction time of 0.01 seconds. On the other hand, MLP was reviewed in much research in the past as the best version of ANN, being able to surpass any other algorithm despite the performance of MLP in this project not being as superior as it is supposed to reach 78.75% at maximum.

None of the models can reach 80% but is still marked as satisfying because the data has so many contents within each observation, while NLP usually handles the task sentence by sentence. Press releases have more than three paragraphs containing economic conditions until the lawsuit and have several keywords that can identify their rating. Another issue is that the data is manually collected and transformed into a specific format for the system to read through and process. Since the system handles the actual data from a real scenario, the class distribution could be unequal. This is especially the case in CRA, as the clients rarely receive a low grade, causing a significant issue for the system as the grade for "adequate" or idB only has six records within the datasets in the span of the previous five years. In a real case scenario, datasets will not always be equally divided; an overall average of 77% accuracy is reasonable to handle primary transformed data.

CONCLUSION

The research achieved the desired goal and what company ABC wanted as well. Models were created and evaluated, and the final output from one of the models was displayed in the form of a dashboard story. Five alternative models are designed to provide options for Company ABC to improve the company's business model architecture. With Company ABC being a newcomer in digital transformation, LR models were suitable for the company to adapt to easy maintenance and application. This supported the NLP technology, with a 78.75% accuracy, a decent result for the early deployment that could be re-modified to fit in if the authority wanted to use the model in different cases.

The TextBlob dashboard output is the desired output for the performance analysis story five years from 2015. It addresses many critical points such as potential fraud clients, the credit rating pattern issue, and some remarkable years of Company ABC wrapped up in a 5-page storyboard as an analysis report. Due to the limited self-collected data, pre-processing is central to the transformation and feature selection analysis to produce eligible datasets from unstructured data. Another limitation is that the data does not have equally distributed classes, making it harder for the model to gain higher accuracy. Additionally, the data is not based on human opinion, so the subjectivity component cannot be used to help improve the model. Regardless, the model is still reasonable in assisting data-driven decision-making, and both the storyboard and alternative models can be used as new parameters within the credit rating assignment meeting.

CONSENT FOR PUBLICATION

Not applicable.

CONFLICT OF INTEREST

The authors declare no conflict of interest, financial or otherwise.

ACKNOWLEDGEMENTS

The authors wish to express their sincere appreciation to the Asia Pacific University of Technology and Innovation (APU) for the opportunity to conduct the research.

REFERENCES

[1]   P. Abrahamsson, O. Salo, J. Ronkainen, and J. Warsta, *Agile software development methods: Review and Analysis,* 2002.

[2]   G.A. Akerlof, "The Market for "Lemons": Quality Uncertainty and the Market Mechanism", *Q. J. Econ.,* vol. 84, no. 3, p. 488, 1970.
[http://dx.doi.org/10.2307/1879431]

[3]   B. Aktan, S. Celik, Y. Abdulla, and N. Alshakhoori, *The impact of credit ratings on capital structure.* ISRA International Journal of Islamic Finance, 2019.
[http://dx.doi.org/10.1108/IJIF-03-2018-0028]

[4]   G. Baber, "The role and responsibility of credit rating agencies in promoting soundness and integrity", *Journal of Money Laundering Control,* vol. 17, no. 1, pp. 34-49, 2014.
[http://dx.doi.org/10.1108/JMLC-09-2013-0031]

[5]   G. Coleman, and R. Verbruggen, "A Quality Software Process for Rapid Application Development", *Software Quality Management,* vol. VI, pp. 241-259, 1998.
[http://dx.doi.org/10.1007/978-1-4471-1303-4_22]

[6]   R. Collobert, "J. Weston, L. Bottou, M. Karlen, K. Kavukcuoglu and P. Kuksa, "Natural Language Processing (Almost) from Scratch"", *J. Mach. Learn. Res.,* 2011.

[7]   Delloite, "The new physics of financial services How artificial intelligence is transforming the financial ecosystem", 2019.

[8]   A.Y. Egwoh, and O.F. Nonyelum, *"A Software System Development Life Cycle Model For Improved Students' Communication And Collaboration".* International Journal of Computer Science & Engineering Survey. IJCSES, 2017.

[9]   U. Fayyad, G. Piatetsky-Shapiro, and P. Smyth, "From Data Mining to Knowledge Discovery in Databases", *AI Mag.,* pp. 37-54, 1996.

[10]   D. Gillmor, "Standard & Poor's Rating Proces", 2015

[11]   S. Grimmelikhuijsen, F.D. Vries, and W. Zijlstra, "Breaking bad news without breaking trust: The effects of a press release and newspaper coverage on perceived trustworthiness", *Journal of Behavioral Public Administration.* 2018.
[http://dx.doi.org/10.30636/jbpa.11.16]

[12] D. Kumar Gupta, and S. Goyal, "Credit Risk Prediction Using Artificial Neural Network Algorithm", *International Journal of Modern Education and Computer Science,* vol. 10, no. 5, pp. 9-16, 2018. [IJMECS].
[http://dx.doi.org/10.5815/ijmecs.2018.05.02]

[13] L.M. Hamilton, and J. Lahne, "Fast and automated sensory analysis: Using natural language processing for descriptive lexicon development", *Food Qual. Prefer.,* vol. 83, 2020.
[http://dx.doi.org/10.1016/j.foodqual.2020.103926]

[14] C.W. Hsu, C.C. Chang, and C.J. Lin, *A Practical Guide to Support Vector Classification.* Department of Computer Science National Taiwan University, 2016.

[15] H. Issa, T. Sun, and M.A. Vasarhelyi, "Research Ideas for Artificial Intelligence in Auditing: The Formalization of Audit and Workforce Supplementation", *J. Emerg. Technol. Account.,* vol. 13, no. 2, pp. 1-20, 2016.
[http://dx.doi.org/10.2308/jeta-10511]

[16] D. Jurafsky, and J.H. Martin, Speech and Language Processing 3rd Edition darft 2019.

[17] S.J. Livingston, B.S.T. Selvi, M. Thabeetha, C.P. Grena, and C.S. Jenifer, "A Neural Network Based Approach for Sentimental Analysis on Amazon Product Reviews", *Int. J. Innov. Technol. Explor. Eng.,* 2019. [IJITEE].

[18] S. Loria, *textblob Documentation.* 2020

[19] W. Mckinney, *pandas: powerful Python data analysis toolkit.* 2020

[20] Moody's, "Moody's - Digital technologies have the potential to spur a global productivity boom", 2019.

[21] L. Munkhdalai, T. Munkhdalai, O. Namsrai, J.Y. Lee, and K.H. Ryu, "An Empirical Comparison of Machine-Learning Methods on Bank Client Credit Assessments", *Sustainability 2019, .*
[http://dx.doi.org/10.3390/su11030699]

[22] G. Park, and H.Y. Lee, "Opportunistic behaviors of credit rating agencies and bond issuers", *Pac. Basin Finance J.,* vol. 47, pp. 39-59, 2018.
[http://dx.doi.org/10.1016/j.pacfin.2017.11.003]

[23] Sklearn, "sklearn.feature_extraction.text.TfidfVectorizer", 2019.

[24] Sklearn, "sklearn.linear_model.LogisticRegression", 2019.

[25] C. Wu, F. Wu, J. Liu, Y. Huang and X, XieM "Sentiment Lexicon Enhanced Neural Sentiment Classification".The 28th ACM International Conference on Information and Knowledge Management (CIKM '19), 2019.

[26] H. Zou, and T. Hastie, "Regularization and Variable Selection via the Elastic Net". Journal of the Royal Statistical Society, 2015.

CHAPTER 3

Recommendations for Implementing an IoT-Based Inventory Tracking and Monitoring System

Muhammad Ehsan Rana[1,*], Kamalanathan Shanmugam[1] and Chan Yu Hang[1]

[1] *School of Computing, Asia Pacific University of Technology and Innovation, Kuala Lumpur, Malaysia*

Abstract: Inventory management is vital in the industry because it allows manufacturers and wholesalers to efficiently store and manage information in the warehouse. Warehouse management provides the facility to control functions such as storing newly shipped products in available locations and tracking inventory information and product distribution for shipping. These complex processes in the warehouse management system require manufacturers and wholesalers to ensure that the warehouse operation is running smoothly and efficiently. The use of the Internet of Things (IoT) for automating industrial and household processes has been increasing rapidly in the last few years. This research focuses on IoT for tracking and monitoring inventory, providing an automated and efficient system for manufacturers and wholesalers. A comprehensive discussion has been conducted on IoT application layers and recommended sensors for inventory tracking and monitoring systems. This research also emphasizes applying IoT in inventory, logistics, and warehousing operations. Researchers have proposed an IoT-based system specifically designed to cater to the shortcomings of the existing inventory management systems.

Keywords: Internet of Things (IoT), Inventory Management, Inventory Tracking and Monitoring, Warehouse Management.

INTRODUCTION

Nowadays, many advanced technologies or systems assist manufacturers in managing inventory products, such as arranging inventory on the shelves or recording inventory information in the warehouses. However, only some of these systems provide holistic visibility of complete inventory information being stored in the warehouse. It is among the critical issues almost every warehouse faces, as manufacturers need an accurate system to track this information. Consequently, manufacturers need to put a lot of effort and time into recording inventory and finding the available space to load new inventory inside the available shelves [1].

* **Corresponding author Muhammad Ehsan Rana:** School of Computing, Asia Pacific University of Technology and Innovation, Kuala Lumpur, Malaysia; E-mail: muhd_ehsanrana@apu.edu.my

Muhammad Ehsan Rana and Manoj Jayabalan (Eds.)

In this research, the authors have emphasised proposing a new advanced inventory system to assist manufacturers in managing inventory information effectively and efficiently. In addition, this system is proposed to contain some unique functionalities to keep track of real-time inventory information in the warehouse. The proposed system is an IoT-based system that consists of sensor devices to identify the inventory information in the inventory store. The inventory information will be displayed on the LCD screen, allowing users to show the recorded inventory on a webpage in real-time. Therefore, users would obtain the latest and updated inventory information easily rather than inspecting and recording each inventory container one by one.

PROBLEM STATEMENT

According to research conducted by Peerless Research Group in 2014, it was analysed that 47% of respondents increased their labour productivity in the range of 10% to 24% after implementing an inventory management system, whereas 16% of respondents received a 25% improvement in labour productivity in their industry. As per the Bureau of Labor Statistics, the turnover rate among warehouse employees is 36%. Furthermore, the logistics industry provides approximately 270,000 jobs annually in the world. Therefore, providing adequate training and skilled labour is always challenging, as specified in the above statistics [2].

Several problems associated with industrial warehouses affect the inventory tracking and monitoring processes directly. A flawed warehouse management process may contribute to many issues, including a substantial profit decrease. It will require the company to have higher expenses in managing and controlling its inventory [3].

If procurement managers cannot control inventory wisely, they cannot ascertain the inventory status to handle customers' needs [4]. Hence, in the worst-case scenario, they will need more inventory to meet their customer needs as they cannot capture the exact inventory status in the warehouse. With an efficient and well-organized inventory management system, manufacturers can keep track of stock and transactions in a warehouse [5].

Most companies need complete visibility of their inventory information. They will have a massive issue of purchasing goods at the wrong time; thus, it will increase unnecessary expenses in the warehouse [6]. Furthermore, it may slow down the warehouse operation process because it needs the manufacturers to put a lot of effort and time into looking for the particular goods, then shipping them out or replenishing the lack of inventory in the warehouse. On the other hand, these problems may decrease the company's profits due to lost sales and higher inventory expenses. The procurement manager does not have complete visibility on which inventory they should purchase [1]. Besides, manufacturers waste significant time searching for available slots and arranging these incoming inventories on placement [7]. Apart from that, one of the common problems in every organisation is having an excessive inventory in the warehouse and being unable to ship it quickly. Thus, the company can keep on losing money by purchasing unnecessary products.

Inventory management has strategic importance for any industry or factory as it needs financial and human resources to record, update, and maintain stock-related data like level, location, status, *etc.* One of the current industry's significant challenges is inaccurate and inconsistent inventory information that might lead to running out of stock or carrying too much stock, eventually incurring high expenses [6]. Based on research conducted in 2016, most industry players face issues due to their ineffective capacity framework and racking arrangement that significantly impact manufacturers' insufficient space to receive more stock [8]. Therefore, it is tough to determine which inventory store can keep the freshly arrived inventory within due time.

USE OF IOT IN INVENTORY TRACKING AND MONITORING

IoT is widely used in healthcare, transportation, home automation, and industrial systems. It is used to communicate and share information via the Internet to conduct tracing inventory, smart reorganisation, real-time monitoring, security, and process control. Using IoT, machines, sensors, and people can connect via the Internet at any given time and place where the infrastructure is available [9].

IoT-based inventory tracking and monitoring systems will significantly help the inventory management business. Using the latest technology trends, an IoT-based inventory management system can utilise data analytics, cloud computing, mobile devices, etc. This can be done to solve the existing issues as well as address the limitations of the current inventory tracking systems.

IOT APPLICATION LAYERS

IoT application layers consist of the sensor, communication, support, and application layers.

Sensor Layer

The lowest layer is called the sensor layer or smart device layer, which consists of smart devices integrated with sensors. Sensors connect with smart devices to process and provide real-time information. Sensors not only measure and detect objects but also convert the reading into an output for the users via a connection to the communication layer [15].

Communication Layer

The communication layer consists of public, private, or hybrid networks designed to support the communication needs for security, bandwidth, and latency [15]. states that sensors may produce a massive volume of data in the communication layer, consisting of wireless or wired network infrastructure to perform as a conveying medium.

Application Support Layer

The support layer processes the data collected from the sensors by maintaining security control, analytics, management of devices, and process modelling with the collaboration of objects with the systems. This is done by giving relevant information about the results to the users.

Application Layer

The application layer contains the IoT application, which performs its domain function and interacts with the user.

RECOMMENDED SENSORS FOR INVENTORY TRACKING & MONITORING SYSTEMS

In IoT-based systems, sensors are indispensable components used to measure object inputs. These inputs contain temperature, motion, position, pressure, light, sound readings, etc. The values obtained through these sensors are transferred to intelligent nodes for further analysis [10].

Temperature Sensor

A temperature sensor is used to detect the temperature or heat. It is used in environmental control, medical, and food processing applications.

Motion Sensor

A Motion sensor focuses on measuring acceleration and vibrations. An example of a motion sensor is a pedometer.

Proximity Sensor

A proximity sensor is typically implemented in applications with high safety, efficiency, and security demands. This sensor is used to detect the motion of an object. They are commonly used in parking systems and other industries with similar requirements.

Humidity Sensor

This sensor detects the humidity in the environment and measures dangerous chemical elements such as carbon monoxide and radiation. Applications can be smart home and security systems.

Magnetic Sensor

A magnetic sensor measures the direction and strength of the magnetic field. Applications are used to track and display an item's position, such as vehicular automation.

Pressure Sensor

It measures the force and weight of an object by detecting touch and contact pressure. Applications are gesture recognition and touchscreen devices.

Sound Sensor

A sound sensor recognises speech, identifies sound, and measures the object's distance by calculating the time taken in echo. Applications are microphones and audio systems.

Optic Sensor

Optic sensors emit, receive, and convert light energy into digital signals. These sensors detect the distance, absence, or presence of an object and electromagnetic energy. Applications include cameras, video images, and mining operations.

APPLYING IOT IN LOGISTIC OPERATIONS

Implementing IoT across the entire logistics value chain will bring a significant impact in terms of benefits in operational efficiency, customer experience, safety, and security. It provides automotive services and processes in the logistic value chain to eliminate the manual interventions that help improve the quality and performance at an accelerated rate of improving the industry process [11].

APPLYING IOT IN WAREHOUSING OPERATIONS

Warehouse plays a vital role in the supply chain industry in storing large-scale products orderly and systematically, allowing operators to manage items efficiently. A warehouse is also used to preserve and store products in massive quantities, either from new arrivals or production, until the items are shipped out from the distribution centre. In addition, a warehouse allows products to be collected, distributed and sorted efficiently. Implementing IoT in the warehouse will provide various benefits to logistics users. Implementing sensor devices in smart inventory management will provide real-time visibility to the inventory levels for monitoring an item's condition and alerting the warehouse manager, thus preventing costly out-of-stock situations. Besides, it will allow the user to analyse which product is required to replenish. Additionally, it will provide visibility, and accurate information, optimise recording product processing, and predictive product analysis [10].

ISSUES ASSOCIATED WITH EXISTING INVENTORY MANAGEMENT SYSTEMS

Nowadays, most industry players still use a manual system to manage their stock data. When stock arrives, they need to manually record each inventory item and seek available storage to load newly arrived inventories. By doing so, it will spend more time and effort recording this information. Thus, it will not be an effective way to manage their inventory information [1]. Besides, humans tend to make mistakes, especially if rushing. Suppose they need to correct a mistake in recording the inventory data. In that case, it will influence the inventory process in the warehouse, and the extra labour and time will be added to re-record it [5]. On the other hand, because producers need to have complete visibility of their stock information, they will make the wrong decision to spend more money to purchase more stocks in the warehouse [4]. Lastly, the redundant process is associated with warehouse management, which requires more time and people to record all the new arrival inventory information and search for the available slot to store these inventories [6].

There are some issues involved in existing inventory management systems, as discussed below:

- Existing inventory management systems do not manage the inventory exhaustively and smartly.
- Current inventory systems do not keep track of the current inventory state and location in real-time, especially when the new inventory arrives.
- These systems do not have a proper way to track and provide basic security in the warehouse.
- The existing system will not function unless the web server and the hardware devices are manually turned on.

- The existing system will not provide accurate and effective tracking of inventory movements, especially in the warehouse's multi-floor building or basement areas.
- Smartcard-based solutions require human intervention in every step, and it costs a lot of effort and time to manage the recording of the items.

Therefore, the current practices portray an ineffective way to manage the daily operations of inventory. Hence, there is tremendous scope for improvement in warehouse inventory management [11].

PROPOSED SYSTEM

There could be different ways to improve the tracking facility in the logistics of a warehouse. One of the suggestions in the tracking facility is to automate the transportation and provide a message notification to minimise human intervention and maintain safe and faster travel of goods [11]. Considering all the abovementioned factors, researchers have proposed an IoT-based system specifically designed to cater to the shortcomings of the existing inventory management systems.

Salient Features of the Proposed System

Using the proposed system, products can be quickly and more efficiently managed in the warehouse. The salient features of the proposed system are listed below:

- The system will not need human intervention to check the inventory status and manually record newly arrived inventory. It will endorse an effective monitoring and tracking process in the warehouse to get an extensive view of the inventory status.
- The system will provide a user-friendly interface for inventory tracking and monitoring by implementing an IoT-based solution. Using the IoT features, available store locations can be located in just one click.
- The system will display the status of inventory using different colours. A red circle will indicate that the store has a full stock of the inventory item. A green circle will determine that the item is out of stock, and a yellow circle will demonstrate that the store is partially filled with that item but is available to add more inventory.
- The system will record the inventory information effectively and efficiently according to the warehouse's inventory shipping routines and display the inventory information using a web-based application.

- The system will reduce the workload of users and overall cost by implementing analysis tools to determine the need to purchase or replenish warehouse items effectively and expand or rent extra storage to store the inventory.
- The system will allow the users to analyse inventory information to figure out best-seller items and the stocks that need quick replenishment.

User Roles In The Proposed System

Manufacturer

- To view complete inventory information in the warehouse.
- To view inventory status using various colours in each store.
- To track real-time inventory information according to inventory shipping in the warehouse.
- To send emails to the respective admin of a store regarding which stores need to be replenished after reviewing the inventory status in the warehouse.
- To receive real-time inventory feedback to specify inventory placement from admin or other manufacturers.

Administrator

- To register new staff and send emails for confirmation.
- To update staff information and send notification emails.
- To view complete inventory information in the warehouse.
- To send emails to other admins for inventory feedback regarding what needs to be purchased or replenished after reviewing the inventory status in the warehouse.
- To track real-time inventory information as per inventory shipping routes in the warehouse.
- To save inventory information and inventory condition and rename inventory stores in the system.
- To view inventory reports containing employee information, inventory information, and inventory feedback information.
- To search inventory information for a specific period.

Shopkeeper

- To register new staff in the system.
- To update staff information and send notification emails.
- To view complete inventory information in the warehouse.
- To send emails to other admins for inventory feedback regarding what needs to be purchased or replenished after reviewing the inventory status in the warehouse.

- To track real-time inventory information as per inventory shipping routes in the warehouse.
- To save inventory information, and inventory condition, and rename inventory store in the system.
- To view inventory reports containing employee information, inventory information, and inventory feedback information.
- To search inventory information for a specific period.

Proposed System Design

The proposed system should deploy the primary target users, manufacturers, administrators, and shopkeepers, to manage the inventory in the warehouse. It is a high-security web-based system that will protect user data and inventory information. Therefore, it must require the users to log in to the system using their username and password. Additionally, this system will automatically verify the username to navigate it to the webpage based on the role registered in the system. For instance, if a manufacturer logs in to the system, it will immediately navigate to the inventory dashboard page. On the other hand, if the admin or shopkeeper logs in to the system, it will navigate to the menu page to select the options: inventory dashboard page, registration, and report information. Moreover, it only allows the admin or shopkeeper to register new staff for the system.

The proposed system will connect with the hardware devices to receive the input data of the inventory information. It will read input from appropriate devices (using sensors) to count inventory items and identify the condition in the inventory container. The proposed system will display inventory information on an LCD screen. It will allow the user to save inventory information based on the information being displayed on the LCD screen. It will provide complete visibility of all warehouse stock items and allow users to monitor inventory information remotely.

The proposed system will show the inventory status, allowing the user to determine whether he needs to replenish or purchase the items in the following order. Users will receive an email after completing the registration or submitting the feedback information. The "Inventory Registration Notification" email will inform the new staff about the registration information after successfully registering them in the system. The system will then send an "Inventory Feedback Notification" email to the user after submitting the feedback information. It will update real-time inventory feedback notifications on the inventory dashboard webpage. Inventory feedback notifications will show the inventory details and the feedback particular to the user.

DATABASE DESIGN

Database Design is an assortment of processes that facilitate the development, planning, maintenance, and implementation of data management systems. Its main objective is to demonstrate the proposed system's logical and physical design models [12].

An ERD shows relationships of entity sets stored in a database and the attributes in these entities that define its properties [13]. It also illustrates a database's logical structure and design [14]. Fig. (**1**) represents the entity-relationship diagram (ERD) of the proposed system.

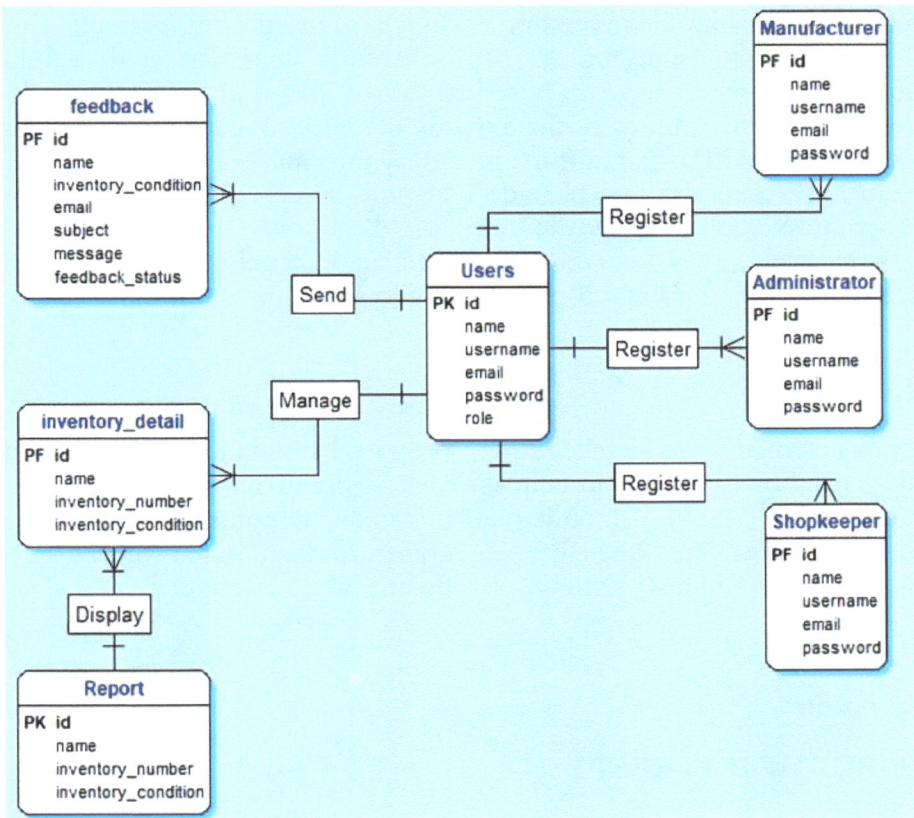

Fig. (1). ERD for Proposed Inventory Tracking & Monitoring System.

Implementation and Adoption Challenges

There are considerable challenges in introducing this system to the industry as they have used conventional methods to manage their inventory for decades. Following are some of the critical challenges in its implementation and adoption.

- Existing staff would be reluctant to use a new system to replace the current system that is well-conversant for them.
- The system interface should be user-friendly to provide an easy switch from the existing to a new application.
- In developing the proposed web-based application, security should be considered.
- The required IoT hardware must be compatible with other components already installed in the warehouse.

CONCLUSION

This paper has comprehensively discussed IoT application layers and recommended sensors for inventory tracking and monitoring systems. Emphasis has been given to applying IoT in inventory, logistics, and warehousing operations. Researchers have proposed an IoT-based system specifically designed to cater to the shortcomings of the existing inventory management systems. The proposed system will track real-time inventory information per inventory shipping routes in the warehouse and provide real-time inventory information based on inventory store conditions. Furthermore, it will not only identify available stores to reserve the newly arrived inventory and provide real-time feedback notifications to the user but will also be able to search inventory information for a specific period.

FUTURE ENHANCEMENTS

Some enhancements can be made to this proposed system as it can be extended to include more functionalities to help establish a more competitive advantage. It is recommended to develop a mobile platform and synchronise it with the proposed web-based system, enabling the target user to keep track of the inventory information in the industry more conveniently and effectively.

CONSENT FOR PUBLICATION

Not applicable.

CONFLICT OF INTEREST

The authors declare no conflict of interest, financial or otherwise.

ACKNOWLEDGEMENTS

The authors wish to express their sincere appreciation to the Asia Pacific University of Technology and Innovation (APU) for the opportunity to conduct the research.

REFERENCES

[1]　V. Khanzode and B. Shah, "A comprehensive review of warehouse operational issues," *Int. j. logist. syst. manag.,* vol. 26, no. 3, p. 346, 2017.

[2]　A. Stringfellow, "Warehouse inventory management: 20 experts reveal the #1 way companies can reduce and control warehouse inventory errors," *Camcode,* 02-Mar-2015. [Online]. Available: https://www.camcode.com/asset-tags/how-to-reduce-warehouse-inventory-errors. [Accessed: 01-Ap--2021]. https://www.camcode.com/asset-tags/how-to-reduce-warehouse-inventory-errors [Accessed: 01-Apr-2021]

[3]　K. Buntak, M. Kovačić, and M. Mutavdžija, "Internet of things and smart warehouses as the future of logistics," *Teh. glas.* (Online), vol. 13, no. 3, pp. 248–253, 2019.

[4]　F. Saleheen, M.H. Miraz, M.M. Habib, and Z. Hanafi, "Challenges of warehouse operations: A case study in retail supermarket", *International Journal of Supply Chain Management,* vol. 3, no. 4, pp. 63-67, 2014. [IJSCM].

[5]　A. C. Moore, "The top 5 warehouse management problems and solutions to fix them," *Business 2 Community,* 21-Oct-2016. [Online]. Available: https://www.business2community.com/product-management/top-5-warehouse-management-problems-solutions-fix-01684147 [Accessed: 01-Ap--2021]

[6]　D. Blanchard, *Supply Chain & Logistics: Top 5 Warehouse Challenges and How to Overcome Them.* 2017.

[7]　B. Sainathuni, P.J. Parikh, X. Zhang, and N. Kong, "The warehouse-inventory-transportation problem for supply chains", *Eur. J. Oper. Res.,* vol. 237, no. 2, pp. 690-700, 2014. [http://dx.doi.org/10.1016/j.ejor.2014.02.007]

[8]　A. Dolgui, and J.M. Proth, Warehouse management and design.*Supply Chain Engineering.* Useful Methods and Techniques, 2010, pp. 419-447. [http://dx.doi.org/10.1007/978-1-84996-017-5_11]

[9]　K. K. Patel and S. M. Patel, "Internet of things-IOT: definition, characteristics, architecture, enabling technologies, application & future challenges," *International journal of engineering science and computing,* vol. 6, no. 5, 2016.

[10]　M. Sankar, and K. Booba, *The usage of internet of things in transportation and logistic industry.* Intelligent Computing and Innovation on Data Science, 2020, pp. 431-438. [http://dx.doi.org/10.1007/978-981-15-3284-9_47]

[11]　S. Shah, M. Bolton, and S. Menon, "A study of internet of things (IoT) and its impacts on global supply chains", *2020 International Conference on Computation, Automation and Knowledge Management (ICCAKM),* 2020. [http://dx.doi.org/10.1109/ICCAKM46823.2020.9051474]

[12]　D.W. Chilson, and M.E. Kudlac, "Database design", *Data Base Adv. Inf. Syst.,* vol. 15, no. 1, pp. 11-19, 1983. [http://dx.doi.org/10.1145/1113500.1113502]

[13]　https://www.lucidchart.com/pages/ER-diagram-symbols-and-meaning [Accessed: 01-Apr-2021]

[14]　J. Garmany, J. Walker, and T. Clark, *Logical database design principles.* Auerbach: Philadelphia, PA, 2005. [http://dx.doi.org/10.1201/9780203505168]

[15]　Y. Cui, F. Liu, X. Jing, and J. Mu, "Integrating sensing and communications for ubiquitous IoT: Applications, trends, and challenges", *IEEE Netw.,* vol. 35, no. 5, pp. 158-167, 2021. [http://dx.doi.org/10.1109/MNET.010.2100152]

CHAPTER 4

Incorporate Artificial Intelligence into the Fitness Field to Curb Diabetes in Malaysia: Current and Future

Wong Xin Yi[1], Mien May Chong[1,*] and Sivaguru A/L Subarmaniyan[1]

[1] *School of Computing, Asia Pacific University of Technology and Innovation, Kuala Lumpur, Malaysia*

Abstract: With the rapid technological change, most people are living an unhealthy lifestyle and consuming processed food. Additionally, most people spend time on their mobile phones instead of working on other activities such as exercise. Beginners should have at least 2 to 3 days of working out per week, and the intermediate should have 3 to 4 days of strength training. A set of stretching exercises is required after each workout. Approximately 3.9 million people aged 18 and above are diagnosed with diabetes in Malaysia. This means that 1 in 5 adults will be diagnosed with diabetes. The prevalence rate has increased from 13.4% in 2015 to 18.3% in 2019. Some of the main factors that can cause a person to acquire diabetes are obesity and consuming excessive amounts of food with high sugar levels. The two types of diabetes are type 1 diabetes and type 2 diabetes. Type 1 diabetes results in the body not producing insulin, whereas type 2 diabetes causes the body to not respond to insulin even though it produces insulin.

Keywords: Artificial Intelligent, Diabetes, Exercise, Fitness, Live-Stream, Obesity.

INTRODUCTION

According to the Health line article [1], beginners should have at least 2 to 3 days of working out per week, and the intermediate should have 3 to 4 days of strength training. A set of stretching exercises is required after each workout.

Malaysia has a higher ranking in obesity among other Asian countries [2]. Within nine years since 2006, the obesity rate has increased from 11.6% to 17.5% in Malaysia. According to the World Health Organization WHO (2019) investigation, 64% of males and 65% of females in Malaysia are overweight or

* **Corresponding author Mien May Chong**: School of Computing, Asia Pacific University of Technology and Innovation, Kuala Lumpur, Malaysia; E-mail: mienmay@staffemail.apu.edu.my

Muhammad Ehsan Rana and Manoj Jayabalan (Eds.)

obese, putting them (mainly those aged 18 and above) in danger of becoming diabetes patients. Moreover, half of the people that fall under this category do not even know they are diagnosed with diabetes [3].

In 2018, Cilisos and Fitness First collaborated and researched why Malaysia had the highest number of obese citizens among all the Asian countries. A total of 3,779 respondents were in the survey from states all around Malaysia: Selangor (40.2%), Kuala Lumpur (25.6%), Penang (7.5%), Sarawak (5.2%), and Johor (4.2%). Almost half of the respondents were 21-29 years old. Expectedly, most people preferred to take the elevator over using the stairs. 33.3% of the respondents said their limit was three flights of stairs [2]. Most people who work in offices spend the entire time sitting during the workday, thus leading to physical and mental health issues [4].

Furthermore, approximately 3.9 million people aged 18 and above are diagnosed with diabetes in Malaysia. This means that 1 in 5 people will be diagnosed with diabetes. The prevalence rate has increased from 13.4% in 2015 to 18.3% in 2019 [5]. Some of the main factors that can cause a person to acquire diabetes are obesity and consuming excessive amounts of food with high sugar levels [6]. The two types of diabetes are type 1 diabetes and type 2 diabetes. Type 1 diabetes results in the body not producing insulin, whereas type 2 diabetes causes the body to not respond to insulin even though it produces insulin [7].

CURRENT SITUATION OF DIABETES CARE IN MALAYSIA

To diminish the case, the Malaysian government introduced the '*Enhanced Primary Health Care (EnPHC)* project in July 2017. The project aims to raise awareness/exposure regarding chronic diseases. Approximately 20 health clinics are located in the Johor and Selangor area. The project requires the citizens to register at the clinic so the track of the population is recorded in the database [3]. However, not all the states in Malaysia have the *ENPHC* health care clinic implemented, such as Negeri Sembilan. Therefore, a fitness monitoring system will be developed to raise awareness of fitness for diabetes.

Countries worldwide have been experiencing the COVID-19 pandemic since the beginning of the year 2020. People need to practice social distancing to prevent the spread of COVID-19 (coronavirus). Actions such as sneezing, coughing, or even close contact can result in a healthy person being infected [8]. Due to the pandemic, fitness centres are forced to close until further notice. Hence, a growing number of e-fitness have come into the market. Examples include following workouts from online conference software like Microsoft Teams and Zoom (Lufkin, 2020). The system will develop a recorded workout video and a live workout session to ensure users can exercise from within their homes. This will be done so that individuals will only struggle and practice exercises if they visit physical fitness centres. Nevertheless, this is still the start of the project research, and the result may vary depending on the functional and non-functional considerations.

Technologies Used in Current Diabetes Care

With the rapid advancement of technology, it is no surprise that it is being used in the diabetic field. There are two main categories: insulin administered by a syringe, pen, or pump and blood glucose monitoring assessed by a meter or continuous glucose monitor. UtilizinUtilisinginge and pen is the safest method for people with diabetes to test the glycemic target [9]. An insulin pen allows the user to administer insulin to the body. The two types of pens are disposable pens and reusable pens. A disposable pen has a prefilled insulin cartridge. This means that once the diabetes patient has finished up the insulin from the disposable pen, the whole pen unit is rendered useless and can be disposed of. On the other hand, a reusable pen has a replaceable insulin cartridge. This means that even if the diabetic patient uses insulin, it is possible to replace the cartridge with a new one.

For hygiene purposes, once the replaceable insulin tube is finished, the patient should discard the needle and replace it with a new disposable one. This allows for more prolonged insulin pen usage and improves the patient's health [10]. The hardware, devices, and software not only manage the blood glucose level but also improve the diabetic's quality of life. This is helpful as patients have to be cautious due to their weaker immune systems [9]. Recently, the technology used regarding diabetes has transformed into a hybrid device that allows the user to monitor glucose and provide insulin simultaneously. At the same time, medical-related devices and software will be tracking them along with allocating diabetes self-management support for better accuracy detection. Additionally, there are more complex and smarter devices that can help further improve the lives of diabetics [9]. For example, the smart insulin pen, a combination of the vial and syringe, can record the dose usage and timing with the push-button injection, ultimately saving the diabetic patient much time.

Problems and Solutions: Why do we have diabetes?

Diabetes always appears in our lives for some reason.

Lack of Exercise and Unhealthy Lifestyles

To avoid getting diagnostic diabetes, exercise and consuming a balanced diet are key factors. However, most people are busy with their hectic lifestyles, causing them to depend on fast/processed food which is unhealthy and increases the chances of getting diabetes. To prevent this, the fitness monitoring management system educates users on the consequences of being unfit and guides them in practising the correct workout posture. Exercising with the proper posture is essential, as not doing so may lead to injuries and result in adverse effects on the spine [11], such as joint imbalance and muscle pain. Moreover, according to the Harvard Medical School [12], exercise helps to decrease blood pressure, serious LDL cholesterol, and triglycerides while maintaining the person's weight on a healthy scale. This strengthens the body's conditions for bones and muscles and helps decrease blood glucose levels whilst simultaneously increasing the body's sensitivity against insulin.

The Lack of an Exercise Routine

From a physiological perspective, if a person wishes to adopt a good habit, there is a theory of doing and repeating the same behaviour for 21 days. This is habit formation. When the habit transformation is in progress (automation), the mind will try to adjust accordingly and attempt to determine the new style of habit [13]. A well-planned 21-day routine is necessary to encourage users to exercise and use the system. However, most people are busy with their schedules, so they barely have any time to work out, as most of their free time is spent on entertainment. A way to remedy this is by using push-up notifications to remind people of their priorities.

RELATIONSHIP BETWEEN DIABETES, ARTIFICIAL INTELLIGENCE (AI) AND FITNESS

As technology improves, artificial intelligence has successfully proven to prevent much pain in patients that used to be a problem. Artificial intelligence and smart medical devices allow professionals to get better ideas for managing chronic diseases [14]. The application of artificial intelligence in the medical field benefits the industry and enhances the quality of life [15]. Some modern machine learning systems are trained to recognise essential variables from unstructured datasets such as video and image datasets [16]. The application of AI in medical science is a low-cost, high-coverage, efficient, and portable technology. It allows experts to judge the symptoms by reading the AI records [15]. Additionally, diabetes mellitus, the glucose homeostasis dysfunction, is the most critical prevalent chronic disease proven to be a big issue for doctors. According to research from Contreras and Vehi [14], when entering the keywords artificial intelligence (AI) and diabetes, the number of research papers matching the criteria in the Google Scholar database is increasing rapidly, as shown in Fig. (**1**).

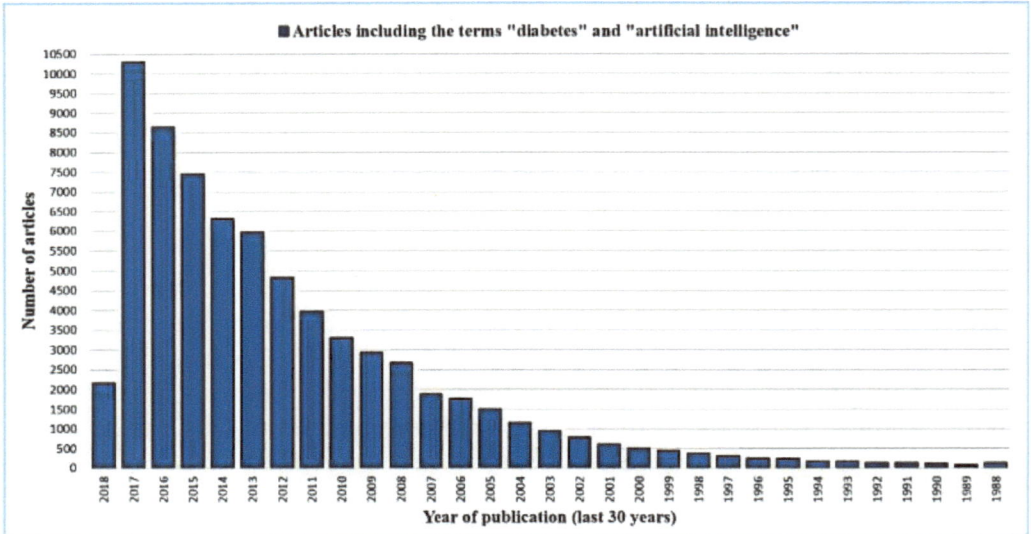

Fig. (1). AI and diabetes papers matching rate in Google Scholar [14].

From the analysis above, researchers have assessed that the concern about diabetes and artificial intelligence is becoming popular. Many individuals or groups want to apply AI technology to solve current life-threatening issues [14]. Moreover, this massive growth includes records and information that could help enhance the performance of intelligent methodologies in dealing with valuable resources in the database. The data is practical to be adequate and strengthen the beneficial management of complex diseases like cancer and diabetes. The glucose monitoring device and the artificial pancreas are the two main tools that allow professionals to collect data by implementing artificial intelligence. Doctors use AI to process refined and difficult understanding methods for diabetes patients. Hence, AI plays a critical role in studying records. AI can learn automatically without any assistance from humans [14]. AI studies knowledge with intelligent behaviour. The more data the AI studies, the less noise in the data, thus producing a more accurate solution. Fig. (2) is a general diagram of how the AI processes the learning algorithm.

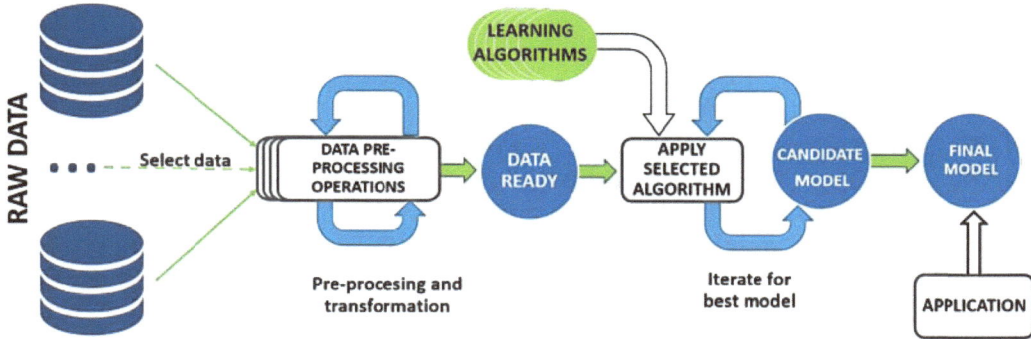

Fig. (2). How the learning algorithm is being processed by AI [14].

Based on the study by Contreras and Vehi [14], blood glucose control strategy, blood glucose prediction, detection of adverse glycemic events, insulin bolus calculators and advisory system, risk and patient personalisation, detection of means, exercise and faults, the lifestyle and daily-life support in diabetes management are the diabetes management topics that utilise the AI technology. For example, when it comes to insulin therapy for diabetes, the insulin bolus calculator advisory system can recommend, measure, and plan the suggested insulin dose for the patient. Moreover, the AI in the system might even be smart enough to support the patient with advice on meal intake, exercise, or medication [14, 17].

Use of AI in the Fitness field

Regular physical exercise can improve the control of blood glucose and prevent/postpone the patient from developing type 2 diabetes [18]. Countries and organisations such as the American College of Sports Medicine and the World Health Organization (WHO) have done science-based research on the guidelines for all ages to practice exercise and working out. Apart from age classification, the research also focused on other dimensions, such as intensity, factors of transportation, and occupation [18]. Once the research was completed, it was shown that the average person should have a minimum of 150 minutes of moderate-intensity aerobic physical activity per week; a minimum of 75 minutes of vigorous exercise for adults.

Based on theory, a long-term exercise plan that you can remain consistent with plays an important role in biological evolution [19]. According to de Moraes Lopes *et al.* (2020), despite AI not being used much in the fitness area, a study has shown that current technology in the market, such as information technology and sensor technology with smart devices, are likely leaning towards the application of AI. Since much information about fitness and AI is being collected, it will be informative on the mining [20]. A recommended system with artificial intelligence is found getting used in the fitness field. Said system is applied to provide suggestions for users (both beginners and existing users) by learning, analysing, and predicting the user's activity [21]. Researchers tend to use suggesting and artificial intelligence in the fitness field as the AI can learn the knowledge required quickly. Furthermore, using AI, the recommendation engine can generate more accurate suggestions to create harmony with the user and encourage them to utilise the system more frequently.

AI and Fitness: For Future Diabetes

Understanding the relationship between the use of ess can help experts warn healthy people, preventing them from getting diabetes. Therefore, a lifestyle, such as a person's physical activity, must be calculated. Proper exercise helps to control the blood sugar level and reduce the risk of the cardiovascular events [15]. According to the machine learning statistic, type 2 diabetes patients benefit from healthy lifestyle choices that can help stabilise the patient. Additionally, a healthy person can decrease the risk of becoming a diabetic by consistently doing proper workout activities [15, 22]. To test whether the concept was workable, Jacobs *et al.* [23] suggested a regression model with integrated machine learning to automatically analyse each patient's exercise level. Patients wore an accelerometer during this research. All records of the patients' patients and glucose levels while exercising were saved. At the end of the research, the 13 type 1 diabetes patients had a sensitivity of 97.2% accuracy (as cited by [15]).

AI can be adopted more in the future with the control of an algorithm known as the reinforcement algorithm. This could ensure that only the informative data is listed and that all the fuzzy designs are not shown. If the algorithm has higher accuracy, the diabetes management system can provide more optimised components for diabetes patients and help them focus more on diabetes therapy. Currently, the diabetes management system can only monitor the basics of the recording, such as diet, physical activity, medication, glucose measurement, and insulin consumption. Many researchers and developers are continuously making more tools and technologies to improve daily-life support for patients. As a result, a more complex -related technology will allow patients to manage their diabetes more easily.

Survey: Result and Discussion

It is essential to determine a suitable research method for a project for calculating measures and wants regarding the proposed system. Moreover, selecting an appropriate research method for gathering data and summarising the requirements of the participants allow both the researcher and reader to understand the research better. The following will be the survey result obtained during the investigation. A total of hundred and twenty-nine (129) responses were received, and the average time for the participants to fill out the form was 09:23 minutes. Microsoft Forms was the primary tool being utilised and distributed for the questionnaire research study.

Malaysia is one of the countries with the most diabetes patients in the world. The collected data in Fig. (3) shows that 64% of the participants are aware of said fact. 47% of the participants do not know about it, showing that most people are up-t--date with the news. Fig. (4) shows how frequently the participant practices physical activity. A Likert scale of 5 has been implemented for this question. On a scale of lowest to highest, the majority of the participants do not exercise, and the average number shown is not even half of five (5); the result for this question has an average number of two point four eight (2.48).

5. Are you aware of Malaysia is one of the countries who has the most diabetes patient?

More Details

- Yes   82
- No   47

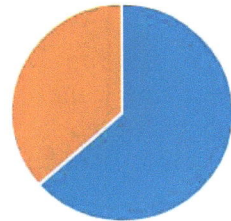

Fig. (3). Survey on Public Awareness Rate towards Diabetes in Malaysia.

9. On a scale of lowest to highest, how often do you exercise?

More Details

129
Responses

2.48
Average Number

Fig. (4). Identify how frequently the participant practices physical activity.

The question in Fig. (**5**) asked the respondents their satisfaction level from the lowest (very dissatisfied) to the highest (very satisfied), regarding the questions listed. For the first sub-question, 44.2% claimed they were confident with the online workout tutorial, 37.2% chose to stay neutral on the sub-question, 7.8% were delighted, 6.2% said they were not satisfied, and 4.7 were very dissatisfied with the online tutorial. The second sub-question in Fig. (**5**) asked if the respondents would accept the proposed live-streaming function. 41.9% of the respondents chose 'satisfied', 44.2% chose to be neutral, 5.4% chose 'satisfied', and 3.1% and 5.4% of the respondents chose 'dissatisfied' and 'very dissatisfied' on the suggested feature.

16. On a scale of lowest to highest...

More Details

■ Very Dissatisfied   ■ Dissatisfied   ▣ Neither Dissatisfied nor Satisfied   ■ Satisfied   ■ Very Satisfied

How is your experience with following the workout session/tutorial online?

How much can you accept the livestream workout with me function as a motivation for you to keep...

100%   0%   100%

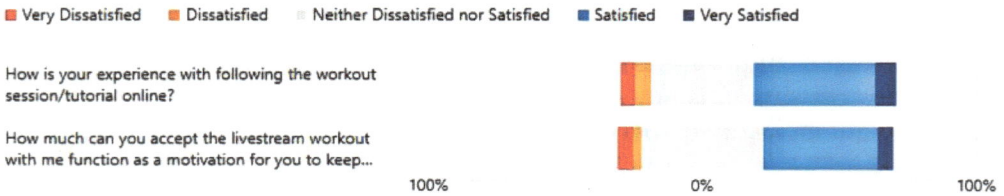

Fig. (5). Public satisfactory level towards the previous online exercise experiences.

Fig. (**6**) is a multi-selection question. Respondents could choose more than one answer as per their wish. From the statistic shown, YouTube is the most popular platform for workout tutorials, with a hundred and eighteen (118) votes, followed by Instagram with twenty-eight (28) votes, Others with twenty-six (26) votes, and Facebook with twenty-four (24) votes. The least amount of votes was for Twitch and Clubhouse, with four (4) and one (1) vote(s) for each. The results were understandable as YouTube has features to attract users to visit the site when they want to have workout sessions. The question in Fig. (**7**) asks to identify the features the respondents would like to see in the future; it is an open-ended question. Sixty-three (63) respondents answered this question, while the rest decided to skip it and proceed to submit. A word cloud is generated for researchers to distinguish the most mentioned words and repeated keywords suggested by the respondents.

12. Which platform you mostly visit for workout tutorials? (you can choose more than one)

More Details

YouTube	118
Twitch	4
Instagram	28
Clubhouse	1
Facebook	24
Others	26

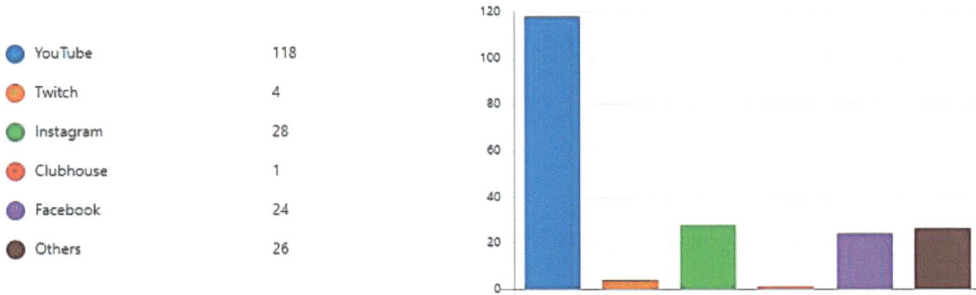

Fig. (6). Identify the public's most visited platform for workout tutorials.

22. What kind of feature you would wish to see in the web application / future?

More Details

63
Responses

Latest Responses

"1 tot 1 session would be better because it is hard for trainee to see if you are ...

"More interaction. Better connectivity "

"Nutrient recommendations"

Fig. (7). Identify the public requirement for future application.

CONCLUSION

An increasing amount of people have concerns about the chronic disease diabetes because it is rather difficult to endure. Luckily, artificial intelligence is now widely used in the medical field. Diabetes patients can take advantage of this and contribute records for better AI improvement with significant consideration of all the emerging areas, including artificial intelligence, diabetes, and fitness, as recorded in this paper.

CONSENT FOR PUBLICATION

Not applicable.

CONFLICT OF INTEREST

The authors declare no conflict of interest, financial or otherwise.

ACKNOWLEDGEMENTS

The authors wish to express their sincere appreciation to the Asia Pacific University of Technology and Innovation (APU) for the opportunity to conduct the research.

REFERENCES

[1]   S. Lindberg, *How Often Should You Work Out?,* 2020. https://www.healthline.com/health/how-often-should-you-work-out [Accessed: 25-Jun-2021]

[2]   CILISOS, "MALAYSIANS ARE THE FATTEST IN ASIA. AND THIS SURVEY WILL TELL YOU WHY," 2018. [Online]. Available: https://cilisos.my/survey-results-hoho-guess-why-17-5-of-malaysian-men-go-to-gyms/ [Accessed: 25-Jun-2021]

[3]   World Health Organization, "Malaysia and WHO call for more investment in primary health care the 21st century," 2019. [Online]. Available: https://www.who.int/malaysia/news/detail/08-04-20-9-malaysia-and-who-call-for-more-investment-in-primary-health-care-the-21st-century [Accessed: 25-Jun-2021]

[4]   S. Dewitt, J. Hall, L. Smith, J.P. Buckley, S.J.H. Biddle, L. Mansfield, and B. Gardner, "Office workers' experiences of attempts to reduce sitting-time: an exploratory, mixed-methods uncontrolled intervention pilot study", *BMC Public Health,* vol. 19, no. 1, p. 819, 2019. [http://dx.doi.org/10.1186/s12889-019-7196-0] [PMID: 31238902]

[5]   *The first-ever Malaysian diabetes index survey uncovers awareness gaps on diabetes amongst Malaysians*   .https://www.astrazeneca.com/country-sites/malaysia/press-releases/the-first--ver-malaysian-diabetes-index-survey-uncovers-awareness.html [Accessed: 21-Jun-2021]

[6]   J.F. Ndisang, A. Vannacci, and S. Rastogi, *Insulin resistance, type 1 and type 2 diabetes, and related complications 2017.* Hindawi, 2017. [http://dx.doi.org/10.1155/2017/1478294]

[7]   C. O'Keefe Osborn, *Type 1 and Type 2 Diabetes: What's the Difference?,* 2020 .https://www.healthline.com/health/difference-between-type-1-and-type-2-diabetes [Accessed: 25-Ju--2021]

[8]   "N. Cone Health- Greensboro", *Social Distancing FAQ: How It Helps Prevent COVID-19 (Coronavirus), and Steps We Can Take to Protect Ourselves,* 2021 .https://www.conehealth.com/services/primary-care/socia--distancing-faq-how-it-helps-prevent-covid-19-coronavirus-/ [Accessed: 25-Jun-2021]

[9]   American Diabetes Association, "7. Diabetes Technology: Standards of Medical Care in Diabetes{\textemdash}2020," *Diabetes Care,* vol. 43, no. Supplement 1, pp. S77--S88, 2020.

[10]   A. Felman, and P.D. Alan Carter, *What are insulin pens and how do we use them?,* 2019 .https://www.medicalnewstoday.com/articles/316607 [Accessed: 25-Jun-2021]

[11]   D. Kim, M. Cho, Y. Park, and Y. Yang, "Effect of an exercise program for posture correction on musculoskeletal pain", *J. Phys. Ther. Sci.,* vol. 27, no. 6, pp. 1791-1794, 2015. [http://dx.doi.org/10.1589/jpts.27.1791] [PMID: 26180322]

[12]   "Harvard Health", *The Importance Of Exercise When You Have Diabetes - Harvard Health,* 2020 .https://www.health.harvard.edu/staying-healthy/the-importance-of-exercise-when-y-u-have-diabetes#:~:text=Exercise [Accessed: 25-Jun-2021]

[13]   J. Kingston, "Engagement and habit formation in the classroom", *TEACH Journal of Christian Education,* vol. 13, no. 1, p. 3, 2019.
[http://dx.doi.org/10.55254/1835-1492.1411]

[14]   I. Contreras, and J. Vehi, "Artificial intelligence for diabetes management and decision support: literature review", *J. Med. Internet Res.,* vol. 20, no. 5, 2018.e10775
[http://dx.doi.org/10.2196/10775] [PMID: 29848472]

[15]   J. Li, J. Huang, L. Zheng, and X. Li, "Application of Artificial Intelligence in Diabetes Education and Management: Present Status and Promising Prospect", *Front. Public Health,* vol. 8, no. May, p. 173, 2020.
[http://dx.doi.org/10.3389/fpubh.2020.00173] [PMID: 32548087]

[16]   D.T. Broome, C.B. Hilton, and N. Mehta, "Policy Implications of Artificial Intelligence and Machine Learning in Diabetes Management", *Curr. Diab. Rep.,* vol. 20, no. 2, p. 5, 2020.
[http://dx.doi.org/10.1007/s11892-020-1287-2] [PMID: 32008107]

[17]   T. Zhu, K. Li, L. Kuang, P. Herrero, and P. Georgiou, "An Insulin Bolus Advisor for Type 1 Diabetes Using Deep Reinforcement Learning", *Sensors (Basel),* vol. 20, no. 18, p. 5058, 2020.
[http://dx.doi.org/10.3390/s20185058] [PMID: 32899979]

[18]   E. Anderson, and J.L. Durstine, "Physical activity, exercise, and chronic diseases: A brief review", *Sports Medicine and Health Science,* vol. 1, no. 1, pp. 3-10, 2019.
[http://dx.doi.org/10.1016/j.smhs.2019.08.006] [PMID: 35782456]

[19]   O. Kuzenkov, A. Morozov, and G. Kuzenkova, "Exploring evolutionary fitness in biological systems using machine learning methods", *Entropy (Basel),* vol. 23, no. 1, p. 35, 2020.
[http://dx.doi.org/10.3390/e23010035] [PMID: 33383722]

[20]   M. H. B. de Moraes Lopes, D. D. Ferreira, A. C. B. H. Ferreira, G. R. da Silva, A. S. Caetano, and V. N. Braz, "Chapter 20 - Use of artificial intelligence in precision nutrition and fitness," D. B. T.-A. I. in P. H. Barh, Ed. Academic Press, 2020, pp. 465–496.

[21]   T.T. Tran, J.W. Choi, C. Van Dang, G. Supark, J.Y. Baek, and J.W. Kim, "Recommender System with Artificial Intelligence for Fitness Assistance System", *2018 15th Int. Conf. Ubiquitous Robot. UR,* 2018 pp. 489-492.

[22]   A. Baum, J. Scarpa, E. Bruzelius, R. Tamler, S. Basu, and J. Faghmous, *Targeting weight loss interventions to reduce cardiovascular complications of type 2 diabetes: a machine learning-based post-hoc analysis of heterogeneous treatment effects in the Look AHEAD trial,* 2017.

[23]   P.G. Jacobs, N. Resalat, J. El Youssef, R. Reddy, D. Branigan, N. Preiser, J. Condon, and J. Castle, "Incorporating an exercise detection, grading, and hormone dosing algorithm into the artificial pancreas using accelerometry and heart rate", *J. Diabetes Sci. Technol.,* vol. 9, no. 6, pp. 1175-1184, 2015.
[http://dx.doi.org/10.1177/1932296815609371] [PMID: 26438720]

CHAPTER 5

An RSA-based Secure E-hailing Application

Loo Jun Hao[1,*], **Nik Sakinah Nik Ab Aziz**[1] and **Nik Nurul Ain Nik Suki**[1]

[1] *School of Computing and Technology, Asia Pacific University of Technology and Innovation, Kuala Lumpur, Malaysia*

Abstract: E-hailing and taxi services play a vital role in the transportation industry. It inadvertently also provides opportunities for malicious hackers to hack into e-hailing applications to gain private user information. With the increase in data breaches, there is a need for an encryption technique to increase the security level and assure the safety of users' data. This study proposed SafeCar, a secure e-hailing application using the RSA algorithm. SafeCar is developed using ASP.NET language. Testing has been done to evaluate the security, input validation, and user satisfaction. The testing results showed that 50% had a very good security level, another 50% with a good security level, 100% user satisfaction, and 67% had very good input validation, with another 33% resulting in good input validation.

Keywords: e-hailing, Encryption, RSA, Security.

INTRODUCTION

Reconnaissance, or recon, is the first and most crucial step for penetration testing or security research. Limited or inaccurate data would lead to the wrong direction in later phases of attack, such as scanning or gaining access, hence the saying, "time spent on reconnaissance is seldom wasted". Reconnaissance is not only for cyber security researchers; privacy-focused users often gather their personal information, also known as a digital footprint, to see if it is exposed to the public. Moreover, they can occasionally check if websites like Haveibeenpwned have breached their accounts. In short, reconnaissance is getting more attention and is easily accessible as online activities have started to become more active. Some initial information gathered in the reconnaissance stage is breached credentials and digital footprints. Breached credentials, especially those not encrypted or hashed, are shortcuts for attackers and the biggest threat to account owners. This is because further reconnaissance and enumeration will not be needed anymore to gain unauthorised access to their accounts. However, in most cases, additional

* **Corresponding author Loo Jun Hao**: School of Computing and Technology, Asia Pacific University of Technology and Innovation, Kuala Lumpur, Malaysia; E-mail: TP045107@mail.apu.edu.my

Muhammad Ehsan Rana and Manoj Jayabalan (Eds.)

information is required to launch an attack successfully. This is where digital footprint recon comes into place. Looking for traces of an individual or organisation left online allows for a broader range of attacks to be launched. For example, gaining information like the working location or friends of the target on social networks allows social engineering to be undertaken. Specific exploits can be launched if the attacker gains mobile device information of the target by searching which platform (Twitter for iOS or Twitter for Android) the target used to send out tweets on Twitter. These are just some examples of how little pieces of information can be gathered to widen the attacking choices of the attacker and the risk exposed to every internet user. Thus, having a tool to automatically collect both digital footprint and breached credentials from several sources would provide convenience to professionals and novice users.

The developer proposed the tool mentioned above that allows users to gather digital footprints from Facebook and Twitter, as well as breach the status of target users with both CLI and GUI.

MATERIALS AND METHODS

Materials required for the project include programming language and libraries used to develop the proposed solution. Python is the chosen programming language, as it is easy to learn and implement and has extensive libraries, including the ones needed for this tool, as shown in Table **1**.

Table 1. Libraries and their purposes.

Library	Purpose
Requests, Beautifulsoup	Scrape information from Facebook and breach checking the website
Tweepy	Work with Twitter API to gather Twitter data
Xlsxwriter	Export gathered data to an Excel file
Argparse	Configure commands and parameters used in CLI
Tkinter	Develop GUI

INFORMATION GATHERING METHODS

Three commonly used methods to gather data from websites are web scraping, API, and browser automation.

Web scraping is also known as web harvesting or data mining. It is a technique to gather desired data by sending HTTP requests, sanitising received HTTP responses, and extracting essential data.

API is known as Application Programming Interface. It is the same as web scraping because both retrieve website data by sending HTTP requests. The difference is that APIs return fetched data in a well-formatted way, usually in JSON or XML format. In contrast, web scraping requires an extra step to sanitise or parse HTTP response to remove unwanted HTML elements, leaving only the desired data [1].

Surveys such as that conducted by [2] on one retail store, TS Stores, showed that out-of-stock issues have caused between 8% and 22% of expected sales of promotional products to be lost. Two of the branches managed by Kim Soon Lee suffered from lost sales amounted to about US $75,000. Previous studies have reported that out-of-stock products can affect a customer's satisfaction with the retailer [3]. If consumers are dissatisfied with a hypermarket, they may be prone to switch their regular store to another. Therefore, hypermarkets may lose their loyal customers and sales opportunities.

Browser automation is used to automate browser activities, such as filling out a form, entering data in a textbox, clicking buttons on a webpage, and so on [2]. The same technique can be used to scrape data from websites. Instead of users who are controlling the browser, the bot or script is the one that automates the predefined user actions on the browser.

However, only **Web scraping and API** are used to gather data as browser automation gathers data significantly slower yet makes no significant difference in the comprehensiveness of data.

Web scraping guarantees the speed of information gathering without compromising much on the comprehensiveness of data. Since it is prone to webpage or HTML structure changes, API can be used to balance out such a risk. On the other hand, web scraping can cover the downside of API's rate limit.

Therefore, both techniques are used to complement each other. Web scraping is used to extract breach status and Facebook data, whereas API is used to extract Twitter data.

SOFTWARE DEVELOPMENT METHODOLOGY

The spiral model was chosen as the software methodology to develop the proposed system. It is a risk-driven iterative development method that loops through four major phases in every cycle: planning, risk analysis, development and testing, and evaluation, as shown in Fig. (**1**).

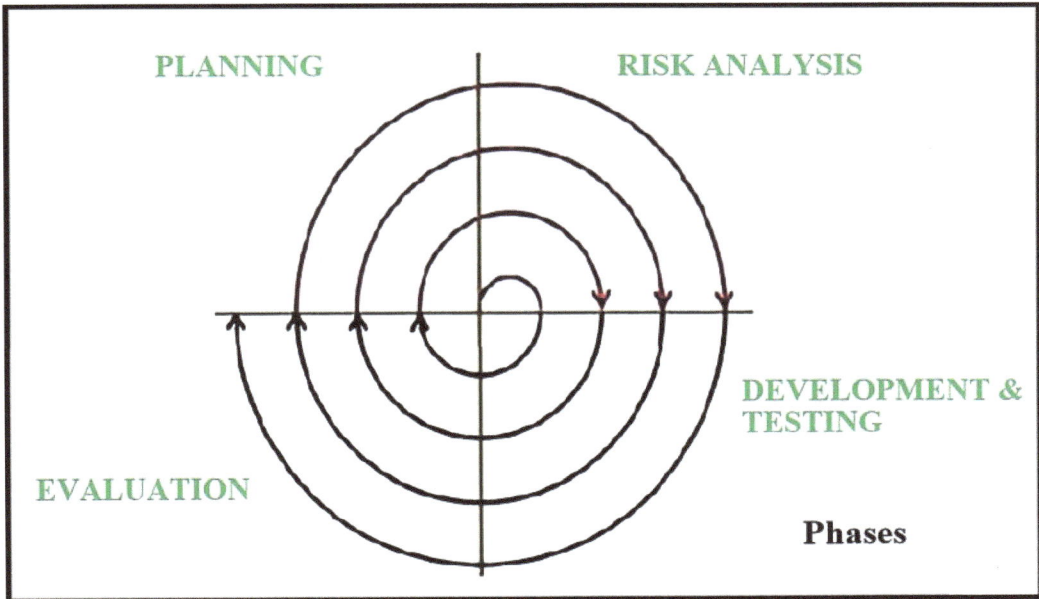

Fig. (1). Spiral model.

The planning phase gathers system requirements and then analyses if it is feasible in terms of budget, resources, and time.

The risk analysis phase identifies potential risks associated with the system and formulates plans to mitigate or reduce the anticipated risks.

The development and testing phase only develops the functionalities decided in the planning phase. Unlike the waterfall model, the spiral model does not produce all the system functions as it is an iterative development method.

Evaluation phase checks if the objective set in the planning phase has been achieved. The end of the evaluation phase only marks the end of a cycle instead of a project. Development of other functions or improvements will be started in subsequent cycles [3].

Two reasons for choosing the spiral model are **flexibility and stability.**

In terms of flexibility, the Spiral model allows changes to be made to the system at any development phase due to its iterative nature. It is hard to predict how much time each function needs to develop successfully. Some of the functions might be developed quicker than expected. In that case, the spiral model allows extra functions to be added. As opposed to other software development methodologies like the waterfall model, functions are being developed one-shot. Any changes to the system might require a considerable rework, which is very costly in terms of time and resources.

Stability-wise, the proposed system is made up of three core functions, which are data gathering, filtering, and exporting. Every function is dependent on the other. Gathering inaccurate data would mean that the filtering and exporting process will be useless, which is simply what garbage in, garbage out means [4]. Therefore, developing and testing each function individually is safer before starting another phase to ensure that it does not affect other functions in the later stages.

RESEARCH METHODS

Observation, interviews, and surveys are the three most frequently used primary research methods. Interviews and surveys are often mistaken for each other. The significant difference between the two is that interviews involve a conversation between the interviewer and interviewee. In contrast, surveys only require respondents to answer the pre-defined questions on a questionnaire [5].

Observation is omitted from the list of choices as it is best used for research that aims to understand user behaviour. However, identifying user behaviour in this project provides less value and insight into the study. For example, it is hard to know whether respondents want to be notified in the case of a data breach by just observing them. Contrary to surveys, this can be easily determined with straightforward questions.

As for interviews and surveys, the latter is chosen due to their efficiency. Online surveys can be completed anytime and anywhere, which is convenient for respondents, whereas participants must reserve their time for interviews. Therefore, according to a research of 1781 respondents, the preferred research method is online surveys [6]. In another study, out of 1542 respondents, 1121 or 72%, preferred online and mailed surveys. Those who opposed this method are participants in the age group over 60, which will not be the targeted users of the proposed system [7]. Thus, surveys are used for primary research as it serves the same purpose as interviews but are more efficient and convenient.

Findings from the survey suggested that the proposed system is necessary (Fig. **2**).

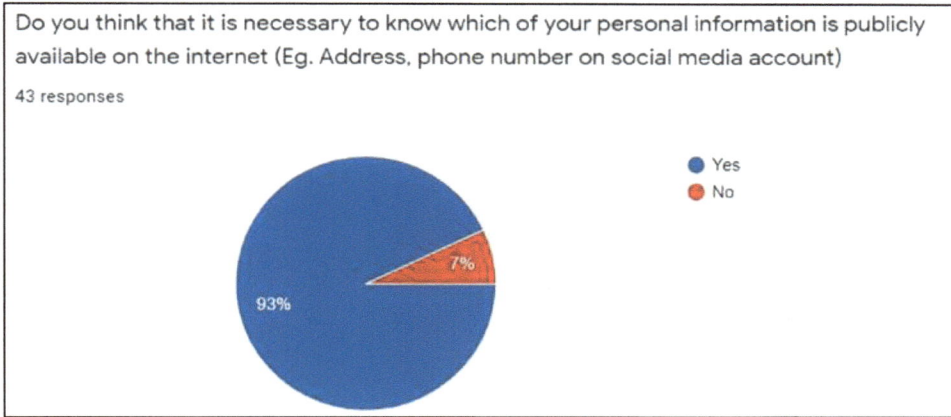

Fig. (2). Result for question 5.

Of 43 respondents, 93% and 98% said it is necessary to know their publicly available information and account breach status, respectively (Fig. **3**). This indicates that the proposed solution is purposeful.

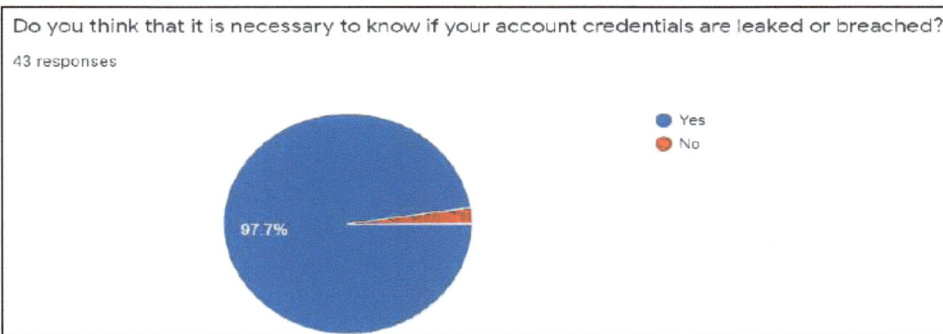

Fig. (3). Result for question 7.

Moreover, it was found that 56% of the respondents have yet to hear of or have the experience of using the digital footprint gathering tool (Fig. **4**). The same applies to the breach status-checking tool, where 47% of the respondents had no experience or idea of such a tool (Fig. **5**). This proves the necessity of having the proposed system provide an additional option to internet users for easier access to reconnaissance.

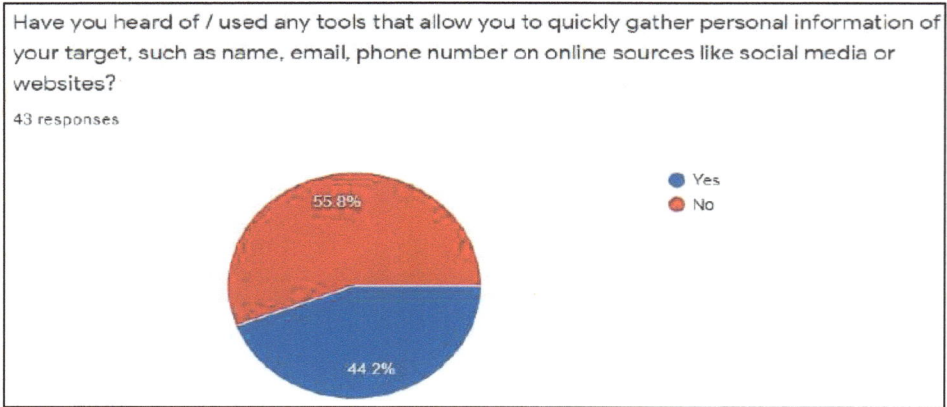

Fig. (4). Result for question 4.

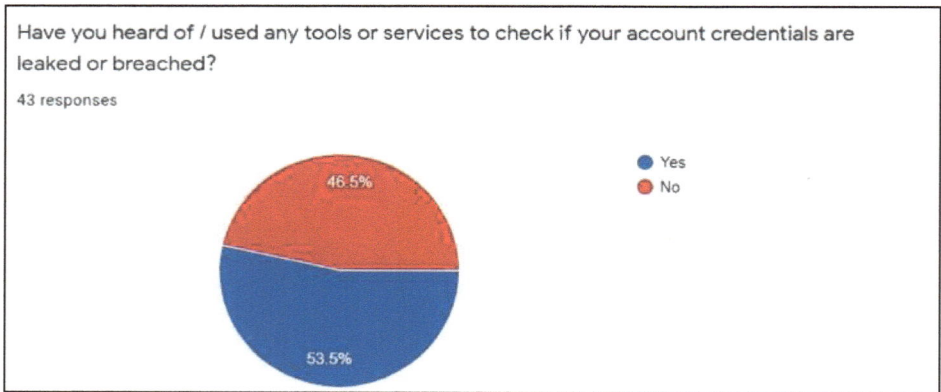

Fig. (5). Result for question 8.

From the survey, participants have chosen speed and comprehensiveness of gathered information as the two most important features of the proposed recon tool. Furthermore, GUI is the preferred way to interact with the system. These user preferences are helpful in system development stages where emphasis can be put on the most requested functions according to users' needs.

SIMILAR WORKS

The focus of these similar works is to obtain features to gather digital footprint, collect breached credentials, and export the result in Excel format.

Table 2. Existing Tools Searching Username.

Tool/Service	Data Gathered	Data size	Export to Excel	Interface	Review
Userrecon (by issamelferkh)	User social media accounts	Searches 75 platforms	No	CLI	Working
Checkusernames (checkusernames.com)	User web services accounts	Searches 160 platforms	No	Website	Working
Sherlock (by sherlock-project)	User accounts	Not mentioned on GitHub website but upon my testing, username is checked against 141 sources	Yes	CLI	Script stopped working at the 141th data source check
Social mapper (by Greenwolf)	User social media accounts	Searches user account on LinkedIn, Facebook, Twitter, Google+, Instagram, Vkontakte, Weibo, Douban	Yes	CLI	Working

Table **2** shows a list of existing tools that provide features to perform a search on the same usernames of any accounts. A decent tool should be able to collect in-depth and more comprehensive data on the target. We can conclude that not much PII could be derived from most of the tools above.

Table 3. Facebook Recon Tool.

Tool/Service	Technique	Data Gathered	Export to Excel	Interface	Review
Ultimate Facebook Scraper (by harismuneer)	Web scraping	1. Profile data 2. User friends 3. User posts 4. User photo 5. Facebook page 6. Facebook group	Yes	CLI	Not tested as this is a paid tool

(Table 3) cont.....

Facebook-scraper (by kevinzg)	Web scraping	Facebook posts on public pages	No	Python Library	1. Only works on public Facebook pages. 2. Unable to scrape posts from Facebook profiles
FaceBook-Scraper (by apurvmishra99)	Selenium – Browser Automation	Facebook posts on public pages and groups	Yes	CLI	Not working. Nothing happened after executing the script
Non-API-FaceBook-Scraper (by LeviBorodenko)	Selenium-Browser Automation	Facebook posts on public pages	Yes	CLI	Working
Facebook Page Post Scraper (by minimaxir)	Facebook API	Facebook posts in public pages that also include data like: 1. Reactions 2. Comments 3. Shares	No	CLI	Not working. The script could only work if the user has access to Facebook API
FBLYZE (by isaacmg)			Yes	Python library	1. The script is built based on Facebook Page Post Scraper by minimaxir. 2. Not working. The script could only work if user has access to Facebook API

Table **3** represents the findings of the Facebook Recon Tool. The common limitation of the scripts above is that only Facebook posts from public pages and groups can be gathered, and none of the tools above offers GUI as an option. Moreover, some advanced features are not free and require additional costs.

Most tools provide CLI compared to GUI, whereas no tool offers both versions. This may give some difficulties to users who prefer GUI instead of CLI.

RESULTS AND DISCUSSION

Core Features And Functionalities

Implementation (GUI)

Screenshots in Figs. (**6** and **7**) show the proposed system developed based on the results gathered from the questionnaire.

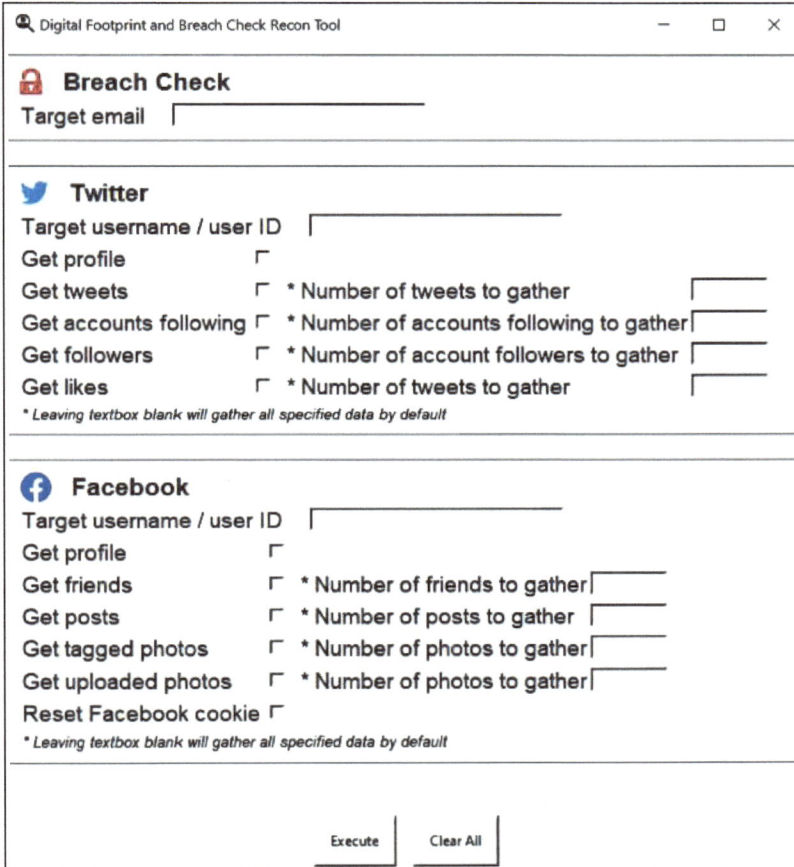

Fig. (6). The main interface of the system GUI.

```
Result                                                         —   □   ×

Gathering data ...

-- [ TWITTER - USER PROFILE ] --
RESULT: User profile found
Username: BarackObama
Profile Name: Barack Obama
Created at: 2007-03-05 22:08:25
Location: Washington, DC
Profile Description: Dad, husband, President, citizen.
URL: http://obamabook.com
Followers Count: 130214088
Accounts Following: 593121
Number of Tweets: 16,157
Profile Image: http://pbs.twimg.com/profile_images/1329647526807543809/2SGvnHYV_normal.jpg
Profile Banner Image: https://pbs.twimg.com/profile_banners/813286/1502508746

######

-- [ DATA EXPORTED TO EXCEL ] --
RESULT: The following data has been exported to : [Output/result-04-14-2021-104359.xlsx] file:
- [Twitter - User Profile]


-- [ DONE ] --
You may find exported results in 'Output' folder in the same directory as Recon tool.

-- [DATA GATHERING PROCESS COMPLETED] --

######
```

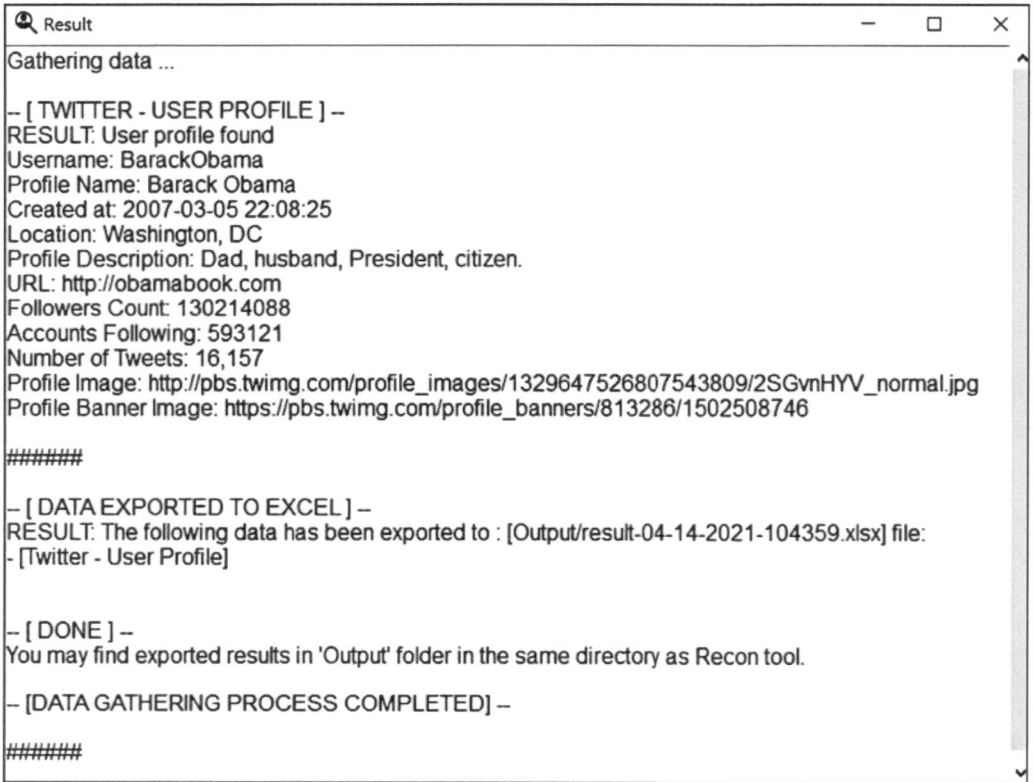

Fig. (7). Sample of result window displaying Twitter profile data gathered.

Fig. (6) displays the system's main interface, where users can enter a username or email of the target user to perform an email breach check or Twitter and Facebook information gathering. Gathered results will be output on the result window, as shown in Fig. (7).

Implementation (CLI)

Table 4 shows some of the commands which explain how users could interact with the CLI system.

Table 4. Breach Check Commands in Facebook and Twitter.

Command	Description	Sample Usage
Breach Check		
-b	Checks for email breach status	-b -e sample@email.com

(Table 4) cont.....

Twitter		
-tt	Gathers user Tweets on Twitter	*-tt -tu twitter_sample_username*
-tp	Gathers user profile info on Twitter	*-tp -tu twitter_sample_username*
-tfg	Gathers accounts followed by user on Twitter	*-tfg -tu twitter_sample_username*
-tfr	Gathers user's follower on Twitter	*-tfr -tu twitter_sample_username*
-tl	Gathers tweets liked by user on Twitter	*-tl -tu twitter_sample_username*
Facebook		
-ff	Gathers user's friends on Facebook	*-ff -fu facebook_sample_username*
-fp	Gathers user's profile info on Facebook	*-fp -fu facebook_sample_username*
-ft	Gathers user's posts on Facebook	*-ft -fu facebook_sample_username*
-fpt	Gathers Facebook photos that user is tagged	*-fpt -fu facebook_sample_username*
-fpu	Gathers Facebook photos uploaded by user	*-fpu -fu facebook_sample_username*

Table 5. Profiles Tested Results.

Facebook Username	Location		Education		Contact info		Basic info (gender, interest in, languages, date of birth)		Work details		Relationship status	Life events		Profile description	Favourite quotes	Family members	
	One	Many	One	Many	One	Many	One	Many	One	Many	One	One	Many	One	One	One	Many
	-	-	-	-	√	-	-	-	-	-	-	-	-	-	-	-	-
	√	-	-	√	√	-	√	-	√	-	-	-	-	-	-	-	-
	-	√	-	-	√	-	-	√	-	-	√	-	-	√	√	-	-
	-	√	-	-	√	-	-	-	-	-	-	-	-	-	-	-	-
	-	√	-	-	-	-	-	-	√	-	√	√	-	√	-	-	-
	-	√	√	-	√	-	√	-	√	-	-	√	-	-	-	-	-
	-	√	√	-	-	-	-	√	-	-	√	-	-	-	-	-	√
	-	-	-	-	-	-	√	-	-	-	-	-	-	-	-	-	-
	-	√	-	√	√	-	√	-	-	√	√	-	√	√	√	-	√
	√	-	-	√	√	-	-	√	-	√	-	-	√	-	√	-	-
	√	-	-	√	-	-	-	-	√	-	-	-	√	-	√	√	-

Testing Results

The system was thoroughly tested in unit testing. Mainly the functions to gather Facebook posts and profile data, as their layout or HTML structure, could be more consistent with other data. The system worked as intended, as proven in user acceptance testing. Most users preferred GUI over CLI since the CLI table was mainly left blank. Table **5** represents the profile-tested results, and Table **6** shows the average score of each criterion in CLI and GUI.

Table 6. Average score of each criterion in CLI and GUI.

Criteria	CLI Score	GUI Score	Average score in CLI and GUI
System design	-	-	-
CLI design is clean	4.50	4.80	4.65
Ease of use	-	-	-
On-screen instructions are helpful	4.50	4.00	4.25
Error messages are helpful	4.00	3.60	3.80
Syntaxes are easy to remember	4.50	-	4.50
Result output is neat and easy to read	4.50	4.20	4.35
Result exported to Excel is easy to read	4.50	4.60	4.55
Performance	-	-	-
System gathers data faster than manual approach	4.00	4.20	4.10
System is not resource intensive	4.00	3.40	3.70
Reliability	-	-	-
System is bug and error free	5.00	4.20	4.60
Data is gathered as stated	5.00	4.40	4.70
Input validations are implemented well	4.50	4.20	4.35
Result	-	-	-
Result gathered is comprehensive	4.50	4.60	4.55

CONCLUSION

The positive side of the system is that it offers a simple all-in-one security tool for professional and novice users. Users can now gather up to 44 data points with a few clicks on GUI or simple commands in CLI. Breach status, Facebook, and Twitter data previously redundant to gather can also be retrieved conveniently and quickly. The objectives of the proposed solution are all accomplished.

On the flip side, the following limitations of the system are identified for future enhancements. Firstly, the current system GUI design only emphasises clarity and simplicity as most of the time is spent developing and debugging the system's functions. However, it can be further enhanced as visually appealing applications will eventually attract more system users. Secondly, the system only gathers breach status and digital footprint from Facebook and Twitter. In future releases, more data sources, such as other breach check websites and social media platforms, should be considered to improve further the depth and types of data gathered. Thirdly, besides exporting the collected results to Excel, other options or formats like PDF, HTML, SQL, etc., should also be available for result exporting. Lastly, as a Python desktop application, the proposed solution requires users to install Python on their devices. Moreover, they can only use or access the tool on devices with the system installed. Thus, the web application should be offered as an alternative for those unfamiliar with or who do not use Python and intend to use the system without installing it individually on devices.

CONSENT FOR PUBLICATION

Not applicable.

CONFLICT OF INTEREST

The authors declare no conflict of interest, financial or otherwise.

ACKNOWLEDGEMENTS

The authors wish to express sincere appreciation to the Asia Pacific University of Technology and Innovation (APU) for giving them this opportunity to conduct the research.

REFERENCES

[1]   R. Mitchell, Web Scraping with Python, 1 ed., United States of America: O'Reilly Media, Inc, 2015.

[2]   A. Jablokow, "Guide To Web Browser Automation," 2018. [Online]. Available: https://blog.ipswitch.com/guide-to-web-browser-automation [Accessed 24 February 2021].

[3]   N. T, "Spiral Model," 2020. [Online]. Available: https://binaryterms.com/spiral-model.html [Accessed 14 July 2020].

[4]   D. Thompson, "Garbage In, Garbage Out," 2016. [Online]. Available: https://www.ibmbigdatahub.com/blog/garbage-garbage-out [Accessed 17 August 2020].

[5]   A. Irvine, "Interviews vs Surveys," 2018. [Online]. Available: https://thesislink.aut.ac.nz/?p=6198 [Accessed 28 September 2020].

[6]   J. Mulder, and M. de Bruijne, "Willingness of Online Respondents to Participate in Alternative Modes of Data Collection", *Surv. Pract.,* vol. 12, no. 1, pp. 1-11, 2019.
[http://dx.doi.org/10.29115/SP-2019-0001]

[7]   D.C. Glass, H.L. Kelsall, C. Slegers, A.B. Forbes, B. Loff, D. Zion, and L. Fritschi, "A telephone survey of factors affecting willingness to participate in health research surveys", *BMC Public Health,* vol. 15, no. 1, p. 1017, 2015.
[http://dx.doi.org/10.1186/s12889-015-2350-9] [PMID: 26438148]

CHAPTER 6

Digital Divide in Primary Schools

Veerakumar Soundrapandian[1,*]

[1] *School of Computing, Asia Pacific University of Technology and Innovation, Kuala Lumpur, Malaysia*

Abstract: The gap in the use of the Internet and computers in society is classified as the level-two digital divide. Research papers from 61 popular journals published between 2005 to 2018 were examined to carry out a Systematic Literature Review (SLR). In addition, renowned organisations' research publications from 2010 to 2018 were used. The adoption of technology, the type of use, the frequency of use, and the effectiveness of use were the main areas of level-two Digital Divide research. This use is further affected by the accessibility determinants of Affordability, Gender, Age, Education Level, Race, and Digital Skills. None of the research used the accessibility determinants as a moderator between availability and use.

Keywords: Accessibility, Adoption, Affordability, Digital Divide, Digital Skills, ICT Use, SLR.

INTRODUCTION

The COVID-19 pandemic has forced many educational institutions worldwide to conduct their teaching and learning online during the yearlong lockdown. This fueled the Digital Divide issue in society, particularly in developing countries among students. The Digital divide is a moving target [1] from Level One, where the availability of Information Communication Technology (ICT) infrastructure is a primary concern [2], to Level Two, which is the *Use* of ICT, to Level Three, which is the *Appropriate-use* of ICT [3]. This Systematic Literature Review (SLR) research delves into the Level-Two Digital Divide using educational technology, computers, and the Internet, which is a part of an unpublished doctoral thesis [4].

In the early days of ICT diffusion, several studies defined the digital divide regarding availability and accessibility only [5 - 8]. Later the use or adoption of ICT received the attention of researchers [9] in developed nations. As the availability issue has been vastly reduced, fixed terrestrial high-speed broadband

---

[*] **Corresponding author Veerakumar Soundrapandian**: School of Computing, Asia Pacific University of Technology and Innovation, Kuala Lumpur, Malaysia; E-mail: veerakumar@apu.edu.my

Muhammad Ehsan Rana and Manoj Jayabalan (Eds.)

at speeds of 25 Mbps/3 Mbps is available for 92.3 per cent of Americans [10] However, the usage issue isn't solved still, and a few researchers view the use as the second-level digital divide [11]. These studies predominantly examine the hours, days, and weeks of computers and Internet usage, taking everyday activities, such as web browsing, social networking, watching videos, listening to music, playing games, checking or sending an email, and uploading or downloading applications into consideration. Without usage, the aims of ICT are unachievable. The Digital Future Report finds that 77 per cent of Americans use the Internet daily, and 17 per cent use it at least once a week [12]. Others measure use by bandwidth usage. Hilbert, in his research, suggested improving "the intensity of usage" [13] by traffic flow per time unit and admitted the absence of internationally recognised measures on effective ICT usage.

ITU [14] has a similar measure of ICT use. For a computer, the measurement consists of nine activities ranging from simple copying or moving a file or folder to an advanced activity of writing a program using a programming language. Twenty-nine Internet activities are used, ranging from getting information about goods or services to online banking. Many of these activities have become partly routine for many users in their daily lives. As Giddens says, human actors maintain stocks of knowledge to perform day-to-day social activities [15].

Similarly, when ICT activities are perceived to be less complicated, and by monitoring how others use them, human actors can follow the same. For example, the WhatsApp messenger application allows short messages, pictures, and videos to be exchanged using Internet-enabled smartphones. Actors in their interaction may routinely observe how other actors use the messenger with few touches and swipes on the smartphone screen to communicate.

Observability, the level of complexity, and the relative advantage in communication lead to the diffusion of the technology [16]. With this in mind, browsing the Internet to read news, watching streaming videos, searching the web for information, and many other primary activities may be accomplished by actors with the existing stock of knowledge, reflexively monitoring the conduct of others but may be incapable of explaining the relative advantage.

Intention to use is a measure of the strength of one's intention to perform a behaviour [17, 18]. According to Ajzen, intention involves belief, target, situation, and time [19]. For instance, a teacher intends to use PowerPoint slides to teach science today. However, Giddens argues that the terms 'intentions', 'motivation', and 'reasons' have different connotations and should be used carefully. Researchers agree that intention and motivation have different meanings. When the behaviour in question is intended, the actor can rationalise the behaviour with discursive consciousness or practical consciousness, but the unintended behaviour is merely a reactive response [20]. Thus, we can conclude that the ICT activities by actors are intended actions like watching an online streaming video or sending a message using WhatsApp. These actions will not happen without having an intention.

Not only for teaching and learning, but education technology is also used as an information search tool, used for school administration, and collaboration with parents [21]. Reinhart examined five types of technology, from basic computer skills to higher-order computer skills, used in classrooms by K-12 teachers in the US. His research deals with whether the teachers use low or high-order technology and the effect of socio-economic factors on the usage [11].

Human actors intentionally or unintentionally change the technology in practice in the course of repeated use and when the knowledge to use increases. In Orlikowski's perspective, repeated practice explains the structuration of technology and use [22]. She illustrates how Americans use tax software to file their returns in her study.

When people routinely use tax preparation software, they draw on its inscribed properties and embedded information content, their experiences with technology, and the understanding of their rights and obligations as taxpayers to enact a set of reporting rules and resources with the software.

METHODOLOGY

This research used evidence-based SLR [23] instead of randomly selecting the journal papers and reports. The research papers published in 61 journals and conference proceedings from 2005 to 2018 were reviewed. A total of 100 journal papers were selected. Of this, 30 percent was from Asia, 22 percent from North America, 15 percent from Europe, 5 from Africa, 3 percent from South America, and 1 percent from Middle Eastern countries where the Digital Divide research was centred. 24 percent of the research delved into the global Digital Divide.

In addition to the above, 25 regional and international organisations reports published from 2010 to 2018 were also reviewed. Finally, 86 reports were used for this research. The significant contribution of the reports came from the Malaysia Communications and Multimedia Commission (MCMC), International Telecommunication Union (ITU), Organization for Economic Co-operation and Development (OECD), National Telecommunications and Information Administration (NTIA), and Global Information Technology Report (GITR).

FINDING

Table **1** below summarises previous Digital Divide research papers examined, where 62 percent investigated the level-two (use) area, exploring the adoption of technology and the frequency of a person logging in to the system. The type of activity carried out, but less research is on technology or software. 42 per cent of the research papers addressed the adoption or subscription of Internet service issues. The hours spent surfing the Internet or computer becomes the frequency of use (25 per cent). The type of activities (34 per cent) one does while using the computer or surfing the internet is also equally researched but is not the appropriate use of technology.

Table 1. Summary of Prior Digital Divide Dimensions 2005 to 2018.

Determinants	# of Papers
Use	**62**
Adoption	42
Frequency	25
Type	34
How Effective	8
Accessibility	**67**
Affordability	48
Gender	35
Education Level	42
Age	30
Race	17
Rural / Urban	23
Digital Skills	29

Affordability characteristics top the accessibility dimension, although several types of research also covered gender, education level, age, race, and location (urban or rural). But, none of them used these characteristics as moderators between availability and use. Besides digital skill popularity among researchers, none of the research used accessibility as a moderator to examine the strength of the relationship between availability and use.

Accessibility

Theoretically speaking, as discussed above, resolving the technology availability issue leads to use. Reflexive monitoring can accomplish essential technology use with practical consciousness and a stock of "mutual knowledge" [20]. However, greater *availability* of ICT infrastructure does not necessarily lead to greater use, and the gaps in technology use still exist. The *accessibility determinants* (refer to Table **2**) act as a moderator between *Availability* and *Use,* where the strength of the relationship between the two variables is affected. The *accessibility* of technology has been used interchangeably with the *availability* of technology by many researchers. On the contrary, the two variables are distinctly different in measuring the digital divide because *availability* is on the supply side, and *accessibility* is on the demand side of the digital divide [24, 25].

Table 2. Accessibility Determinants.

Variables	Definition
Affordability	A person's economic standing to subscribe and purchase technology [24, 26, 27].
Education	The education level of a person influences technology use [28 - 31]
Gender	Inequality of opportunities between males and females in education, employment and entrepreneurship influences the use of technology [32 - 43].
Age	The age of a person can affect accessibility to use technology [30, 41, 42, 44 - 48].
Race	A person's race affects the accessibility to technology use [47 - 49].
Digital Skills	The ability to use computers and the Internet in digital communications, information processing, and education technology [26, 50, 51].

Here, *accessibility* is the ability of a person to access ICT [30, 52 - 56]. Many researchers concluded that affordability, education level, gender, age, digital skills, and race of consumers determine the ability to access technology [36, 41, 42, 52, 57 - 61]. Thus, accessibility poses another major factor in the Digital divide [14].

Table **3** illustrates the *accessibility* determinants and their definitions. Despite the number of characteristics, this research will only probe those that impact the primary school significantly and ignore some features, such as disability. The majority of the research in *accessibility* have centred on affordability characteristic. In contrast, gender, education level, and age characteristics have a considerable amount of literature but relatively less research on race and rural-urban factors.

Table 3. Digital Skills Definition.

Source	Definition
OECD (2013)	".. the ability to use technology to solve problems and accomplish complex tasks."

(Table 3) cont.....

Source	Definition
Ferrari (2013)	"The ability to critically analyse and assess digital information, problem-solving through digital tools, creation and recreation of content and so forth".
Development Economics (2013)	"… as the attributes that allow individuals and businesses both to use digital equipment and to access, create or share digital information via the internet and thereby benefit from opportunities in the modern economy."
WDM Consultants (2011)	… As a multifaceted concept which encapsulates four skill clusters: (1) Digital Technical Skills; (2) Digital Information Processing Skills; (3) Foundational Skills; and (4) Transversal Skills.
Ilomaki (2011)	"The ability to retrieve, assess, store, produce, present, and exchange information, and to communicate and participate in collaborative networks via the internet."

Affordability

When Michael Powel was US FCC chairman, he compared the digital divide to a Mercedes divide; not everyone can afford a Benz car. People may have the intention to drive a Benz car, the car is available in the market for everyone to purchase, but not everyone can own one, making the Benz car inaccessible. Developed nations have higher accessibility to ICT use than developing and underdeveloped countries [62]. The top ten in the Network Readiness Index for the year 2014 are all from developed nations. Finland and Singapore top the list [63].

For the two billion people earning less than US $60 per month in 51 developing countries, the Internet is inaccessible; broadband cost for ordinary citizens forms 40 per cent of their monthly income. Clark and Gomez researched 25 developing countries and suggested that affordability is critical to effectively using ICT [64]. Conversely, the affordability issue looms in developed countries as well. The US Census Bureau survey finds that 7 per cent of American households have not subscribed to the Internet because of cost [49] and 33 per cent of the non-broadband adopters cite monthly cost as the prime reason for not having the home service. Digital Future Report found similar reasons for not using the Internet [12]. The majority find that they are disadvantaged in job seeking, government services, and other vital areas of life [65].

The socioeconomic disparity exists between nations and within a country, predominantly urban and rural areas [66]. Srinuan study in ICT access and use between Bangkok's metropolitan and rural regions supports the digital gap [24]. In America, 76 per cent of those without fixed broadband live in rural areas [67]. Economically backward Malaysian states lag in internet penetration, and urban dwellers tend to own computers and subscribe to broadband more than rural dwellers. This apprehension is evident in the economic growth of the thirteen states in Malaysia. Selangor, Kuala Lumpur, and Penang are highly developed and industrialised. In contrast, conditions like Kelantan, Terengganu, Sabah, and Sarawak [68] are very much backward, with many only living with essential amenities [69].

Rich and poor are the structures of current society. The intended consequences of conscious human actions are to reduce this socio-economic inequality so that all will be at the same level playing ground to reap the technology benefits. The initiatives taken only sometimes achieve the objectives, and as Giddens says, such initiatives result in unintended consequences, too. The liberalisation of the telecommunication sector did not significantly improve the quality and reduce the cost of broadband service in developing countries [14, 70]. It is unclear how smartphone subsidies could increase accessibility to mobile Internet subscribers.

Malaysia had a 61.5 per cent affordability index ranking in 2014 [70], down from 68.8 per cent in 2013, where it occupied the number one spot [71], but has yet to meet the 5 per cent of monthly income for affordability benchmark set by the UN Broadband Commission. Malaysia is in the top position with an 82.44 per cent Affordability Drivers Index (ADI) score [27]. Regarding affordability, the cost of accessing ICT, Malaysia ranks 48th out of 148 nations [63], and the unlimited broadband services are USD 26.89 per Month for 1MB bandwidth [28]. Economically prosperous nation citizens pay only 1 per cent to 2 per cent of their monthly income for accessing the Internet [70]. Thus, the median monthly income would have to be RM 10,000 to meet this standard, but the actual Malaysian monthly median income is RM 2,308 [72]. The affordability of students, teachers, and the school will affect the autonomy of use when they cannot afford a broadband subscription or purchase a computer for their home use.

The Malaysian government has deregulated the wireless telecommunication sector for increased competition, privatised the fixed-line telephone company, invested substantially in telecommunication companies, and provided subsidies for citizens [73]. For example, youths received US $65 for purchasing smartphones in 2013 (A4AI, 2013) and 3.4 billion investment in UNIFI broadband service to provide high-speed broadband and subsidise private household subscriptions [74]. However, questions also arise on how many poor people take advantage of accessing the Internet at the 426 1Malaysia Internet services touted to have 398,204 members [75].

Gender

Inequality of opportunities between males and females in education, employment, and entrepreneurship is evident, looking at the OECD report pressing the need to tackle these areas *via* their gender initiatives to empower females [54, 76]. Many studies find that the accessibility of ICT between males and females differs and is a cause of concern in third-world countries [36 - 40, 77]. Even in developed nations such as Singapore, having 73 per cent Internet penetration after Japan, South Korea, Taiwan, and Brunei Darussalam [78, 79], there are significant differences in Internet access by males and females [80]. Contrary to this, Srinuan research in Thailand [24], Li and Ranieri research in China, and [81] research in Europe found a gender difference in Internet accessibility to be insignificant and at least diminishing in urban areas [65]. Moreover, the Pew Research Centre found that female broadband adoption in the US has increased to 88 per cent compared to 89 per cent for males [82]. Thailand, Jamaica, and Ireland have more women Internet users than men, and Finland and Russian Federation have diminishing gender gaps. Still, the gap is much higher in countries, such as Croatia, Turkey, and Morocco [83]. Still, in 2017 global internet access for men was 51 per cent compared to 45 per cent for women.

Gender plays a crucial role in Malaysian primary schools, as 70.4 per cent of the teachers are females [46]. How this female dominance influences technology accessibility in schools is unknown, even though current research in developed nations and urban areas indicates a diminishing trend for gender effect on accessibility [65, 84]; the trend is unclear in developing countries and rural areas.

Education Level

Studies have shown that the education level of a person influences accessibility [9, 29, 53, 54, 85]. Computer ownership, Internet use, and broadband adoption increase as the education level of a person increases. ITU finds that 90 per cent of people having a college degree or more use the Internet, whereas only 37 per cent of people not having a high school diploma use the Internet [86]. From no diploma to college graduates, Internet use for checking or sending an email, web browsing, downloading applications, and social networking increases [49]. Parents' education level has also been found to have influenced the way children access the Internet [87].

As for Malaysian primary school teachers, 72.9 per cent are graduates, 27.1 per cent are non-graduates, and 4 per cent are untrained teachers. Among the National, Chinese, and Tamil schools, the graduate teachers who are degree holders are 74.6 per cent, 65.1 per cent, and 72 per cent, respectively [35].

Age

Despite being highly educated, the age of a person can affect accessibility. The younger generation of digital natives, people who grew up with technologies such as computers, cell phones, and the Internet, are likely to have higher accessibility than "digital immigrants" [84, 88]. Several types of research confirm age as one of the determining factors in adopting technology [41 - 43, 86]. Lee *et al.* conclude that age impacts the type of broadband accessibility and the type of "online informational activity" [78].

In Malaysia, Internet household uses 21.4 per cent of people between the ages of 20-24, then starts to decline significantly for ages 30-34, and those above 40, use was only 8 per cent in 2016. Ironically, 88.2 per cent of primary school teachers are above the age of 29, and 49.7 per cent are above the age of 39 [35]. It is still being determined whether the general public statistics of age and usage will have the same effect on primary school teachers.

Race

Another characteristic of the accessibility of technology is race [47, 65]. The disparity among various races is evident, predominantly minority races in a country that lags in technology use. According to the NTIA report, household computer ownership, Internet use, and broadband adoption differ among the major races in America. Though Asian Americans (85 per cent) and Whites (79 per cent) lead in Internet household use, African Americans (62 per cent), Hispanics (64 per cent), and American Indians or Alaska Natives (58 per cent) lag behind [49].

Digital Skills

Digital skills are also known as IT knowledge, IT literacy [89], and ICT competence [39]. It describes a person's ability to use computers and the Internet in digital communications and information processing [21, 90]. Lack of digital skills can result in the high possibility of losing available economic opportunities, the increased chance of non-employability in organisations, and the high probability of ending in poor health [26, 31, 34, 91]. The mere use of technology may not be the end, as teachers need to possess the right digital skills for appropriate use. The Digital Skills for the UK economy reported, "A learner's digital education will depend on the digital competencies and skills of those teaching them". Yet, a survey finds that 60 per cent of UK primary school teachers have no confidence in handling ICT curriculum [51].

New technologies change the skills required, causing the less skilled to experience low wage growth [76], which can lead to income inequality. ITU report says that one-third of users lack basic digital skills such as copy and paste, while just 41% have standard skills such as basic spreadsheet formulas. Interestingly, even young students who have grown up using Internet technologies tend to be passive consumers, focused on social media, unable to create content, and typically not venturing beyond accessing the information provided by their teachers [34, 92 - 94].

For the development of the information society, WSIS+10 shareholders have identified several priority areas. One of them is the promotion of simplified devices and applications having text-free interfaces so the less skilled can use digital devices [95]. Teachers should have the opportunity to acquire the skills necessary to access information, analyse and create media, and the capacity to use education technology. Media and Information Literacy (MIL) is vital for teachers to realise their rights to freedom of information and expression to foster students' lifelong learning.

In defining the digital divide, many international organisations, too, have yet to underestimate the digital skills required to use computers and the Internet [14, 49, 54, 63, 83]. Table 3 presents digital skills definitions.

Some studies on the digital divide have focused on digital skills classifying the users according to usage skills possessed, and concluded that basic digital skills are positively related to Internet use [89]. Whereas Lee *et al.* classified digital skills into instrumental skills as "the ability to manoeuvre various Internet options". Creative skills as "the ability to make inventive content to express group or self-identity" [78]. Networking skills as "the ability to search for, synthesise and disseminate information". Li and Ranieri's study espouse that the more educated the parents, the more opportunities there are for children to acquire digital skills [40].

Aesaert conducted similar research on 560 primary school students in Flanders, Belgium [90]. They classified digital skills into higher-order competencies and technical computer skills. Further, They broke them into 56 items ranging from browsing the Internet, search engine manoeuvring, identifying relevant information, sending an email, and basic file operations. This prior research explored the students' digital skills rather than the teachers' digital skills in integrating technology into teaching.

Table 4 illustrates the international and regional organisation reports addressing the digital skills required for using technology.

Table 4. Digital Skills Dimension in Reports.

Source	Contributions	Issues
International Telecommunication Union [28]	Measured by adult literacy rate, gross secondary enrolment, and gross tertiary enrolment	I need to measure Digital Skills directly.
Digital skills for the UK economy [50]	I am categorising Digital Skills into basic skills needed by every citizen, Digital skills required in the workplace, and skills needed by ICT professionals.	I am measuring the Digital Skills shortage in the UK only.
Economic Planning Unit [96]	Developing ICT Skills in Malaysia	Not identifying the type of Digital Skills required
United Nations E-Government Survey [82]	ICT skills	Not identifying the type of Digital Skills required
UK Digital Skills Taskforce [51]	Digital Skills required in various sectors and provided recommendations	This applies to the UK and developed countries
Europe's Digital Progress Report (EC, 2016)	Digital Skills are categorised as 1. Basic Skills and Usage of the Internet 2. Advanced Skills and Development for ICT employment.	This applies to European countries.

CONCLUSION

Realising the contribution of ICT to the economy, many countries have taken positive measures to reduce the Level-One Digital Divide between the Internet and computers *available* for everyone. Though developed nations have succeeded in bridging the gap, to a large extent, compared to developing countries, the Level-Two Digital-Divide gap persists. Even when technology is available, adoption is still being determined. The cost of accessing the technology deters the poor. Not all have the digital skills and the education required for a basic level of use. Moreover, the usage gap occurs between different age groups where the digital immigrant's technology adoption is lower than digital natives. Gender still plays a role in developing countries, but the gap is closing when more educational and economic opportunities are available. Finally, the literature review found that the minority race in a country uses technology less than the majority race.

CONSENT FOR PUBLICATION

Not applicable.

CONFLICT OF INTEREST

The authors declare no conflict of interest, financial or otherwise.

ACKNOWLEDGEMENTS

The authors express sincere appreciation to the Asia Pacific University of Technology and Innovation (APU) for giving them this opportunity to conduct the research.

REFERENCES

[1]   M. Hilbert, "The bad news is that the digital access divide is here to stay: Domestically installed bandwidths among 172 countries for 1986–2014", *Telecomm. Policy,* vol. 40, no. 6, pp. 567-581, 2016.
[http://dx.doi.org/10.1016/j.telpol.2016.01.006]

[2]   V. Soundrapandian, and K. Lumpur, "Systematic Literature Review of Level-One Digital Divide", *Compusoft. Int. J. Adv. Comput. Technol.,* vol. 9, no. 9, pp. 3824-3830, 2020.

[3]   V. Soundrapandian, and T.P. O'Daniel, "Redefining Digital Divide in the Malaysian Primary Schools", *JARDCS,* vol. 11, no. 1, pp. 1429-1436, 2018.

[4]   V. Soundrapandian, Digital Divide Determinants and Impact In The Malaysian Primary Schools [Unpublished doctoral thesis], 2020.

[5]   M.F. Guillén, and S.L. Suárez, "Explaining the global digital divide: Economic, political and sociological drivers of cross-national Internet use", *Soc. Forces,* vol. 84, no. 2, pp. 681-708, 2005.
[http://dx.doi.org/10.1353/sof.2006.0015]

[6]   D.L. Hoffman, and T.P. Novak, *Bridging the Digital Divide : The Impact of Race on Computer Access and Internet Use*, 1998.

[7]   "Deepening Digital Divide and Widening Spatial Gaps in Indonesia 2005-2009", *Chin. J. Psychol.,* pp. 483-500, 2009.
[http://dx.doi.org/10.1016/j.spinee.2008.06.275]

[8]   M.Z.M. Zain, H. Atan, and R.M. Idrus, "The impact of information and communication technology (ICT) on the management practices of Malaysian Smart Schools", *Int. J. Educ. Dev.,* vol. 24, no. 2, pp. 201-211, 2004.
[http://dx.doi.org/10.1016/j.ijedudev.2003.10.010]

[9]   NTIA, "Exploring the digital nation," Natl. Telecommun. Inf. Adm., 2013, [Online]. Available: https://www.ntia.doc.gov/

[10]   FCC, "2018 Broadband Deployment Report," Federal Communications Commission, 2018. https://www.fcc.gov/reports-research/reports/broadband-progress-reports/2018-broad-and-deployment-report

[11]   J.M. Reinhart, E. Thomas, and J.M. Toriskie, "K-12 Teachers: Technology Use and the Second Level Digital Divide", *J. Instr. Psychol.,* vol. 38, pp. 181-193, 2011.

[12]   DFR, "Surveying the Digital Future," 15th. Annu. Study Impact Digit. Technol. Am., 2017.

[13]   M. Hilbert, "Technological information inequality as an incessantly moving target", *J. Am. Soc. Inf. Sci. Technol.,* pp. 1-26, 2013.

[14]   ITU, "Manual for Measuring ICT Access and Use by Households and Individuals," Int. Telecommun. Union, 2014, [Online]. Available: http://www.itu.int/

[15]   A. Giddens, "Structuralism, post-structuralism and the production of culture," Social theory and modern sociology. pp. 73–108, 1987

[16]   E. M. Rogers, Diffusion of innovations. 1995.

[17]   M. Fishbein and I. Ajzen, Belief. Attitude, Intension and Behavior. Addison-Wesley Publishing

Company, 1975.

[18] G. DeSanctis, and M.S. Poole, "Capturing the Complexity in Advanced Technology Use: Adaptive Structuration Theory", *Organ. Sci.,* vol. 5, no. 2, pp. 121-147, 1994.
[http://dx.doi.org/10.1287/orsc.5.2.121]

[19] I. Ajzen, "The theory of planned behavior", *Organ. Behav. Hum. Decis. Process.,* vol. 50, no. 2, pp. 179-211, 1991.
[http://dx.doi.org/10.1016/0749-5978(91)90020-T]

[20] A. Giddens, *Central Problems in Social Theory : Action, Structure, and Contradiction in Social Analysis. by Anthony Giddens*, 1979.
[http://dx.doi.org/10.1007/978-1-349-16161-4]

[21] R. Vanderlinde, K. Aesaert, and J. van Braak, "Institutionalised ICT use in primary education: A multilevel analysis", *Comput. Educ.,* vol. 72, pp. 1-10, 2014.
[http://dx.doi.org/10.1016/j.compedu.2013.10.007]

[22] W.J. Orlikowski, "Using Technology and Constituting Structures: A Practice Lens for Studying Technology in Organizations", *Organ. Sci.,* vol. 11, no. 4, pp. 404-428, 2000.
[http://dx.doi.org/10.1287/orsc.11.4.404.14600]

[23] B. Kitchenham, O. Pearl Brereton, D. Budgen, M. Turner, J. Bailey, and S. Linkman, "Systematic literature reviews in software engineering – A systematic literature review", *Inf. Softw. Technol.,* vol. 51, no. 1, pp. 7-15, 2009.
[http://dx.doi.org/10.1016/j.infsof.2008.09.009]

[24] C. Srinuan, *Understanding the digital divide: Empirical studies of Thailand.* Chalmers University of Technology, 2012.

[25] B. Furuholt, "Bridging the Digital Divide : Sustainable Supply and Demand of Internet Access in Developing Countries," Aalborg University, 2008.

[26] WEF, "Our Shared Digital Future Building an Inclusive, Trustworthy and Sustainable Digital Society," 2018. doi: November 25, 2016.

[27] A4AI, "Affordability Report," Alliance for Affordable Internet, 2018.

[28] ITU, "Measuring the Information Society Report 2015," International Telecommunication Union, Geneva, 2015.

[29] MCMC, "Communications & Multimedia Blueprint 2018-2025," 2018. [Online]. Available: https://www.mcmc.gov.my/

[30] NTIA, "National Telecommunications and Information Administration," 2018. [Online]. Available:https://www.ntia.doc.gov/blog/2018/initial-estimates-show-digital-economy-accouned-65-percent-gdp-2016

[31] OECD, "Bridging the Rural Digital Divide," 2018. [Online]. Available: https://www.oecd-ilibrary.org/science-and-technology/bridging-the-rural-digital-divide_852bd3b9-en

[32] OECD, "Secretary-General's Report to Ministers 2014," Organ. Econ. Co-operation Dev., 2014, [Online].   Available: http://www.oecd-ilibrary.org/economics/secretary-general-s-report-to-ministers-2013_sg_report-2013-en

[33] EPU, "Labor market for an advanced nation," Econ. Plan. Unit, 2015, [Online]. Available: http://rmk11.epu.gov.my/index.php/en/muat-turun-dokumen

[34] ITU, "Measuring the Information Society Report Volume 1," Int. Telecommun. Union, vol. 1, 2018, [Online]. Available: https://www.itu.int/en/ITU-D/Statistics/Documents/publications/misr2018/MIS-2018-Vol-1-E.pdf

[35] MOE, "Quick Facts 2018," Putrajaya, 2018.

[36]   A. Acilar, "Exploring the digital divide in a developing country", *Issues in Informing Science and Information Technology,* vol. 8, pp. 231-244, 2011.
[http://dx.doi.org/10.28945/1415]

[37]   G. Foteinou, "e-exclusion and the gender digital divide", *Comput. Soc.,* vol. 40, no. 3, pp. 50-61, 2010.
[http://dx.doi.org/10.1145/1862406.1862410]

[38]   T.N. Friemel, "The digital divide has grown old: Determinants of a digital divide among seniors", *New Media Soc.,* pp. 1-19, 2014.

[39]   G. Gudmundsdottir, "From digital divide to digital equity: Learners' ICT competence in four primary schools in Cape Town, South Africa," Int. J. Educ. Dev. using ICT, vol. 6, no. 2, pp. 84–105, 2010.

[40]   Y. Li, and M. Ranieri, "Educational and social correlates of the digital divide for rural and urban children: A study on primary school students in a provincial city of China", *Comput. Educ.,* vol. 60, no. 1, pp. 197-209, 2013.
[http://dx.doi.org/10.1016/j.compedu.2012.08.001]

[41]   J. De Hann, "A Multifaceted Dynamic Model of the Digital Divide", *IT Soc.,* vol. 1, pp. 66-88, 2004.

[42]   M.K. Eamon, "Digital Divide in Computer Access and Use between Poor and Non-Poor Youth", *J. Sociol. Soc. Welf.,* vol. 31, no. 2, pp. 91-112, 2004.

[43]   J.J.P-A. Hsieh, A. Raj, and M. Keil, "Understanding Digital Inequality", *Comparing Continued Use Behavioral Models of the Socio-Economically Advantaged and Disadvantaged,* vol. 32, no. 1, pp. 97-126, 2008.

[44]   J.J.P-A. Hsieh, A. Rai, and M. Keil, "Understanding Digital inequality: Comparing continued use behavioral models of the socio-economically advantaged and disadvantaged", *Manage. Inf. Syst. Q.,* vol. 32, no. 1, pp. 97-126, 2008.
[http://dx.doi.org/10.2307/25148830]

[45]   ITU, "Mobile_cellular_2000-2012," Int. Telecommun. Union, 2013.

[46]   MOE, "Quick Facts Malaysia Educational Statistics," Ministry of Education Malaysia, Putrajaya, pp. 1–45, 2016.

[47]   F.M. Hess, and D.L. Leal, "A Shrinking "Digital Divide"? The Provision of Classroom Computers across Urban School Systems", *Soc. Sci. Q.,* vol. 82, no. 4, pp. 765-778, 2001.
[http://dx.doi.org/10.1111/0038-4941.00058]

[48]   J. B. Horrigan, "Lifelong Learning and Technology," 2016. [Online]. Available: http://www.pewinternet.org/2016/03/22/lifelong-learning-and-technology/

[49]   NTIA, "Exploring the Digital Nations: Embracing the Mobile Internet," 2014. [Online]. Available: https://www.ntia.doc.gov/

[50]   ECORYS, "Digital skills for the UK economy," 2016. http://www.ecorys.com/ (accessed Jan. 05, 2017).

[51]   UDST, "Digital Skills for Tomorrow's World," 2014. [Online]. Available: http://www.ukdigitalskills.com/wp-content/uploads/2014/07/Binder7-REDUCED2.pdf

[52]   T.N. Hohlfeld, A.D. Ritzhaupt, A.E. Barron, and K. Kemker, "Examining the digital divide in K-12 public schools: Four-year trends for supporting ICT literacy in Florida", *Comput. Educ.,* vol. 51, no. 4, pp. 1648-1663, 2008.
[http://dx.doi.org/10.1016/j.compedu.2008.04.002]

[53]   ITU, "Measuring the Information Society Report 2016," Geneva, Oct. 2016. [Online]. Available: www.itu.int

[54]   OECD, "Society at a Glance 2014," 2014.
[http://dx.doi.org/10.1787/soc_glance-2014-en]

[55] World Bank, "World Development Report: Digital Dividends," Washington DC, 2016.

[56] S.S. Kleinman, "Understanding the Digital Divide: Implications for College Teaching", *Transformations,* vol. 6, no. 1, pp. 51-108, 2001.
[http://dx.doi.org/10.1093/ilj/6.1.52]

[57] "J. a G. M. Van Dijk, "The evolution of the digital divide: The digital divide turns to inequality of skills and usage,"", *Digit. Enlight. Yearb.,* vol. 2012, pp. 57-75, 2012.
[http://dx.doi.org/10.3233/978-1-61499-057-4-57]

[58] V. Venkatesh, and T.A. Sykes, "Digital Divide Initiative Success in Developing Countries : A Longitudinal Field Study in a Village in India", *Inf. Syst. Res.,* vol. 7047, pp. 1-22, 2012.

[59] G.D.M. Wijers, "Determinants of the digital divide: A study on IT development in Cambodia", *Technol. Soc.,* vol. 32, no. 4, pp. 336-341, 2010.
[http://dx.doi.org/10.1016/j.techsoc.2010.10.011]

[60] K. Barzilai-Nahon, "Gaps and Bits: Conceptualizing Measurements for Digital Divide/s", *Inf. Soc.,* vol. 22, no. 5, pp. 269-278, 2006.
[http://dx.doi.org/10.1080/01972240600903953]

[61] H.B. Gündüz, "Digital Divide in Turkish Primary Schools: Sakarya sample", *Turk. Online J. Educ. Technol.,* vol. 9, no. 1, pp. 43-53, 2010.

[62] M. Hilbert, "The end justifies the definition: The manifold outlooks on the digital divide and their practical usefulness for policy-making", *Telecomm. Policy,* vol. 35, no. 8, pp. 715-736, 2011.
[http://dx.doi.org/10.1016/j.telpol.2011.06.012]

[63] WEF, "Global Information Technology Report 2014," World Econ. Forum, p. 369 p., 2014, [Online]. Available: http://reports.weforum.org/global-information-technology-report-2014/

[64] M. Clark and R. Gomez, "Cost and other barriers to public access computing in developing countries," Proc. 2011 iConference - iConference '11, pp. 181–188, 2011.

[65] J. B. Horrigan and M. Duggan, "Home Broadband 2015," 2015.

[66] T. Correa, I. Pavez, and J. Contreras, "Beyond access: A relational and resource-based model of household Internet adoption in isolated communities", *Telecomm. Policy,* vol. 41, no. 9, pp. 757-768, 2017.
[http://dx.doi.org/10.1016/j.telpol.2017.03.008]

[67] FCC, "Eighth Broadband Progress Report," Washington, 2012. [Online]. Available: http://transition.fcc.gov

[68] C. Horn, and E. Rennie, "Digital access, choice and agency in remote Sarawak", *Telemat. Inform.,* vol. 35, no. 7, pp. 1935-1948, 2018.
[http://dx.doi.org/10.1016/j.tele.2018.06.006]

[69] EPU, "Tenth Malaysia Plan 2011-2015," Econ. Plan. Unit, 2010, [Online]. Available: www.pmo.gov.my/dokumenattached/RMK/RMK10_E.pdf

[70] A4AI, "The Affordability Report 2014," Alliance for Affordable Internet, Washington, 2014.

[71] A4AI, "The Affordability Report 2013," Alliance for Affordable Internet., 2013.

[72] DOSM, "Salaries & Wages Survey Report, Malaysia 2018," 2018. [Online]. Available: https://www.dosm.gov.my/v1/index.php?r=column/cthemeByCat&cat=155&bul_id=aWJZRkJ4UEdK cUZpT2tVT090Snpydz09&menu_id=L0pheU43NWJwRWVSZklWdzQ4TlhUUT09

[73] TheStar, "TM and Govt to invest RM3," The Star Online, Kuala Lumpur, Dec. 27, 2015.

[74] MCMC, "Communications & Multimedia: Pocket Book of Statistics Q4," Cyberjaya, 2015. [Online]. Available: https://www.mcmc.gov.my/

[75] MCMC, "Communications & Multimedia: Pocket Book of Statistics," Kuala Lumpur, 2014. [Online].

Available: https://www.mcmc.gov.my/

[76] ADB, "Asian Development outlook 2018," 2018. [Online]. Available: https://www.adb.org/sites/default/files/publication/411666/ado2018.pdf

[77] H. Leslie Steeves, and J. Kwami, "Interrogating Gender Divides in Technology for Education and Development: the Case of the One Laptop per Child Project in Ghana", *Stud. Comp. Int. Dev.,* vol. 52, no. 2, pp. 174-192, 2017.
[http://dx.doi.org/10.1007/s12116-017-9245-y]

[78] H. Lee, N. Park, and Y. Hwang, "A new dimension of the digital divide: Exploring the relationship between broadband connection, smartphone use and communication competence", *Telemat. Inform.,* vol. 32, no. 1, pp. 45-56, 2015.
[http://dx.doi.org/10.1016/j.tele.2014.02.001]

[79] P.H. Cheong, "Gender and Perceived Internet Efficacy: Examining Secondary Digital Divide Issues in Singapore", *Womens Stud. Commun.,* vol. 30, no. 2, pp. 205-228, 2007.
[http://dx.doi.org/10.1080/07491409.2007.10162513]

[80] L. Gurung, "The Digital Divide: An Inquiry from Feminist Perspectives", *Dhaulagiri,* vol. 12, pp. 50-57, 2018.
[http://dx.doi.org/10.3126/dsaj.v12i0.22179]

[81] J.H.B. Lengsfeld, "An Econometric Analysis of the Sociodemographic Topology of the Digital Divide in Europe", *Inf. Soc.,* vol. 27, no. 3, pp. 141-157, 2011.
[http://dx.doi.org/10.1080/01972243.2011.566745]

[82] UN, "United Nations E-Government Survey 2014," United Nations Dep. Econ. Soc. Aff., 2014, [Online]. Available: http://unpan3.un.org/egovkb/

[83] UNDES, "United Nations E-Government Survey 2014," United Nations Department of Economic and Social Affairs, 2014.

[84] M. Van Volkom, J.C. Stapley, and V. Amaturo, "Revisiting the Digital Divide : Generational Differences in Technology Use in Everyday Life", *N. Am. J. Psychol.,* vol. 16, no. 3, pp. 557-574, 2014.

[85] C. Berrío-Zapata, and H. Rojas-Hernández, "The digital divide in the university: The appropriation of ICT in Higher Education students from Bogota, Colombia", *Comunicar,* vol. 22, no. 43, pp. 133-142, 2014.
[http://dx.doi.org/10.3916/C43-2014-13]

[86] ITU, "Measuring the Information Society," Int. Telecommun. Union, 2013, [Online]. Available: https://www.itu.int

[87] S. Zhao, "Parental education and children's online health information seeking: Beyond the digital divide debate", *Soc. Sci. Med.,* vol. 69, no. 10, pp. 1501-1505, 2009.
[http://dx.doi.org/10.1016/j.socscimed.2009.08.039] [PMID: 19765874]

[88] M. Dornisch, "The Digital Divide in Classrooms: Teacher Technology Comfort and Evaluations", *Comput. Schools,* vol. 30, no. 3, pp. 210-228, 2013.
[http://dx.doi.org/10.1080/07380569.2012.734432]

[89] E. Ferro, N.C. Helbig, and J.R. Gil-Garcia, "The role of IT literacy in defining digital divide policy needs", *Gov. Inf. Q.,* vol. 28, no. 1, pp. 3-10, 2011.
[http://dx.doi.org/10.1016/j.giq.2010.05.007]

[90] K. Aesaert, D. van Nijlen, R. Vanderlinde, and J. van Braak, "Direct measures of digital information processing and communication skills in primary education: Using item response theory for the development and validation of an ICT competence scale", *Comput. Educ.,* vol. 76, pp. 168-181, 2014.
[http://dx.doi.org/10.1016/j.compedu.2014.03.013]

[91] OECD, "Skills Outlook 2013," Organ. Econ. Co-operation Dev., 2013, [Online]. Available:

https://www.oecd.org/skills/piaac/Skills volume 1 (eng)--full v12--eBook (04 11 2013).pdf

[92]   C. Jones, R. Ramanau, S. Cross, and G. Healing, "Net generation or Digital Natives: Is there a distinct new generation entering university?", *Comput. Educ.,* vol. 54, no. 3, pp. 722-732, 2010.
[http://dx.doi.org/10.1016/j.compedu.2009.09.022]

[93]   A. Margaryan, A. Littlejohn, and G. Vojt, "Are digital natives a myth or reality? University students' use of digital technologies", *Comput. Educ.,* vol. 56, no. 2, pp. 429-440, 2011.
[http://dx.doi.org/10.1016/j.compedu.2010.09.004]

[94]   W. Ng, "Can we teach digital natives digital literacy?", *Comput. Educ.,* vol. 59, no. 3, pp. 1065-1078, 2012.
[http://dx.doi.org/10.1016/j.compedu.2012.04.016]

[95]   ITU, "WSIS+10 High-Level Event," Int. Telecommun. Union, 2014, [Online]. Available: http://www.itu.int/

[96]   EPU, "Driving ICT in the Knowledge Economy," Econ. Plan. Unit, pp. 2011–2015, 2015, [Online]. Available: http://rmk11.epu.gov.my/pdf/strategy-paper/Strategy Paper 15.pdf

CHAPTER 7

Intrusion Detection System for the Internet of Medical Things (IoMT)

Ameer A.N. Alasaad[1], Nor Azlina Abd Rahman[1,*] and Yusnita Yusof[1]

[1] *School of Technology, Asia Pacific University of Technology and Innovation, Kuala Lumpur, Malaysia*

Abstract: In this paper, the authors proposed the design of an Intrusion Detection System (IDS) that can be used in the healthcare sector to increase cybersecurity. This sector is facing high cyber threats. Similar IDS systems will be reviewed in the following pages, followed by the justifications of why the authors decided to design the IDS to be Signature-based. The experimental results showed that the developed IDS could successfully capture the network traffic, record the logs and show an informative alarm screen with a few other options within the dashboard to assist the user in handling the situation and assure the hospital network security.

Keywords: Healthcare IoT, HIDS, Hospital Security, Intrusion Detection System (IDS), Internet of Medical Things (IoMT), NIDS.

INTRODUCTION

Recently, technology has been playing a significant role in improving medical devices. Many medical devices are smart, meaning they are computer-related and connected to a database or more in the hospital network. The benefits are increasing, as well as the risk or fear of cyber-attacks. IoMT, The Internet of Medical Things, is a term for all smart medical devices and programs linked to a healthcare centre's network. In other words, IoMT is a medical device that can connect to a network to start communication and data transmission between smart devices. "Healthcare IoT" is considered another description of IoMT [1]. Since the IoMT is advancing so fast to provide more comfort to the patients and to make the hospital's staff work efficiently, the need to ensure the privacy and security of all the sensitive data are increasing symmetrically.

Many sectors respond to IoT technology very fast, unlike the healthcare sector. However, the Internet of Medical Things (IoMT) is now getting ready to move to

---

[1] **Corresponding author Nor Azlina Abd Rahman:** School of Technology, Asia Pacific University of Technology and Innovation, Kuala Lumpur, Malaysia; E-mail: nor_azlina@apu.edu.my

Muhammad Ehsan Rana and Manoj Jayabalan (Eds.)

the next level in keeping people safe and guaranteeing better medical services whilst reducing healthcare costs. Allied Market Research came out with a report predicting that the IoMT market will reach around $137 billion globally by 2020. It is worth mentioning that about 3.9 million smart medical devices are connected and monitor many areas of a patient's body [2].

Statistics, according to the Herjavec Group, which provides a special report from cybersecurity venture editors, show that there are more than 93% of healthcare groups faced a cybersecurity breach and data leakage within the years from 2017 to 2020. Moreover, the healthcare organisations that have experienced cyber-attacks over five times in three years are actually above 57% of the healthcare sector [3]. Regarding the IoMT insecurity, the CISO of Northwell Health, one of the nation's largest healthcare systems, Kathy Hughes, said that the IoMT devices have small operating systems and the security features and functions are bolt-ons rather than built-in, which makes those devices suspectable for cyber-crimes and threats. Real cases and difficult situations happened recently. A medical centre in California, US, lately shut down due to a ransomware attack that infected the clinics so harshly.

Additionally, (ENT) a hearing centre located at Battle Creek, Mich., collapsed and closed its doors for good since the database was hacked and the data was permanently erased. In some cases, recovering and dealing with post-attack troubles is challenging to get operations back to normal [4]. The usage of IoT devices, in general, is rapidly increasing, causing cybersecurity threats to grow alongside it.

Fig. (**1**) shows the increase in the IoT market globally from 2017 to the upcoming five years. Aside from that, ransomware attacks against healthcare sectors are expected to increase x5 in 2021, according to the cybersecurity ventures report [5].

To maximise data protection, healthcare IT specialists need to understand the cyber threats they are dealing with. Apart from the fact that the cyber-attack can cause financial consequences, it also might put the patient's life on the line. This is possible if the medical device's function is interrupted. Implementing an Intrusion Detection System (IDS) will assist the team in putting an end to many vulnerabilities.

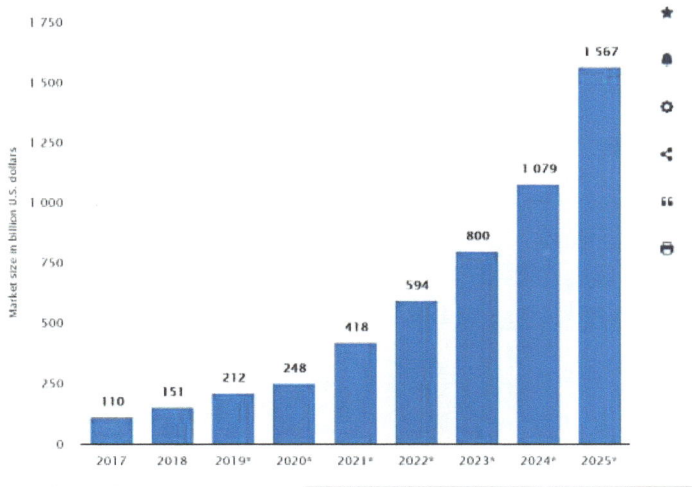

Fig. (1). Market size of the IoT [5].

REVIEW OF IDS SYSTEMS

In this section, a few similar systems will be studied with brief explanations about the features and limitations of each one of them. This step will provide a strong base for a better understanding of the challenges' nature related to developing this project.

Snort

Snort is considered the leading industry in IDS tools and systems. It is a well-known product from Cisco, and there are versions to be installed on both Windows and Linux operating systems. Snort allows the user to run the system in three different modes, as shown in Fig. (**2**):

- Sniffer mode
- Packet logger
- Intrusion detection

One benefit is that Cisco Systems support it since it is one of Cisco's products. However, it has its disadvantages as well, which include the difficulty of updating the rules you set in the system as it needs to be done manually and the fact that it requires so many configurations to setup Snort, which makes it slightly complicated to use if the person has no experience with such tools [6].

Services / Snort / Alerts　　　　　　　　　　　　　　　　　　　　　　　　　　　❓

| Snort Interfaces | Global Settings | Updates | Alerts | Blocked | Pass Lists | Suppress | IP Lists | SID Mgmt | Log Mgmt | Sync |

Clear all interface log files

Alert Log View Settings

| Interface to Inspect | WAN ⬍ | ☐ Auto-refresh view | 1000 | | 💾 Save |
| | Choose interface.. | | Alert lines to display. | | |

| Alert Log Actions | ⬇ Download 🗑 Clear |

Alert Log View Filter　　　　　　　　　　　　　　　　　　　　　　　　　　　➕

Last 1000 Alert Log Entries

Date	Pri	Proto	Class	Source IP	SPort	Destination IP	DPort	SID	Description
2017-07-23 20:49:52	1	UDP	A Network Trojan was Detected	66.240.205.34 🔍 ⊞	1066	🔍 ⊞	16464	1:31136 ⊞ ✖	MALWARE-CNC Win.Trojan.ZeroAccess inbound connection
2017-07-22 06:15:49	2	UDP	Potentially Bad Traffic	163.172.17.76 🔍 ⊞	54465	🔍 ⊞	5060	140:26 ⊞ ✖	(spp_sip) Method is unknown
2017-07-21 09:26:30	2	UDP	Potentially Bad Traffic	163.172.22.169 🔍 ⊞	52428	🔍 ⊞	5060	140:26 ⊞ ✖	(spp_sip) Method is unknown
2017-07-21 01:03:28	2	UDP	Potentially Bad Traffic	163.172.17.76 🔍 ⊞	46834	🔍 ⊞	5060	140:26 ⊞ ✖	(spp_sip) Method is unknown
2017-07-20 20:36:37	2	UDP	Potentially Bad Traffic	163.172.22.169 🔍 ⊞	54788	🔍 ⊞	5060	140:26 ⊞ ✖	(spp_sip) Method is unknown
2017-07-20 08:31:30	2	UDP	Potentially Bad Traffic	163.172.17.76 🔍 ⊞	59571	🔍 ⊞	5060	140:26 ⊞ ✖	(spp_sip) Method is unknown

Fig. (2). Snort [6].

Suricata

Another similar system is called Suricata, as shown in Fig. (**3**). It is an open-source tool and is considered NIDS, specifically an IDS using detection based on Signature. Suricata has a lot of instructions and standards that can identify malicious traffic attempts. It has the feature of auto-detect for the protocols to match any port. This NIDS can be run as passive or active NIDS, sometimes called NIPS (Intrusion Prevention System). Suricata has an advantage over Snort, as it offers capture accelerators and other features. On the other hand, the disadvantage of this system is the apparent lack of guideline documents, making it challenging to troubleshoot an issue in the system if the user is not very familiar with Suricata [6].

SolarWinds Security Event Manager

SolarWinds Security Event Manager (SEM) can be considered a HIDS system installed on Windows. However, it can capture logs from other operating systems, such as Mac OS, Linux, and Unix. SEM has advantages, such as its ability to process live data, take active responses to deal with an event, and analyse the log files. However, the limitation of SolarWinds Security Event Manager (SEM) is that it cannot work as NIDS alone. It only can perform as NIDS partially with support from Snort tools [7]. Fig. (**4**) demonstrates the screenshot of SEM.

Fig. (3). Suricata [6].

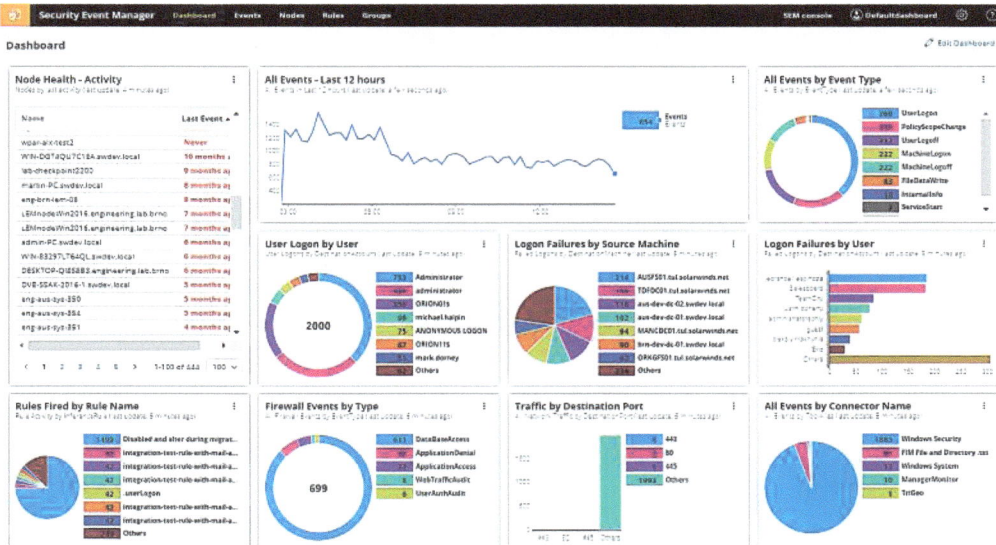

Fig. (4). SolarWinds Security Event Manager [7].

An intrusion detection system can recognise unauthorised behaviour or misuse/abuse of a computer system. The first steps of inventing this system came after analysing packets transferred from one network to another carrying a header to let the packet reach the correct device. When the packet arrives at the network, all devices within this network will be able to notice the packet, but since the address in the packet's header does not match the devices, the devices ignore the packet. This happens until the packet finds a match between a device and its header address. After that, the device will finally be able to receive and view the packet. Network experts studied that if one machine decides not to ignore the packets coming into the network, then this machine will be able to monitor and maybe control traffic within the network. Over time, a few research studies were the beginning of the invention of the Intrusion Detection System (IDS) to avoid any breach of the computer security main corners: Confidentiality, Integrity, and Availability (CIA). The Intrusion Detection System records the logs and then identifies and escalates any potential incidents [8]. Fig. **5** shows the activities of a typical signature-based IDS.

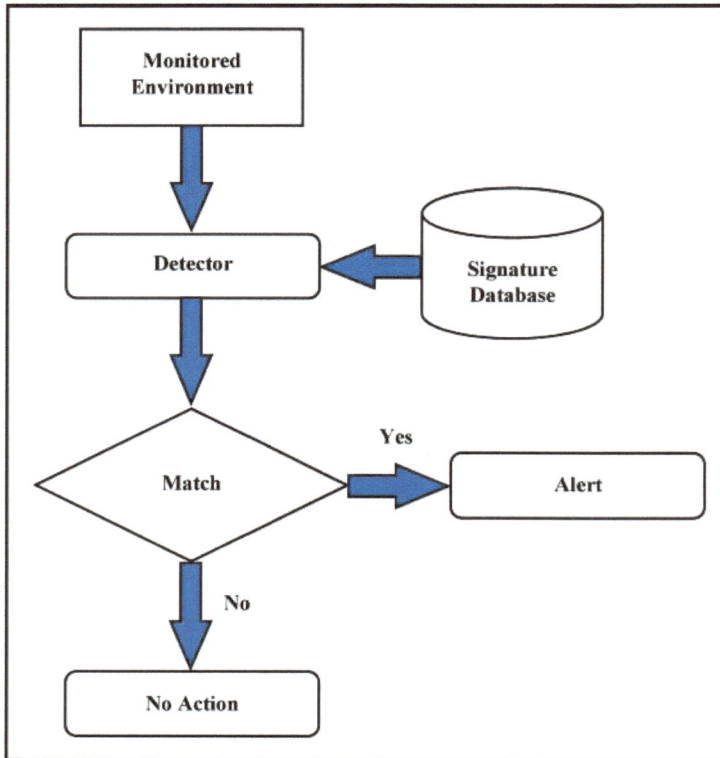

Fig. (5). Signature-based IDS [9].

Generally, any Intrusion Detection System should be able to fulfill a few critical issues:

- IDS should be able to proceed independently without any need for direct human management.
- IDS must be error-tolerant; in other words, the IDS must avoid any crash or rebuilt database in case of restart.
- IDS must monitor and record abnormal events and differentiate them from normal situation.
- In the case of adding new programs and applications, IDS should be able to adapt to the changing of the system behaviour to minimise false positive alarms.

To explain the point in-depth, the reader should understand that the monitored system generates massive logs, so IDS should be effective by producing very low false positive and negative alerts. Table **1** explains these alerts and each one's meaning.

Table 1. types of alarms in IDS [10].

	Positive	*Negative*
True	*Alerts when there is a harmful/illegal traffic*	*Silent when traffic is normal/legal*
False	*Alerts when traffic is normal/legal*	*Silent when a harmful incident happen*

The efficient IDS have high true positive, low false positive, high true negative and low false negative incidents, as shown in the table [10].

TYPES OF IDS

The two types of IDS discussed in this section are HIDS and NIDS.

Host-based Intrusion Detection System (HIDS)

It is essential to mention that HIDS was the initial sort of Intrusion Detection System. The monitored system here is a computer, node, or host. While technology is advancing very fast, many HIDS performances have improved to monitor the network. However, there is still a need for HIDS, specifically in some cases. This type of IDS can be considered the internal system to observe the performance of the device or host and report to the owner/administrator any suspicious activity in the system. For instance, HIDS can identify harmful programs. Moreover, it can detect any access to the system resources with suspicious intent and any modification to the registry that can be dangerous to the computer.

One of the benefits of this type of Intrusion Detection System is that it can check the encrypted packets simply because it reviews the communication before it gets encrypted. Furthermore, HIDS can check stream communication even if some sessions are uniting or fragmentation attacks because it views the recombined sessions as complete. HIDS does not require any additional hardware, but the downside of it is the high cost to implement it and the performance issues that might happen.

Network-Based Intrusion Detection System (NIDS)

Unlike previous HIDS, the Network-based IDS is designed to detect unauthorised parties trying to gain access to the network with multiple hosts and devices. The administrator is encouraged to act by blocking some IP addresses or eliminating malicious files once an alert is received from the NIDS.

The general advantages of using NIDS are detecting network-based attacks such as DoS attacks and the low cost of implanting NIDS. On the other hand, the major disadvantages are the possibility of losing packets due to the continuous changes in the traffic volume, the disability to analyse encrypted communication, and the need for additional hardware (especially for large networks).

There are two common locations to assign a NIDS:

• IDS using a switch spanning port

The IDS has to be connected to a switch through a SPAN port. A SPAN port can be configured to push all the packets through this port. The switch will then send a copy of the total traffic to the IDS to be inspected and monitored. The disadvantage of applying the IDS this way is pressuring the switch to work twice to deliver the traffic to the IDS.

• IDS using a network tap

In this method, the IDS works as a checkpoint for all the data passing through the wire. Taps for networks are not popular when designing a typical network. However, these taps are available to purchase if needed. This method is suitable if the administrator would like to implement IDS temporarily [10].

Fig. (6) shows a comparison between HIDS and NIDS.

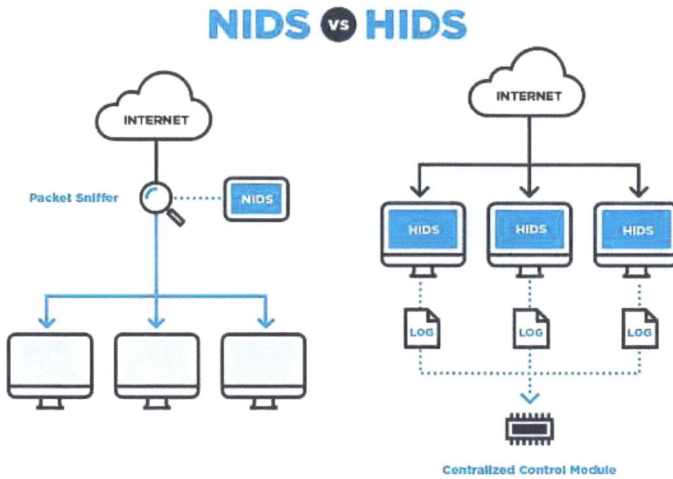

Fig. (6). IDS Vs HIDS [7].

TYPES OF DETECTION

Regardless of the IDS type, there is another classification for the method by which the packets are detected.

Signature-Based Detection

In this detection technique, the IDS checks the packets and detects if there is a match between the compared packet and a bunch of rules and patterns called Watch List. Those rules were defined previously.

The advantages of this method are:

- The simplicity of processing the data.
- Quick and immediate response against known attacks.
- The false positive rate is low.

On the other hand, the disadvantages are:

- Restricted ability to detect a zero-day attack.
- The need for frequent updating of the signature database.

Anomaly-Based Detection

For the Anomaly-based IDS, there is a need to create a reference called a baseline. In the baseline, the activities and regular usage of the users within the network will be determined. After that, the IDS will detect any traffic that seems unmatched with the baseline; thus, the IDS will alert the administrator.

The advantages of the Anomaly-based detection method are:

- The ability to detect zero-day attacks at an early stage.
- The false negative rate is low.

On the other hand, the disadvantages are:

- Slow functioning of new networks since it needs time to create the baseline.
- The false positive rate is high.
- Low detection capabilities for the known attack.

There are other classifications for the IDS based on many categories, such as the operating system hosting the IDS and the list going on with different classifications. One of the classifications is based on the incident response method: Passive and Active IDS. The passive IDS monitors, analyses, and records the logs and then alerts the administrator in case of a possible threat or intrusion. However, the active IDS can take action towards the event that has been detected. For instance, the active IDS can stop the traffic when suspicious and take the entire system to a safe mode if the risk is severe [10].

At the end of this deep research study about the many types of IDS systems and the functionality of each one, the developer of this project decided to develop and implement Network Intrusion Detection System to ensure the entire hospital network was secure and safe. The reason for this was so the developer would build IDS that monitored all the traffic within the network. Moreover, the type of detection will be signature-based, which means the developer will create a Watch List for known threats, and based on that, the alarms will be generated if any match. The reason why the developer has chosen signature-based IDS is to minimise false positive alarms. Thus, the monitoring will work with more efficiency. Figs. (**7** and **8**) demonstrate a screenshot from the designed IDS dashboard.

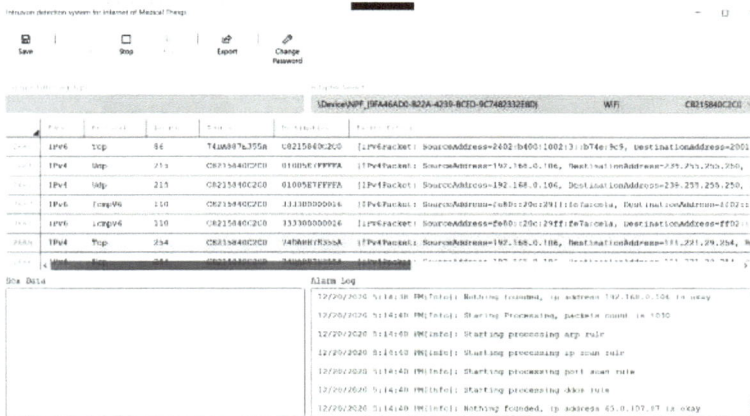

Fig. (7). Network monitoring running.

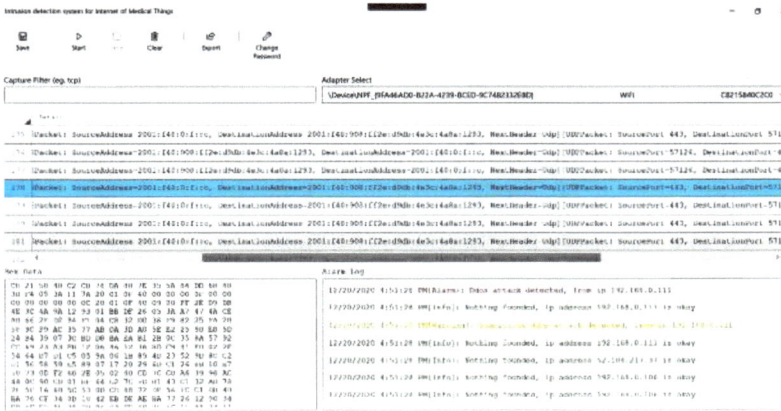

Fig. (8). Alarms generated.

REQUIREMENT ANALYSIS

The data for this project has been gathered via a questionnaire research method. All the participants are above 18 years old and have a background in IT. A group of them work in the healthcare field, so their response is based on real-life evaluations.

In Your Opinion, How Secure Is Iomt (Internet Of Medical Things)?

The third question reflects on the requirements and features of this project, as shown in Fig. (**9**). It helps the developer understand the need for the proposed IDS system by gathering feedback about the security level of the IoMT devices. The majority, 53% of the participants, said IoMT devices have a minimum level of security; in other words, there is a low threshold to stopping hackers from breaching the devices and systems. There is also 14.5% (12 persons) who believe that there is an apparent lack of security which is a critical issue for such sensitive devices. This information supports the need to enhance the security of the IDS proposed system. However, 27 respondents said the IoMT devices have a high level of protection.

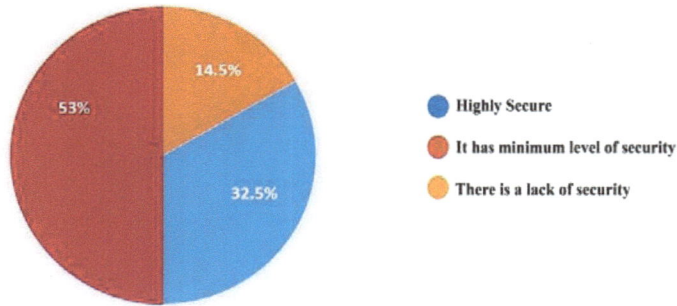

Fig. (9). Question 3 of the survey conducted.

Fig. (**10**) shows that security is the most serious concern among the developers of IoT, which include IoMT devices as well. Therefore, 65% of the participants believe in the need to ensure privacy and security before using such new and trendy technology with critical and sensitive matters like healthcare.

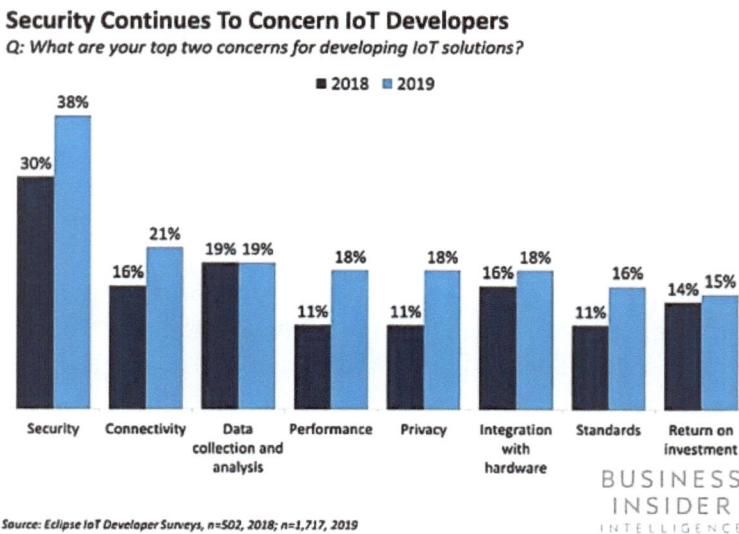

Fig. (10). Security concerns IoT developers [11].

Which Level of Confidentiality do You Think the Patient's Medical Records Should be at?

To have a clear picture of the awareness of privacy needs when it comes to the medical records and files of the patients, this question was added to the survey. The level of confidentiality is measured on a scale from 1 to 5, where 1 means Unclassified, 2 means Sensitive, 3 equals Confidential, 4 means Secret, and 5 represents the answer Top secret. The analysis in Fig. (**11**) shows that most participants believe that the patient records and data should be at the Secret and Top-secret levels. The importance of privacy can be noticed in this collected data.

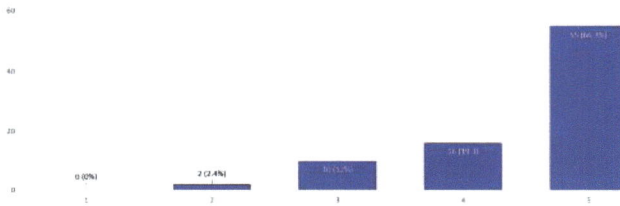

Fig. (11). Question 4 of the survey conducted.

More than 70% know the importance of keeping patient records undisclosed and private. On the other hand, cyber threats against medical records have been increasing worldwide as of late, parallel with technology getting advanced over time. Fig. (**12**) shows statistics about the vast number of medical record breaches.

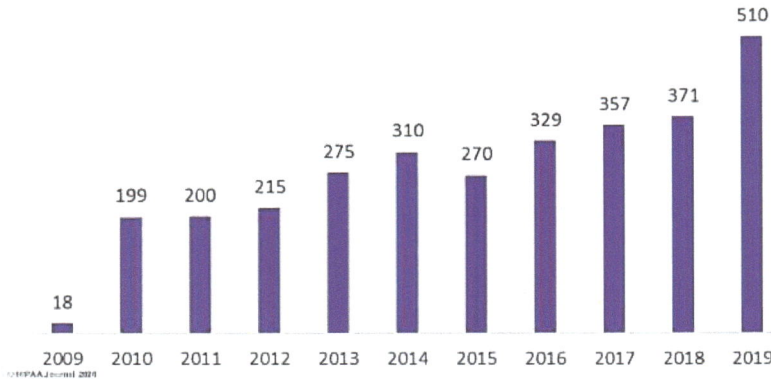

Fig. (12). Healthcare data breaches of 500 or more records [12].

As per Fig. (**13**), more than 100 thousand people were affected by medical records breaches between 2014 and 2016. However, the number of affected individuals started to increase again from 2018 onwards, which is why most participants in this survey said that medical records should be considered top-secret data with maximum confidentiality.

INDIVIDUALS AFFECTED BY HEALTHCARE DATA BREACHES

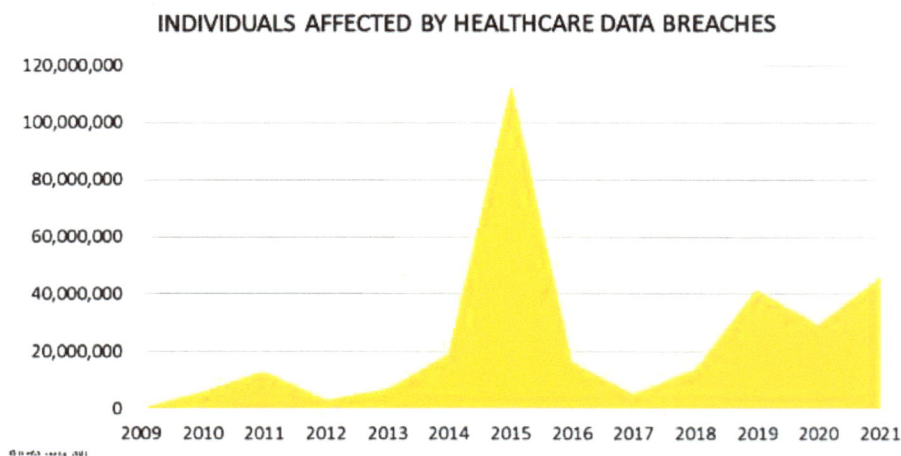

Fig. (13). Individuals affected by healthcare data breaches [12].

All Hospital Network Devices have Potential Threats that must be Monitored

This question reflects the requirements for developing the proposed system. It is crucial to get feedback for the people working in the field. This is to understand whether it is better to build HIDS to secure a few IoMT devices or if there is a persistent need to build NIDS since every single device within the hospital network is threatened. A scale from 1 to 5 is shown in Fig. (**14**), where 1 represents Strongly disagree, and 5 represents Strongly agree. The analysis showed that 43 participants strongly agree with the statement in question 8, followed by 26 who agree, 14.5% who are unsure, and only 2 who disagree. Those who disagree believe only a few IoMT devices need to be protected from cyber threats.

The fact that the entire traffic of 98% of the whole IoT device is unencrypted makes it challenging for the cybersecurity staff to deal with all potential cyber threats, exposing personal and confidential data on the network.

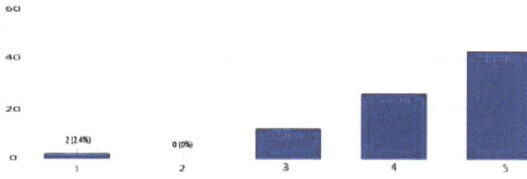

Fig. (14). Question 8 of the survey conducted.

According to the research team in Palo Alto, many cyber-attacks are threatening IoT devices, all of which are severe. Fig. **(15)** shows that the reader can recognise cyber-attacks that threaten IoMT devices. On top of that, the hospital network usually has different departments with different types of devices for other functions. For instance, some devices work at clinics that are different from computers used for billing and the database that contain patient records. Thus, each device will usually have a separate remote entry method resulting in the threats not being the same [13].

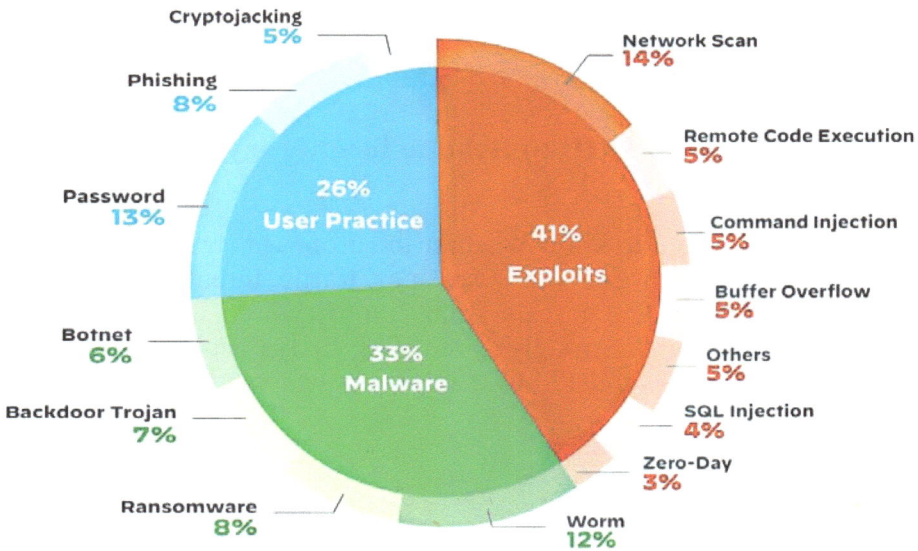

Fig. (15). IoT Devices Vulnerable to Severe Attacks [13].

The statistics in Fig. **(16)** shows that there are many threats to the IoMT, especially a Denial-of-Service attack, which is usually an attack that infects the entire network. Therefore, along with the users' opinions, the developer of this IDS system is considering building Network Intrusion Detection System (NIDS) and making the detection signature-based to eliminate known threats such as DDoS attacks. The DDoS rule is to be added to the watch list as a fundamental rule.

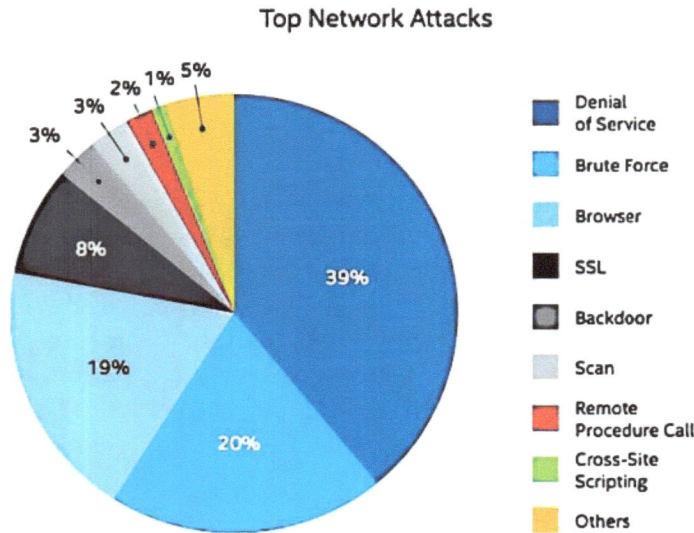

Fig. (16). Top network attacks [14].

Intrusion Detection System (IDS) Helps to Identify any Suspicious Activity in the Hospital Network

This question is justified to know whether the proposed IDS will be an effective and efficient solution to end the suspicious traffic threatening the hospitals' network. This question has a scale from 1 to 5, where 1 represents Strongly disagree, and 5 represents Strongly agree. The analysis in Fig. (**17**) shows that most respondents chose Agree (34.9%) and strongly agree (39.8%) to confirm the statement.

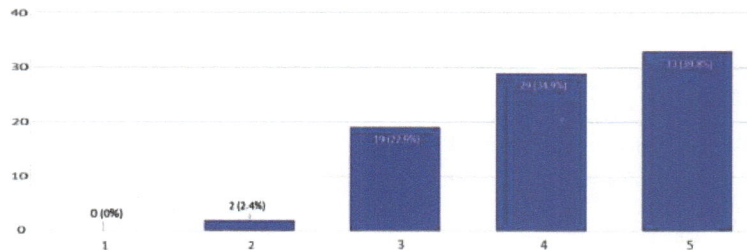

Fig. (17). Question 9 of the survey conducted.

Intrusion Detection System (IDS) has two types, Passive and Active. The passive IDS warns the admin immediately once any abnormal event occurs. On the other hand, the Active IDS is designed with automation to take action that speeds up the response time to an incident. Nevertheless, both types of IDS carry out one main and vital role: keeping network traffic controlled and protected as shown in Fig. **(18)**. Furthermore, extracting log details for deep study and investigation adds valuable experience to the security team. This is to make sure such evil intents to exploit vulnerabilities will not happen again, increasing the security level of the hospital network to be faster than a network without IDS implementation. This supports the researcher and end-users view to protect the healthcare field, which most needs such security features.

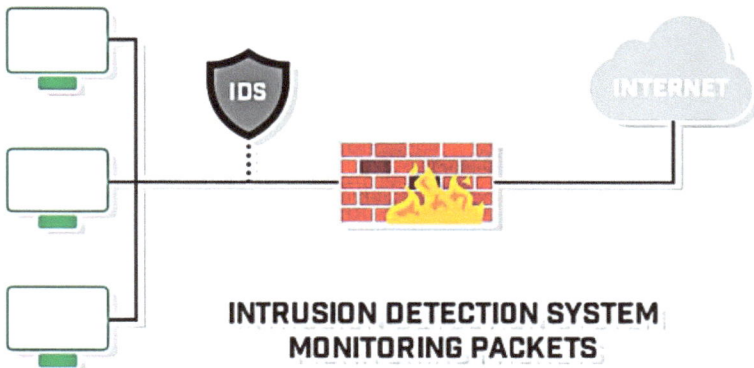

Fig. (18). IDS monitoring network traffic [15].

CONCLUSION

This research paper conducted a study within the Internet of medical things (IoMT) as a technology that is advancing very fast. However, cyber threats are also increasing rapidly worldwide, and IoMT devices have been targeted multi-times and still suffer from such. The paper provided a clear understanding of the problem, the current status, and the exact role and contribution the proposed IDS will deliver. A few areas need to be studied further in the future to improve and enhance the performance of IDS in the healthcare field. For instance, the involvement of Machine Learning with IDS to make it efficiently active, 5G technology in the near future and its impact on IoMT privacy and security, and finally, awareness of cyber threats against smart medical devices and humans' role to protect the IoMT from any harmful actions that might disturb its smooth functionality.

The Intrusion Detection System has several functions and features, such as filtering captured Logs and alarms, but there is a need to mention that the signature-based IDS depends on a Watch List. This makes regular updates of the rules in the list essential to maintain a high-security level from various cyber-attacks. Further enhancements can be added to the future system, such as having a section for statistics and graphs to assist the IT staff in understanding and gathering additional information about the health status of the network.

CONSENT FOR PUBLICATION

Not applicable.

CONFLICT OF INTEREST

The authors declare no conflict of interest, financial or otherwise.

ACKNOWLEDGEMENTS

The authors wish to express sincere appreciation to the Asia Pacific University of Technology and Innovation (APU) for giving them this opportunity to conduct the research.

REFERENCES

[1]   A. DelVecchio, "IoMT (Internet of Medical Things) or healthcare IoT," 2015. [Online]. Available: https://internetofthingsagenda.techtarget.com/definition/IoMT-Internet-of-Medical-Things [Accessed 10 April 2021].

[2]   B. Marr, "Why The Internet Of Medical Things (IoMT) Will Start To Transform Healthcare In 2018," 2018. [Online]. Available: https://www.forbes.com/sites/bernardmarr/2018/01/25/why-the-internet-of-medical-things-iomt-will-start-to-transform-healthcare-in-2018/?sh=5c1a6d7d4a3c [Accessed 10 April 2021].

[3]   D. Milkovich, "15 Alarming Cyber Security Facts and Stats," 2020. [Online]. Available: https://www.cybintsolutions.com/cyber-security-facts-stats/ [Accessed 11 April 2021].

[4]   S. Morgan, *The 2020 Healthcare Cybersecurity Report.* Herjavec Group, 2020.

[5]   intellectsoft, "Top 10 Biggest IoT Security Issues," 2020. [Online]. Available: https://www.intellectsoft.net/blog/biggest-iot-security-issues/ [Accessed 10 April 2021].

[6]   dnsstuff, "What Is an Intrusion Detection System? Latest Types and Tools," 2019. [Online]. Available: https://www.dnsstuff.com/intrusion-detection-system [Accessed 11 April 2021].

[7]   S. COOPER, "Intrusion Detection Systems Explained: 13 Best IDS Software Tools Reviewed," 2020. [Online]. Available: https://www.comparitech.com/net-admin/network-intrusion-detection-tools/ [Accessed 9 April 2021].

[8]   T. Rains, *Cyber-security Threats, Malware, Trends, and Strategies.* Packt, 2019.

[9]   R. Agrawal, "A study of methodologies used in intrusion detection and prevention system (IDPS)", In: *research gate,* 2012.

[10]   LIU HUA YEO, XIANGDONG, SHALINI, "UNDERSTANDING MODERN INTRUSION DETECTION SYSTEMS," *College of Technology, Eastern Michigan University,* p. 9, **2018**

[11]   Insider Intelligence, "The security and privacy issues that come with the Internet of Things," 2020. [Online]. Available: https://www.businessinsider.com/iot-security-privacy [Accessed 10 April 2021].

[12]   hipaajournal, "Healthcare Data Breach Statistics," 2021. [Online]. Available:

https://www.hipaajournal.com/healthcare-data-breach-statistics/ [Accessed 10 April 2021].

[13]   L. O'Donnell, "More Than Half of IoT Devices Vulnerable to Severe Attacks," 2020. [Online]. Available: https://threatpost.com/half-iot-devices-vulnerable-severe-attacks/153609/ [Accessed 10 April 2021].

[14]   Help Net Security, "Trends in Internet trust exploits, IoT, cyber espionage and privacy`," 2014. [Online]. Available: https://www.helpnetsecurity.com/2014/12/09/trends-in-internet-trust-exploit--iot-cyber-espionage-and-privacy/ [Accessed 10 April 2021].

[15]   Blog Team, "Understanding Intrusion Detection and Prevention Systems," 2018. [Online]. Available: https://www.accessagility.com/blog/understanding-intrusion-detection-and-prevention-systems [Accessed 12 April 2021].

CHAPTER 8

Cyber Security State of Industrial Internet of Things (IIoT)

Ali Ahmed Mohammed Ali Alwashali[1], Nor Azlina Abdul Rahman[2] and **Mohammad Haziq Roszlan[2,*]**

[1] *School of Computing & Technology, Asia Pacific University of Technology and Innovation, Kuala Lumpur, Malaysia*

[2] *Forensic and Cyber Security Research Centre, Asia Pacific University of Technology and Innovation, Kuala Lumpur, Malaysia*

Abstract: Cybersecurity is a critical component of technology and must be considered during the early stages of the development of any system. Cyber security issues and challenges faced by IIoT are discussed in this paper. The first section of this paper focuses on Industrial Control System (ICS) environments where IIoT are deployed to understand the nature of business and technology companies with IIoT networks, followed by a comparison to understand the difference between Operational Technology (OT) and Information Technology (IT) networks and how both can be used to serve the need of business requirements. This paper evaluates the state of cyber security in industrial networks and IIoT and the safety and privacy concerns found in the literature. Solutions and improvement techniques introduced to cyber security functions mainly focus on prevention, detection, and response. Moreover, IoT organisational and operational security and cyber threat intelligence are also discussed. Finally, an approach is presented on how to conduct a security assessment on IIoT environments safely.

Keywords: Countermeasures, Cyber security, IIoT, Industrial control system (ICS), Operational technology, Vulnerability.

INTRODUCTION

IoT provides a layer of intelligence on top of physical machines and devices by connecting them to share resources. The idea of connecting things could be as simple as automating tasks, such as opening a garage door, or more complex, like controlling the entire business operation of a factory. The number of devices in 2020 connected to the internet is estimated to be 20 billion ("Gartner Says 8.4 billion Connected 'Things' Will Be in Use in 2017, Up 31 Percent From 2016)

---

* **Corresponding author Mohammad Haziq Roszlan**: Forensic and Cyber Security Research Centre, Asia Pacific University of Technology and Innovation, Kuala Lumpur, Malaysia; E-mail: mhaziqroszlan@gmail.com

Muhammad Ehsan Rana and Manoj Jayabalan (Eds.)

[1]. This report focuses on the state of security in the industrial internet of things and the underlying infrastructure that controls them.

The adoption of the industrial internet of things enables industries to integrate physical systems and IT applications to facilitate and orchestrate entire production lines to reduce human manual intervention. The difference between conventional IoT devices and industrial IoT is in the environment where they are deployed and the application's target. Conventional IoT devices usually target consumers, while IIoT targets the industrial sectors. Furthermore, Industrial IoT is used in critical environments, making reliability and safety their highest priority.

In terms of security, TrendMicro zero-day initiative team conducted intensive research in two years (2015-2016) to assess the state of ICS security. The research revealed 250 zero-day vulnerabilities that could be used to attack critical infrastructure [2]. Moreover, it is believed that the state of ICS security is insecure. Only one company was able to discover serious security problems and the average time required to patch vulnerabilities. Fig. (**1**) shows the number of days needed by each vendor affected in the research to patch vulnerabilities.

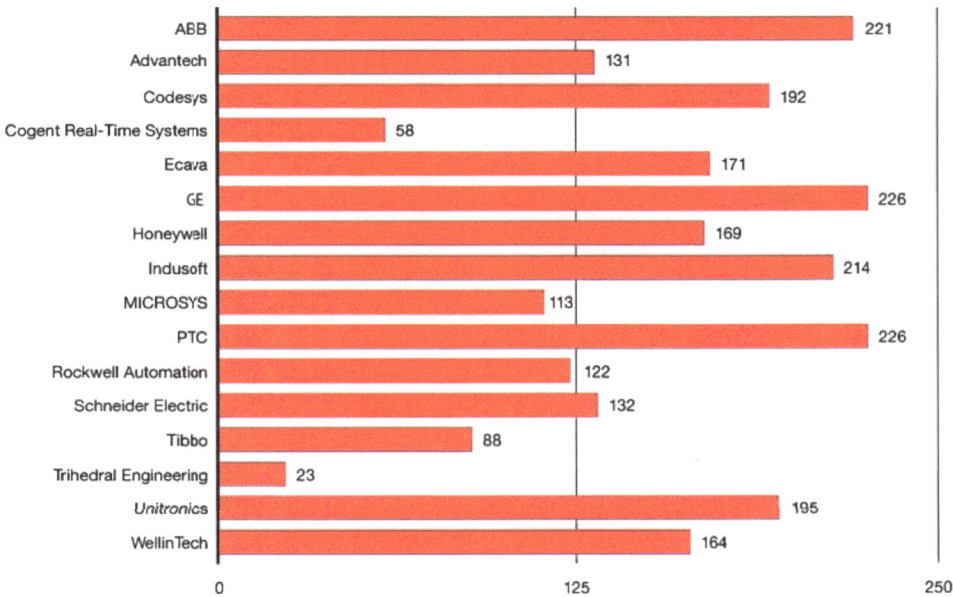

Fig. (1). Average patch time by Vendors [2].

According to the national vulnerability database (NVD) maintained by NIST, 2020 does not have any fewer vulnerabilities than previous years, as there are 365 new ones. Most of the published vulnerabilities can be exploited remotely. The servility of the published vulnerabilities is shown in Fig. (**2**).

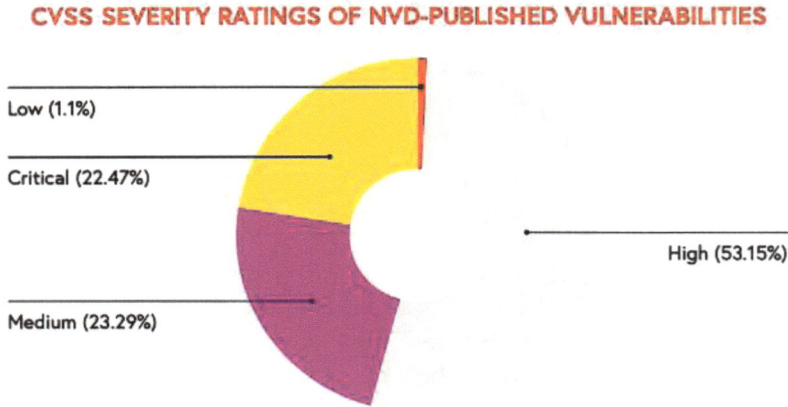

CVSS SEVERITY RATINGS OF NVD-PUBLISHED VULNERABILITIES

Low (1.1%)

Critical (22.47%)

High (53.15%)

Medium (23.29%)

Fig. (2). 2020 vulnerability severity [3].

The US ICS-CERT team also published 139 advisories for hardening the security of ICS [3].

Industrial Control System Environment

The architecture of any control system is divided into three primary levels: field level, control level, and production control level. The field level consists of sensors and actuators. Sensors either control the actuators or send data for storage and processing. The control level is placed at a higher field level. It receives data from sensors and sends commands to actuators. The interaction between devices controlled on this level uses intelligent language to define the rules and decision-making parameters. A programmable logic controller is an excellent example of a control-level device. Devices at the production control level control all the lower levels of devices and provide a high overview of the entire production process. Human Machine Interface is an example of a production control system. The production control level is where IT systems are interfaced with OT networks [4].

IoT in Electrical Sector

The electrical sector was one of the first industries to embrace the internet of things to build smart power grids. IoT will act as a layer of connected devices built on the power grid network.

The definition of the smart grid is derived from the fact that the distributed IoT devices across the power grid network send the gathered data to an IT system for processing, where AI and big data will be used to assess the network and predict demand [5].

Applications of IIoT in Smart Grid

- Power monitoring across plants
- Prediction sensors of demand and supply
- Smart meters at the consumer side to exchange data with the station
- Operation continuity and disaster recovery
- Control power generation and consumption
- Asset management

A Prime component in the smart grid is the advanced metering infrastructure that requires a communication medium for data exchange between smart meters and AMI [5]. Table 1 shows the differences between Information Technology and Operational Technology.

Table 1. Differences between Information Technology and Operational Technology.

-	IT	OT
Focus	Data	Physical World
Risk Impact	Business operation	Health and Safety
Network connectivity	Interconnected	Traditionally isolated systems
Timeliness	Tolerant	Critical
Physical effect	None	High
Security Solution	Mature	Less mature than IT
Support	Diversified	Only one vendor. In some cases, security professionals are not allowed due to legal and license issues
Technology Lifetime	Three to five years	Ten to fifteen years and more
Operating System	On top of a typical OS	Commercial custom OS and software
Protocol Example	HTTP	Modbus
System Resources	No resources constrain	Lack of enough resources to adopt security measures such as logging and encryption

VULNERABILITY AND RISK ASSESSMENT

Bou-Harb and Neshenko reviewed more than 100 pieces of research in the field of IoT security. According to the review published, despite the trend in IoT security research, many operational challenges in IoT remain unsolved, reducing confidence in IoT security [4, 5]. Vulnerabilities affecting IoT devices must be addressed to improve the underlying technology and mitigate exploitation's impact. In some cases, patching the system solves the problem for a specific vulnerability but does not solve the original challenge. Some IoT devices do not provide a mechanism to update the system and improve security. They only offer complex and inefficient ways to update vulnerabilities by installing a higher firmware version. In large-scale applications, IoT needs to have a way to automate vulnerability discovery and patching [6].

Safety and Security

In ICS environments, Safety measures and assessment frameworks are more mature than the frameworks in the field of information security. ICS environment faced safety issues before IT even accepted cyber security as a real threat. Adopting IoTs in an industrial environment introduces new operational methods that tend to automate and fully computerise operations. This weakens the frameworks and safety measures that were well tested and delivered to human factors when production systems used to be controlled and operated manually [7].

IIoT Vulnerabilities

In smart grid architecture, the example of IIoT is the smart meters devices deployed at the customer's side to facilitate communication between the customer and power provider. Through smart meters, power providers receive data about the status of the network, usage, billing, and much other information. Physical access to smart meters at the customer's location risks the integrity of the devices and data sent to the data centre collecting the customer's data [8]. Two attack surfaces against smart meters, namely attack against physical, cyber systems and communication networks. Gaining physical access to the meter can result in different attack scenarios.

- Injecting false data
- Spoofing identity
- Electricity theft
- Denial of services

Despite the application domain, a common issue faced by all IoT devices is the system's and hardware's limited resources. Moreover, smart meters are deployed on a large scale to reach millions of devices and cost requirement mandates lowering the cost of each meter. Security mechanisms are affected directly by limiting software and hardware capabilities allowing said attack scenarios to be possible and easy to perform. Similarly, a meters communication network that links meters with collectors through wireless networks can also be exploited. Data collectors receive data from meters in scales ranging from a few hundred to millions. Some attack scenarios against communication networks

- Distributed denial of service
- Connection Disruption between meters and data collectors
- Confidentiality attacks of data transmission
- WiFi and ZigBee-specific attacks
- Malicious data injection

ICS Vulnerabilities

The advancement of IT security directly influences the state of ICS security. The plethora of IT attack techniques and vulnerabilities affect ICS security. Rather than ICS zero-day vulnerabilities, attack groups would use vulnerabilities in technologies [9]. Furthermore, the evolution of IIoT in ICS has widened the attack vector to exploit critical infrastructure [9]. Research shows how IoT devices deployed in many environments, including the electrical industry, can perform highly sophisticated attacks [10]. The paper mapped the simulated attack phased to real APT attacks against devices in ICS environments such as PLC, SCADA, HMI, *etc.*

HMI represents the heart of any ICS. Attacks on HMI devices will lead to massive attacks since they are used to control IIoT in fields. Unfortunately, companies focus most of the security on field devices rather than HMI. The research conducted by Trend Micro demonstrates the sensitivity of HMI devices and the lack of security mechanisms. As discussed below, four types of security weaknesses were the most prevalent to be used during cyber-attacks.

Memory Corruption

This vulnerability can lead to buffer overflow and give the attacker full control of the system. The vulnerability occurs when the attacker accesses the memory location of insecure code to change the execution flow of the code. One example of insecure functions (Fig. **3**) causing buffer overflow is _sprintf. ZDI reported the issues to vendors, and while they fixed most of them, it is impossible to replace all insecure functions causing the same problem fully. It's estimated that thousands of _sprintf functions across software and devices are left insecure.

```
.text:100015D6 loc_10015D6      ; CODE XREF: BwSvcFunction+44j
.text:100015D6                  ; DATA XREF: .text:off10001B08o
.text:100015d6 push offset aRpc_dllBwcmd_g ; jumptable 10001124
case 20011
.text:100015DB call      sub_10001BB0
.text:100015E0 move      ebx, [esp+0F8h+arg_8]
.text:100015E7 add       esp, 4
.text:100015EA lea       edx, [esp+0F4h+WindowName]
.text:100015EE push      ebx
.text:100015EF push      offset aS      ; "%s"
.text:100015F4 push      edx            ; char *
.text:100015F5 call      _sprintf
```

Fig. (3). Insecure code in Advantech WebAccess HMI Solution.

Credential Dump

Passwords are stored in cleartext. A leak of passwords can be leveraged to move laterally in the environment and compromise more devices. Suppose the admin user password was leaked; the attacker can access all other devices the admin has rights on. In some cases, one account can access the entire network, which is catastrophic in ICS environments. The example discussed in the research is General Electric (GE) MDS PulseNET system. The software contained a hardcoded password in the code. Vendors put in the password for support purposes, but attackers can use the password to log in to any system without any vulnerability needed. Hardcoded passwords cannot be changed or removed by the administrator. Only vendors can access the code. The same is published in CVE-2015-6456 with 9/10 severity.

Insecure Configuration

Insecure default configuration was another common issue in most systems controlling HMI, which directly controls many field devices such as IIoT. Vulnerability CVE-2016-6486 in Siemens SINEMA Server is a case study in this category of vulnerabilities. Less privileged users can add themselves to higher-privileged user groups and control the system. No proper validation is made to make sure the limited user does not modify the list of ACL in the first place.

Code Injection

Hackers can instruct the device to perform malicious activities like adding a user or modifying sensitive OS files. Injection techniques are not limited to conventional SQL or command injection. They exist in any interpreting engine and are not limited to a specific OS or language. Gamma scripting in the Cogent DataHub system is a propriety language used to develop applications that control complex SCADA systems.

AMI Privacy Concern

Concerns are raised about the massive collection and access of personal data by sensors deployed as part of a smart grid system. Applications introduced by the smart grid mandate collecting customer data that is considered personal. For example, smart meters are designed to collect real-time data about home appliances accurately. This is done to maintain a repository of information for processing at smart grid stations. Analysing the data collected can be used to adjust the power consumption of each appliance and predict failures. Furthermore, it helps customers access their billing information and reduce the cost of power usage at a granular level. The concerning part of the massive data collection is the ability to generate profiles of individual activity inside homes through the usage pattern of various machines and appliances. It is even possible to identify the type of appliances and machines used in running time [11]. An Italian researcher could predict the usage of home appliances such as a washing machine, TV, fridge, toaster, and others. Fig. (**4**) shows the appliances with 90% accuracy.

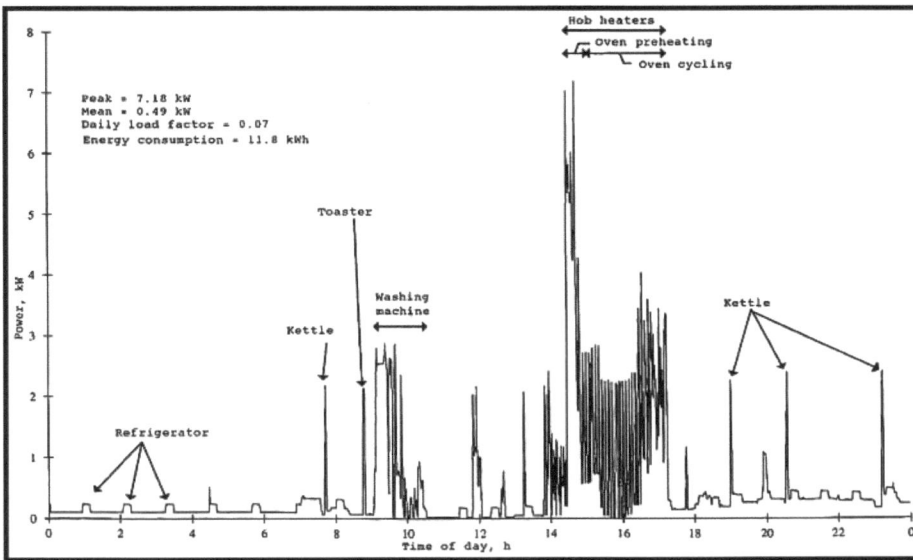

Fig. (4). Accurate prediction of home appliances.

In extreme cases, law enforcement can use data generated by the smart grid and IIoT to build a massive real-time surveillance system.

IMPROVING IIOT SECURITY

Three core functions in OT or IT cyber security programs are prevention, detection, and response. Each one contributes to the overall cyber security posture of an organisation. However, difficulties in improving cyber security functions vary based on the nature of the business and the type of technology. Environmental loss and safety are prime security goals of OT networks but not in IT. Therefore, more than mature cyber security programs in IT environments is needed to be used in IIoT environments. Prevention, detection, and response (Fig. 5) are the three main functions constituting a cyber security program. They support each other, and each one contributes to the efficiency of the other. Good detection capabilities enable incident discovery and early investigation. Subsequently, findings of incident response improve prevention during post-incident activities to ensure the same thing does not occur again in the environment.

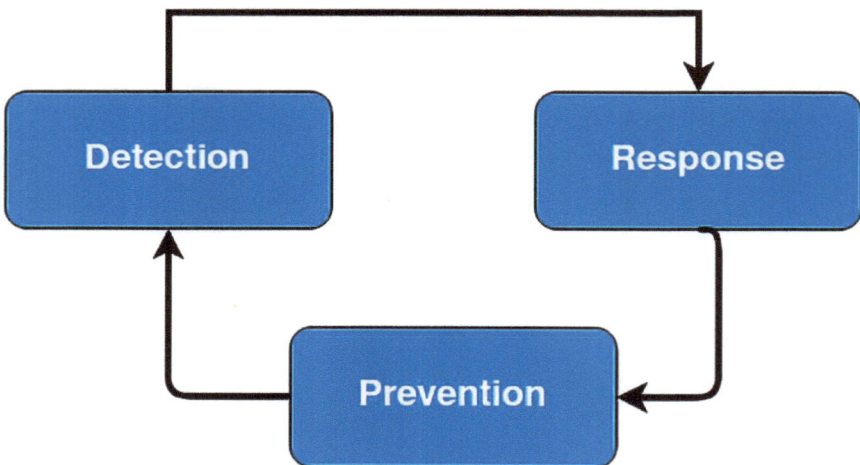

Fig. (5). Cyber security functions.

Improving Prevention

IIoT Security researchers focus on devising new security mechanisms that fit the requirements and applications of IIoT. Cryptography and access control have been the trending research topics for IIoT security. Cryptography research trends gravitate towards filling the gap of developing algorithms that fit constant devices such as IoT. A thorough literature review on lightweight cryptography algorithms and protocols was published [12]. The national institute of standards and technology also took the initiative to guide researchers to develop lightweight encryption algorithms [13]. The same is also discussed in ISO/IEC 29192 standards [14].

The second area of research is access control mechanisms and their implementation, which is a challenging topic in IIoT. The researcher discussed the requirements for access control systems in IIoT environments and mapped proposed models to the four layers of IoT/IIoT systems: Cloud, Fog Mist, and Edge [15]. Additionally, another researcher conducted extensive research on models and frameworks that can be tailored to fit the different layers of abstraction in IIoT systems [16].

Improving Detection

A detailed white paper on the four types of threat detection in IIoT networks was published [17]. According to Sergio, detection is the most crucial function of cyber security. Threats should be detected in the early stages of the attack to reduce the damage caused to the network.

- Configuration Detection
- Modelling
- Indicators
- Behavioural

Configuration detections rely on what is known about the infrastructure configuration to spot the anomalies. For instance, the protocol used to communicate between devices. PLCs never communicate with clients in the network or any configuration changes. The approach to becoming effective requires experts in operations and infrastructure devices to know when the network or device deviates from the typical configuration. Despite the challenge of documenting and maintaining the configuration state of the infrastructure, it is encouraged to use detection by configuration deviation due to the static nature of IIoT networks because the configurations are less likely to be frequently changed.

Modelling employees' big data and machine learning to profile normal behaviour of IIoT. The method focuses on building a model that describes the device's normal behaviour over time. Machine learning algorithms have applications in this area and can produce effective results. Apart from the security benefits of modelling, it has applications for predicting operating failures. The same is discussed in detail, focusing on IIoT protocols in the research published by [18].

Indicator methods provide specific information about threats, commonly known as indicators of compromise. It is specific information about previously seen attacks. While not effective on its own, it can complement other detection mechanisms. Even though they provide the most accurate way to describe and share attack information and attack scoping, they are the quickest and easiest to be changed by attackers.

Lastly, threat behavioural focus on the attacker's behaviour and exploit methods. Adversaries are studied to build a knowledge base of all tactics seen. Response plans are built on tactics knowledge to recover and solve incidents faster. A good example is using malicious project files with PLCs to operate the environment. Attackers frequently use this tactic in ICS attacks [19]. is a knowledge base for attacks against industrial control networks. There are currently 81 techniques documented and mapped into 10 categories. ATT&CK ICS philosophy paper describes the motivation and components of the framework [20].

Detection of IIoT attacks using Honeypots

Honeypots are IoT devices deployed in the field to monitor any incoming attacks. In a typical scenario, IoT honeypots do not offer real operational services and are only deployed for monitoring. Honeypot is triggered when attackers try to interact with them. The following list contains research on how to use a honeypot for detection in ICS environments, whereas some researchers provide a real honeypot that can be used for situational awareness of the network.

Researchers proposed many IoT-specific honeypots and frameworks that focus on cyber threats in IoT environments and support protocols used by OT networks. IoTPOT is an [21] example of an IoT honeypot developed by [22]. The author also developed a sandbox solution to analyse malware that attacks honeypots. Information collected by honeypot and malware is extracted during the initial attack phase of honeypot to help mitigate future attacks and provide insight into ongoing attack patterns. Siphon is another IoT honeypot developed by [23]. The authors developed the platform to attract hackers to attack IoT. They deployed the platform at 16 different places around the world, aiming to collect data about attacks that try to spread through IoT devices. The mimicked services range between IoT devices, IP cameras, printers, and physical devices. Other honeypot platforms are proposed by researchers, such as HosTaGe, Crysys honeypot, and HoneyPhy. These platforms also use their application in cyber threat intelligence to study the patterns of attacks in physical locations like a city or country. The data collected can be of great use for threat research and intrusion analysis. For example, two sets of IoT honeypots can be deployed inside companies' environments and outside the network in the same country or in the cloud. The data collected from both sets can be analysed to differentiate targeted attacks and large-scale random internet attacks.

ORGANISATIONAL AND OPERATIONAL SECURITY

IIoT's high interoperability and the high number of devices connected to one network make it more challenging for companies to maintain organisational and operational security. No one fits all framework for people, processes, and technology. Many businesses in information technology have achieved a reasonable degree of success in security resilience by adopting organisational and operational measures. Endpoint Visibility in the network is critical when those endpoints are IIoT devices. Asset management becomes challenging for unpatched or improperly configured devices. This becomes even worse when the enterprise security team cannot determine whether IoT devices have been breached or involved in malicious activity. If inventory management is not enforced with best practices, it will not be sure if the proper protection is applied. Ponemon Institute published a study that showed that 65% of incidents happened due to a lack of visibility [24]. Ponemon Institute and Devo Technology Study reveal that 65% of cybersecurity analysts consider quitting due to lack of visibility [10].

Security orchestration, automation, and response (SOAR) technology can help compensate for some of the workloads that IoT necessitates because it consolidates technologies and employee big data to understand the flow and patterns of the network. Endpoint detection and response is a central tool for threat detection but has yet to be found to be mature technology in IIoT platforms [25]. No one fits all framework in operational security, so companies should tailor operational security frameworks to meet business requirements. People, technology, and processes are the three main pillars of any operational security [26]. Although the many frameworks divide the importance of security operations into the three functions of People, technology, and processes, without people, none of the technologies or processes would be implemented and counted for success. Hence, people are the most critical function that should be carefully selected, managed, and trained.

The security operation is concentrated around building teams. The security operation team is usually divided into three tiers (also known as layers). Tier 1 is the team receiving alerts; they query SIEM to aggregate data and eliminate false positives. Tier 2 are incident responders; they perform investigations on received escalated alerts from tier 1. Tier 3 are the experts in the team, with most of their time spent on threat hunting. While building a team in the industrial environment, choosing people who can spend time with engineers in the field is vital. Moreover, they should understand operations and complex interconnections, mainly when IIoT is found. The team should know how to support someone on the field during outages or security issues.

The processes that establish guides for daily operations are part of organisational security. Processes in the form of documents contain the details of incident escalation, line of communication, incident classification, and many other essential activities in security operations. This helps operators and security personnel to refer to the documents and automate tasks if possible. Policies can be converted into operational playbooks and more detailed documents [27].

CYBER THREATS INTELLIGENCE AND INFORMATION SHARING

Cyber Threat Intelligence is the field that focuses on providing processed information called intelligence that prevents the mitigation of cyber-attacks. The product of CTI can be as raw data or specific to cyber-attacks, known as indicators of compromise. Information sharing is part of cyber threat intelligence functions. During cyber incidents, companies that provide CTI commercial services publish technical reports explaining the incident's root cause and preventive mechanisms. The 2016 Ukraine power incident is an example to stress the importance of information sharing. The ESET company published the first report, "Industroyer: Biggest malware threat to critical infrastructure since Stuxnet, "and the second CRASH OVERRIDE by Dragos and many others. Other companies track cyber-criminal groups for years before publishing a complete analysis of their cyber capabilities and tactics employed during their attack campaigns [28]. The availability of information related to any attack enabled companies to act proactively. Cyber threat intelligence platforms are developed to consolidate different data sources to be available for searching by defenders.

IoT Threats Intelligence Platform

Developed an IoT-specific platform for sharing threat intelligence information called Siot. The main development objective is to automate the collection and aggregation of threat information targeting IoT devices. Siot is not the first platform that shares the same objective in the field of cyber threat intelligence; other platforms, such as MISP, do the same [29]. However, they are not explicitly focused on IoT threats like Siot (Fig. 6).

Siot uses backscatter and probing algorithms to extract intelligence from the collected data of large networks. The research community can use the data to avoid similar attack techniques in the future. In addition, the platform can relate the intelligence gathered to specific countries, business sectors, or ISP. The data is ranked based on the number of compromised IoT devices and abnormal activities. Each rank comprises severity from 1 to 10. Nonetheless, the ranking system may not be accurate, and it is subjective to the collected data availability and authenticity. The authors should have mentioned any feature that enables users to aggregate the data based on the data source in case a data source is not trusted or the data provided is not up to a certain quality.

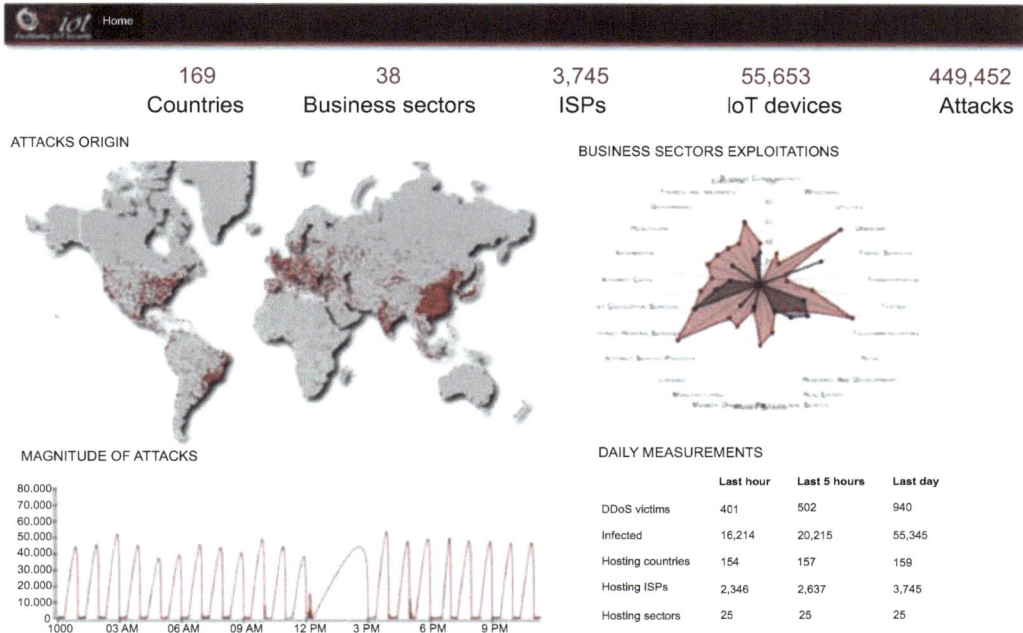

Fig. (6). Siot Platform [25].

Siot core components (Fig. 7) are:

- Data aggregation module
- Data processing module
- User Interface (dashboards)

The core functionality of the data aggregation module is the extraction of IP addresses to be queried on other platforms, such as Shodan, using API. A data processing module processes the extracted data to identify possible targeted or compromised IoT devices within the environment. Users interact with Siot through a web interface called a dashboard on the client's side. It uses D3 JavaScript to generate graphs to represent data.

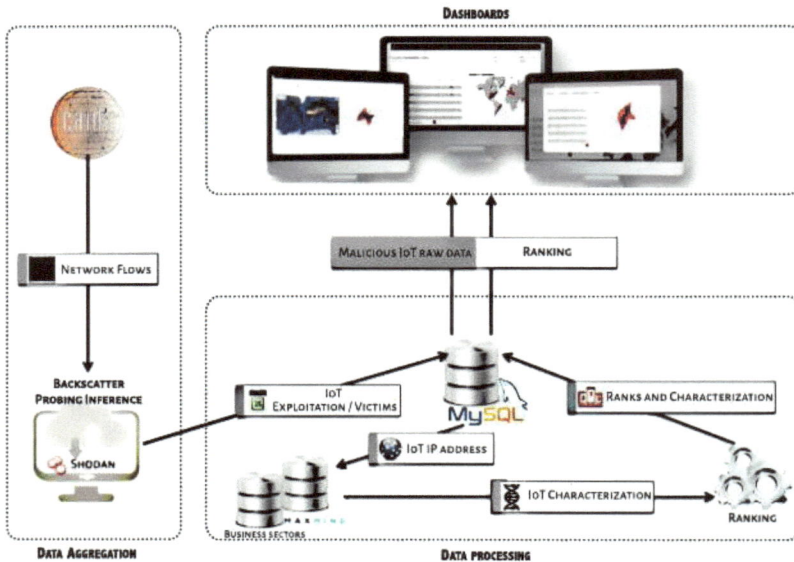

Fig. (7). Siot Components [5].

SECURITY ASSESSMENT APPROACH FOR IIOT NETWORKS

("A Hands-On Introduction to Mandiant's Approach to OT Red Teaming," 2020) FireEye red team published an article discussing the approach they are following when performing red teaming exercises against OT networks and a case study from one of their engagements. Although the case study is not about a power grid network, the attack scenario applies to any OT network, including a power grid OT network. The only difference is the last phase of the attack, which is specific to the target system. The case study presented can be related to previous information mentioned in the report (Fig. **8**).

According to the FireEye team, the initial access to the control server was through weakly implemented password protection. According to the case study, the team needed only 6 seconds to crack the password harvested from the network. The same is discussed as a significant vulnerability found by TrendMicro in chapter 2. The typical approach is to leverage IT systems for initial compromise before moving to OT devices. This can also be related to what Drago's publication mentioned earlier, that it is rare to find attackers using ICS zero vulnerabilities and IT attacks to gain access [11].

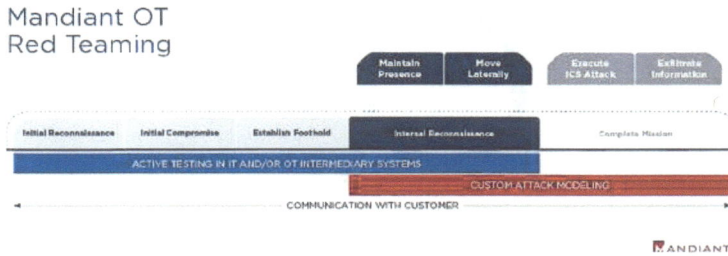

Fig. (8). Mandiant Approach [11].

The engagement is divided into two main phases. The first phase performs active testing of OT and IT systems to gain first access to the networks. The second phase builds a custom attack modelling focusing on OT devices being targeted. The initial phase used IT cyber-attack techniques, such as LLMNR protocol attacks to harvest passwords from the network by performing man-in-the-middle attacks. Tools such as Wireshark, Hashcat, and Responder, along with many other publicly available tools, were used.

The first phase provides the team with access to a critical server. The second phase starts to model a custom attack that fits the object and type of OT device compromised. The modelling simulates the goal of real attacks by developing a custom model that requires deep knowledge of ICS controls. The target OT devices are industrial steaming boilers for chemical companies. The objective is to simulate an attacker that intends to cause the highest physical damage to the environment. The team must gain access to the logic file where the operation flow of the boiler is written. Modifying the logic with a successful exploit of another component can result in lowering the water amount below the safe threshold and disabling heat management and safety components.

CONCLUSION

This research paper discusses operational challenges in IoT, vulnerabilities in IIoT, and several countermeasures for protecting the system. Based on what is discussed in this paper, the researcher can conclude that:

- Attackers can gain access to Operational Technology networks with limited knowledge of Industrial Control System (ICS)
- Achieving sophisticated attacks that result in physical damage and massive impact may require deep knowledge of ICS. An attacker may arbitrarily perform random steps that can cause damage.

- IT security influences OT security due to the high integration between IT and OT networks

CONSENT FOR PUBLICATION

Not applicable.

CONFLICT OF INTEREST

The authors declare no conflict of interest, financial or otherwise.

ACKNOWLEDGEMENT

This research is supported by the Asia Pacific University of Innovation and Technology.

REFERENCES

[1]   https://www.gartner.com/en/newsroom/press-releases/2017-02-07-gartner-says-8-

[2]   https://documents.trendmicro.com/assets/wp/wp-hacker-machine-interface.pdf

[3]   https://www.claroty.com/2020/08/25/what-you-need-to-know-about-ics-rivulnerability-landscape/

[4]   E. Bou-Harb, and N. Neshenko, *"Cyber Threat Intelligence for the Internet of Things," Springer International Publishing.* Availanle, 2020. [online] [http://dx.doi.org/10.1007/978-3-030-45858-4]

[5]   Bou-Harb, E., Neshenko, N., "Generating and Sharing IoT-Centric Cyber Threat Intelligence," Cyber Threat Intelligence for the Internet of Things, pp. 77–84, May 31, 2020.

[6]   Tekeoglu, A., Tosun, A.Ş., 2016. A Testbed for Security and Privacy Analysis of IoT Devices, in: 2016 IEEE 13th International Conference on Mobile Ad Hoc and Sensor Systems (MASS). Presented at the 2016 IEEE 13th International Conference on Mobile Ad Hoc and Sensor Systems (MASS), pp. 343–348. [http://dx.doi.org/10.1109/MASS.2016.051]

[7]   Stouffer, K., Lightman, S., Pillitteri, V., Abrams, M., Hahn, A., "Guide to Industrial Control Systems (ICS) Security," NIST Special Publication (SP) 800-82 Rev. 2, 2015 [online]. Available: 10.6028/NIST.SP.800-82r2 [Accessed 11 Oct 2020]

[8]   Wei, L., Rondon, L.P., Moghadasi, A., Sarwat, A.I., "Review of Cyber-Physical Attacks and Counter Defense Mechanisms for Advanced Metering Infrastructure in Smart Grid," IEEE/PES Transmission and Distribution Conference and Exposition (T&D), pp. 1–9, April 16 -19, 2018

[9]   Thomas Pope, Thomas Pope, "The Real Risk to ICS Environments Using Threat Intelligence to Improve Compliance and Risk Management," Dragos, Nov , 2019 [online]. Available: https://www.dragos.com/resource/the-real-risk-to-ics-environments-using-threat-inte-ligence-to-improve-compliance-and-risk-management/ [Accessed 11 Oct 2020]

[10]   https://www.businesswire.com/news/home/20190729005244/en/Ponemon

[11]   https://www.fireeye.com/blog/threat-research/2020/08/hands-on-introduction-tomandiant-appro-ch-to-ot-red-teaming.html

[12]   Agrawal, M., Zhou, J., Chang, D., "A Survey on Lightweight Authenticated Encryption and Challenges for Securing Industrial IoT," Security and Privacy Trends in the Industrial Internet of Things, pp.71–94, May 14, 2019.

[13]   "Analysis of the Cyber Attack on the Ukrainian Power Grid, 2016," *ATT&CK® for Industrial Control Systems,* 2020 [online]. Available: https://collaborate.mitre.org/attackics/index.php/Main_Page [Aaccessed 16 Oct. 2020]

[14]   D. Nathans, *Designing and Building Security Operations Center.* Syngress, 2015, pp. 125-149. [http://dx.doi.org/10.1016/B978-0-12-800899-7.00006-9]

[15]   https://www.dragos.com/wp-content/uploads/Dragos-Insights-into-Building-an-ICS-Security-Operations-Center.pdf [Aaccessed 16 Oct. 2020]

[16]   Faisal, M.A., Cardenas, A.A., Wool, A., "Profiling Communications in Industrial IP Networks: Model Complexity and Anomaly Detection," Security and Privacy Trends in the Industrial Internet of Things, Advanced Sciences and Technologies for Security Applications, pp. 139–160, May 14, 2019.

[17]   Stellios, I., Kotzanikolaou, P., Psarakis, M., Alcaraz, C., Lopez, J., "A Survey of IoT-Enabled Cyberattacks: Assessing Attack Paths to Critical Infrastructures and Services," IEEE Communications Surveys Tutorials, vol. 20, no. 4, pp. 3453–3495, July 12, 2018, [online], Available from: 10.1109/COMST.2018.2855563 [Aaccessed 16 Oct. 2020].

[18]   "Lightweight Cryptography | CSRC | CSRC," CSRC | NIST, 2017 [online]. Available: https://content.csrc.e1a.nist.gov/projects/lightweight-cryptography [Accessed 26 Oct 2020].

[19]   "ISO/IEC 29192-2:2019," ISO, 2019 [online]. Available: https://content.csrc.e1a.nist.gov/projects/lightweight-cryptography [Accessed 26 Oct. 2020).

[20]   Stavros Salonikias, Antonios Gouglidis, Ioannis Mavridis, Dimitris Gritzalis, "Access Control in the Industrial Internet of Things", Security and Privacy Trends in the Industrial Internet of Things, pp 95-114, May 14, 2019 [Online]. Available: https://link.springer.com/chapter/10.1007/978-3-030-12-30-7_510.1007/978-3-030-12330-7_5 [Accessed 26 Oct 2020].

[21]   Ouaddah, A., Mousannif, H., Abou Elkalam, A., Ait Ouahman, A., "Access control in the Internet of Things: Big challenges and new opportunities," Computer Networks, vol. 112, pp. 237–262, Jan 15, 2017[online]. Available: 10.1016/j.comnet.2016.11.007 [Accessed 26 Oct 2020].

[22]   Sergio Caltagirone, Robert M. Lee, n.d., "The Four Types of Threat Detection With Case-Studies in Industrial Control Systems (ICS)," Dragos, July 31, 2018 [online]. Available: https://www.dragos.com/resource/the-four-types-of-threat-detection-with-case-studies-in-industrial-control-systems-ics/ [Accessed 26 Oct 2020].

[23]   Guarnizo, J., Tambe, A., Bhunia, S.S., Ochoa, M., Tippenhauer, N., Shabtai, A., Elovici, Y., "SIPHON: Towards Scalable High-Interaction Physical Honeypots," arXiv, Jan 10, 2017 [online]. Available: https://arxiv.org/abs/1701.0244610.1145/3055186.3055192 [Accessed 26 Oct 2020].

[24]   Pa, Y.M.P., Suzuki, S., Yoshioka, K., Matsumoto, T., Kasama, T., Rossow, C., "IoTPOT: A Novel Honeypot for Revealing Current IoT Threats," Journal of Information Processing vol. 24 no.3, pp. 522–533, 2016 [online]. Available: 10.2197/ipsjjip.24.522

[25]   Wagner, C., Dulaunoy, A., Wagener, G., Iklody, A., "MISP: The Design and Implementation of a Collaborative Threat Intelligence Sharing Platform," The 2016 ACM on Workshop on Information Sharing and Collaborative Security, WISCS '16, pp. 49–56 [online]. Available: 10.1145/2994539.2994542 [Accessed 26 Oct 2020].

[26]   "How to Prepare Your Security Operations for the Continuing IoT Upsurge," Siemplify , 2019 [online]. Available: https://www.siemplify.co/blog/how-to-prepareyour-security-operations-for-the-continuing-iot-upsurge/ [Accessed 28 Oct.20]

[27]   "Securing Industrial Control Systems," springerprofessional.de., 2018 [online]. Available: https://www.springerprofessional.de/securing-industrialcontrolsystems/16720118 [Accessed 11 Oct. 2020].

[28]   Ghasempour, A., "Internet of Things in Smart Grid: Architecture, Applications, Services, Key Technologies, and Challenges," Inventions, vol. 4, no. 22, March 26. 2019 [online]. Available:

10.3390/inventions4010022 [Accessed 11 Oct. 2020].

[29] Ghasempour, A., "Optimum number of aggregators based on power consumption, cost, and network lifetime in advanced metering infrastructure architecture for Smart Grid Internet of Things," 13th IEEE Annual Consumer Communications Networking Conference (CCNC), pp. 295–296, Jan. 9 -12, 2016 [online]. Available: 10.1109/CCNC.2016.7444787

CHAPTER 9

Machine Learning for Browser Privacy

Kelvin Tan[1] and **Rajasvaran Logeswaran**[1,*]

[1] *School of Computing, Asia Pacific University of Technology and Innovation, Kuala Lumpur, Malaysia*

Abstract: Online privacy is an Internet user's control of how much personal information is shared with a third party. Unfortunately, some third parties, such as data brokers, collect user data without permission to resell the data to other parties. Browser tracking allows each Internet user to be uniquely identified, and in-depth user profiles are built. Browser fingerprinting is one of the most effective methods of browser tracking. It uniquely identifies each user through their devices' configuration, even for users using the same device models. Using Virtual Private Networks, the Tor browser and specific browser extensions as a countermeasure against browser fingerprinting are not widespread, so it often results in a compromised user experience. Researchers have proposed various classification machine learning approaches to improve browser privacy; some focus on recognising and blocking advertisements and website scripts that track users. In contrast, others identify potential vulnerabilities in browser security configurations. There is a need for more research in machine learning, especially natural language processing, to enhance browser privacy.

Keywords: Browser Fingerprinting, Machine Learning, Online Privacy, User Interest Profiling.

INTRODUCTION

With the increased time spent on the Internet, user data is of great interest to marketers and advertisers. Browser tracking uniquely identifies each user and collects data regarding their browsing activities. The massive amount of collected user data leads to highly sophisticated and effective machine learning models that classify users into market segmentation for targeted marketing purposes. This paper examines the current research in browser tracking, and the machine learning approaches on user data, as well as the research in the countermeasures through privacy-enhancing technology (PET) and machine learning approaches.

---

* **Corresponding author Rajasvaran Logeswaran:** School of Computing, Asia Pacific University of Technology and Innovation, Kuala Lumpur, Malaysia; E-mail: Loges@ieee.org

Muhammad Ehsan Rana and Manoj Jayabalan (Eds.)

ONLINE PRIVACY

Privacy is a human right that controls how much access other individuals have over themselves. As humans are social beings, privacy, as part of social communication, has evolutionary roots in personal and social boundaries [1]. However, online privacy is an evolutionary mismatch, as online communication is very different from its face-to-face counterpart, and people are much less concerned about privacy in an online setting. This phenomenon is known as the privacy paradox.

On the other hand, some researchers, such as [2] and [3], explain that online privacy is a form of social contract or power-responsibility equilibrium, where people are less concerned about online privacy if they believe that the government, online businesses, and firms will honour their end to the contract by ensuring that the users' data is handled safely. This social contract can lead to mutual benefits. In fact, by disclosing information such as personal preferences, customers can save money through highly customised product recommendation systems [4]. However, customers will start withholding personal information if an online business uses such information to price discriminate.

DATA BROKER

Both approaches to online privacy, whether explained from the perspective of evolution or social contract, assume that disclosure of personal information is a consensual process. Data brokers are private companies that collect personal information from social networks and browsing history [5]. These companies operate covertly and exchange this information with other data brokers and governments.

By applying machine learning to such data, invaluable information such as a user's preferences and other behavioural patterns are obtained. Not only is such information highly sought by marketers, but governments often hire data brokers. As governments and large corporates benefit immensely from such arrangements, there are almost no consequences to the practice of making immense profits from selling someone's data without their permission.

While the reason for banking, financing parties, or law enforcement to purchase the services of data brokers can be for more benign reasons, such as fraud detection, some clients (such as politicians) use such information to influence the general public for personal gains [6]. Each click, like, and post is collected and aggregated to build a highly detailed profile so each person can be labelled and categorised. Naturally, such services not only attract a wide variety of clients but also attract other crime syndicates. Although one would think that data brokers would hold deeply onto their resources, data breaches happen, leading to financial fraud, identity theft, and other scams [5].

Unfortunately, because these companies operate covertly, many people are unaware of their existence. They are not held accountable for data breaches where there was not even a social contract or any consensus in the first place. Victims of such cases end up financially devastated and are often left with little to no assistance while these private companies continue to make a profit.

CURRENT RESEARCH IN BROWSER FINGERPRINTING

In web browsing, third parties infer the browsing habits of first parties (Internet users) over time. Some third parties are necessary, such as essential and optimisation third parties, who collect such information to improve user experience [7]. Others, such as malware third parties, redirect third parties and tracking third parties, are responsible for viruses, redirects, and embedded tracking.

Targeted online advertising evolved from simple ad banners. Today, many online advertisements are personalised according to the users' interests, which is made possible by collecting and analysing a user's browsing activities and habits. IP addresses, cookies, and browser fingerprinting are used to identify an Internet user uniquely. An IP address is assigned for each device connected to the Internet [8]. While a device's IP address may change over time, it was found that IP addresses are often retained and reused, which could lead to long-term tracking. Online advertisers often overlook IP address tracking, although it is difficult for Internet users to modify their IP address.

On the other hand, browser fingerprinting is more commonly used and discussed. Browser fingerprinting is a process where information about a device, such as the hardware and browser configuration, is collected *via* a web browser. In more advanced fingerprinting, attributes are collected from browser features, such as canvas and webGL, which also provides information about the device's graphics [2].

A similar but rarer technique used is the AudioContext, where audio signals are collected instead. Browser extensions are also used in browser fingerprinting [9]. The type and nature of extensions that are installed can often reveal information such as age group, religion, politics, ethnicity, health, and sexual orientation, through techniques such as inference attacks. Said attacks occur when the extensions' textual descriptions are analysed using natural language processing (NLP). Even minor details, such as font metrics and battery status, can be used against an Internet user's interest [10]. Although different Internet users may purchase the same devices, their configurations, such as cookies, cellular connections, time zones, and form fields, change and diverge over time. This enables techniques such as rule-based algorithm, LSH algorithm, and autoencoder to identify unique Internet users [11, 12].

CURRENT RESEARCH IN USER INTEREST PROFILING

A user's online activities can often reveal information about themselves, such as their likes and dislikes, which are of great interest to marketers and advertisers. Vast amounts of web browsing data are typically collected through tracking methods, such as IP address and browser fingerprinting, which are used for machine learning to obtain personal information with great accuracy. Using K-Means++ on Tweets from Kenyan Twitter users, the researchers in [13] received a kappa score of 0.592, which means there was a strong agreement between the model and human evaluators in classifying the users.

Similarly, the Click-through rate (CTR) can also provide information about user interests [14]. For example, if a user has purchased a product after watching its advertisement, chances are that the user will not make another purchase. User interests and, to a certain extent, purchase behaviour may change according to the season. To trace positive and negative interests and their dynamic changes over time, a deep-based dynamic interest perception network (DIPN) was proposed, which received the highest AUC (area under the curve) performance compared to other CTR models.

To predict the possibility of a user clicking an advertisement and whether the user will click a specific type of advertisement, long short-term memory (LSTM) was employed [15]. The users' page visits were collected as a temporal sequence to train the LSTM model. For both user click and user interest prediction, which are binary classification and multi-class prediction tasks, respectively, LSTM had the highest AUC.

Thus, from the massive amount of highly identifiable user data received through sophisticated browser fingerprinting, state-of-the-art user interest profiling can generate monetisable and invaluable information about each Internet user from web browsing activities that can be as simple as mouse clicks. This is made through the seamless integration of advanced user tracking methods such as browser fingerprinting and machine learning algorithms for user interest profiling.

BROWSER FINGERPRINTING COUNTER MEASURES

There is an arms race between developing new fingerprinting techniques and countermeasures [10]. Security companies are improving fingerprinting techniques for fraud prevention purposes. Countermeasures against browser fingerprinting can be divided mainly into two categories, those implemented by the user and those operated by the web browser [16].

According to [16], User-based countermeasures can be in the form of choosing and configuring one's browser. While Tor is a famous browser with features such as limiting fonts, disabling plugins, and canvas by default to counter fingerprinting, it comes at the cost of user experience due to its slow browsing speed. Only less than 1% of web users employ the Tor browser.

Web extensions are another option, as some extensions provide features such as blocking scripts and spoofing fonts and attributes. However, web extensions are limited by browser choice, as not all browsers support extensions, and the functionalities allowed depend on the browser vendors. It can also compromise the browsing experience through false positives. It leads to what is known as the fingerprinting paradox, where the installation of such extensions unintentionally creates yet another attribute to help web trackers identify the user. Users can also use countermeasures to disable Java and Flash scripts and all cookies, typically using ad blockers [9].

On the other hand, browser-based countermeasures are implemented by browser vendors [16]. A method commonly used is minimising fingerprint attributes to the bare minimum of the information required for the functioning of websites. For example, they only allow WebRTC API access for websites that support video chats. Alerts and notifications can also be used by asking if the user wants to use said website's video chat features before enabling access to WebRTC API. Some browsers also reduce the accuracy of information related to time, location, and the device's battery level. Each browser fingerprinting countermeasure discussed has its weaknesses, often at the expense of user experience. Thus, there is a need for more research in this aspect.

In [16], it was explained that key players in browser vendors, such as Google, are unlikely to act against their interest in making enormous profits out of browser fingerprinting. Even operating systems, such as Windows and Android, take part in browser fingerprinting by providing a unique identifier for each device to support personalised ads. Thus, an approach was proposed to give users control over their cookies and UBI (Unique Browser Identifier).

However, only some Internet users are technologically savvy and have the privacy literacy to implement user-based countermeasures against browser tracking. Due to practical concerns, even among technologically savvy Internet users, the adoption of privacy-enhancing technology (PET), such as Virtual Private Networks (VPNs) and the Tor browser, is not widespread [17, 18]. This is because some PET can be challenging to implement and may compromise user experience.

MACHINE LEARNING AND BROWSER PRIVACY

FP-INSPECTOR, a browser fingerprinting countermeasure that uses machine learning, was proposed by [19]. It has two major components. Firstly, the detection component uses static and dynamic JavaScript analysis after the syntactic and semantic features are extracted, which are then used to train a supervised machine learning classifier. The mitigation component then uses a layer of restrictions to the fingerprinting scripts. The combination of static and dynamic classifiers yielded a recall and precision of 93.8% and 93.1%, respectively.

Some researchers also proposed embedding deep learning models within web browsers as a countermeasure to browser tracking. The authors of [20] developed PERCIVAL, which is an ad blocker that uses deep learning to use image identification on ads. In terms of disk space, it only takes 1.75 MB. Because it uses image identification and not natural language processing, it works on ads of different languages. It was also tested on first-party ads like those from Facebook and Google. PERCIVAL also replicated EasyList rules at a 96.76% accuracy. PERCIVAL was implemented on Chromium and Brave at a performance overhead of 4.55% and 19.07%, respectively.

On the other hand, Deep Tracking Detector (DTD) uses deep learning to analyse the URL string properties to detect tracking [21]. It was tested on the top 100,000 websites listed by Alexa, and the accuracy was more than 97%. Because DTD runs its classification locally, it offers various benefits. In addition to being lightweight, it does not require the browser to download the source code and potentially malicious resources before DTD's analysis can be done. Unlike a fixed blocklist in most ad blockers, DTD can also generalise to new tracking domains.

According to [22], third parties are exploiting Canonical Name Records, or Alias (CNAME) records found in the user's Domain Name System (DNS). A machine learning-based in-browser app was designed to counter CNAME cloaking-based tracking, an advanced tracking technique that bypasses browser filter lists. The dataset used was a list from Alexa containing 300,000 websites with CNAME cloaking-based tracking. Ten supervised classification models were employed.

Extra trees achieved an F1 score of 0.931 in classifying requests with CNAME tracking. A blocklist was automatically built, which outperformed other well-known blocklists.

Another browser privacy approach that uses a classification machine learning approach was proposed by [23]. Since most browsers accept first and third-party cookies by default, a browser extension was developed to assess the security configuration for potential vulnerability against attacks from cross-site scripting, insecure data transfer, form-fill, and WebGL. A decision tree algorithm, J48, was used to classify 5 classes of browser security configuration from very bad to very good. A 0.971 and 0.969 for precision and recall were obtained, respectively.

NATURAL LANGUAGE PROCESSING AND BROWSER PRIVACY

Internet users frequently encounter privacy policies. However, they are usually lengthy and challenging to comprehend. PrivacyCheck, a browser extension for summarising privacy policies, was introduced in [24]. Using natural language processing, it analyses privacy policies to answer 20 User Control and General Data Protection Regulation (GDPR) questions. PrivacyCheck also has a component known as the Competitor Analysis Tool (CAT) database that summarises privacy policies in different market sectors to give users recommendations for other websites with better privacy policies. Although the researchers could obtain up to 87% accuracy using the Multinomial Naive Bayes model, it was too large for the browser extension. Replacement with Logistic Regression, which was ten times smaller, caused the accuracy to drop to 56%. PrivacyCheck v2 came with the improvement of having a front-end client that connects to its back-end server *via* REST API [25]. LightBGM was selected for its small size and increased accuracy to 60% in this version.

On the other hand, Opt-Out Easy is an extension that uses natural language processing on privacy policies to present opt-out choices, excluding users from practices such as tracking when enabled [26]. As opt-out decisions tend to be hyperlinks hidden behind lengthy privacy policies, BeautifulSoup extracted the hyperlinks, which are then tokenised using the NLTK library. Using the Logistic Regression classifier, opt-out categories are classified into targeted advertising, communication, cookies, analytics, and sharing with third parties. The F1 values for these classes ranged between 0.70 and 0.85.

CONCLUSION

In short, the use of browser fingerprinting to track Internet users and build detailed user interest profiles has become rampant. While user profiling is often used for benevolent purposes such as personalised services and enhanced security, it has also led to unethical practices, which include viruses, redirects, and even criminal activities, such as financial fraud and identity theft. Additionally, private companies known as data brokers, who often operate covertly, collect user data without permission and resell it to clients, such as advertisers, marketers, governments, and other data brokers, for massive profits.

As browser fingerprinting has provided these parties with immense user data and the ability to track each user with great accuracy, sophisticated user interest profiles are built through machine learning. Even user clicks provide invaluable information to these parties. On the other hand, research on browser fingerprinting countermeasures is lacking. The use of Tor browser, VPN, and browser extensions are rarely used and have their weaknesses, often at the expense of user experience.

Researchers have proposed various machine learning classification approaches towards browser privacy. These machine-learning approaches focus on recognising website fingerprinting scripts, advertisement images, compromised browser security configurations, and tracking attempts. The use of natural language processing for browser privacy is limited and primarily focused on summarising privacy notices.

CONSENT FOR PUBLICATION

Not applicable.

CONFLICT OF INTEREST

The authors declare no conflict of interest, financial or otherwise.

ACKNOWLEDGEMENT

The authors wish to express their sincere appreciation to the Asia Pacific University of Technology and Innovation (APU) for the opportunity to conduct the research.

REFERENCES

[1]   A. Shariff, J. Green and W. Jettinghoff, "The Privacy Mismatch: Evolved Intuitions in a Digital World", *Current Directions in Psychological Science,* 2020. [*Online] Available from: https://www.researchgate.net/publication/346049634_The_Privacy_ [*Accessed 15 February 2021]

[2]   S. Kruikemeier, S.C. Boerman, and N. Bol, "Breaching the contract? Using social contract theory to explain individuals' online behavior to safeguard privacy", *Media Psychol.,* vol. 23, no. 2, pp. 269-292, 2020.
[http://dx.doi.org/10.1080/15213269.2019.1598434]

[3]   R. Bandara, M. Fernando, and S. Akter, "Addressing privacy predicaments in the digital marketplace: A power☐relations perspective", *Int. J. Consum. Stud.,* vol. 44, no. 5, pp. 423-434, 2020.

[http://dx.doi.org/10.1111/ijcs.12576]

[4]   S. Ichihashi, "Online privacy and information disclosure by consumers", *Bank of Canada Staff Working Paper,* vol, 22, 2019. [*Online] Available from: https://www.econstor.eu/handle/10419/210763 [*Accessed 15 February 2021]

[5]   G. Birckan, M.L. Dutra, D.D.J. de Macedo and A.F.G. Viera, "Effects of data protection laws on data brokerage businesses", *Transactions on Scalable Information Systems,* vol. 7, no. 27, 2020. [*Online] Available from: https://www.researchgate.net/publication/343261077_Effects_of_data_protection_laws_on_data_brok erage_businesses [*Acessed 15 February 2021]

[6]   G. Birckan, M.L. Dutra, D.D.J. de Macedo and A.F.G. Viera, "Personal Data Protection and Its Reflexes on the Data Broker Industry", In Mugnaini R. (eds) Data and Information in Online Environments, DIONE 2020. Lecture Notes of the Institute for Computer Sciences, Social Informatics and Telecommunications Engineering, vol. 319, Springer, Cham, 2020 10.1007/978-3-030-50072-6_9

[7]   X. Hu, G.S. de Tangil and N. Sastry, "Multi-country Study of Third Party Trackers from Real Browser Histories", *2020 IEEE European Symposium on Security and Privacy,* pp. 70-86, 2020. [*Online] Available from https://conferences.computer.org/eurosp/pdfs/EuroSP2020-2psedXWK6U4prXdo7t91Gm/508700a070/508700a070.pdf [*Accessed 18 February 2020]

[8]   V. Mishra, P. Laperdrix, A. Vastel, W. Rudametkin, R. Rouvoy and M. Lopatka, "Don't count me out: On the relevance of IP address in the tracking ecosystem", *The Web Conference* 2020, Taipeï, Taiwan, April 2020, pp. 808-815, 2020

[9]   S. Karami, P. Ilia, K. Solomos and J. Polakis, "Carnus: Exploring the privacy threats of browser extension fingerprinting", Proceedings of the Symposium on Network and Distributed System Security, 2020, San Diego: NDSS. [*Online] Available from: https://www.ndss-symposium.org/w--content/uploads/2020/02/24383-paper.pdf [*Accessed 12 March 2021].

[10]   P. Laperdrix, N. Bielova, B. Baudry and G. Avoine, "Browser fingerprinting: A survey", *arXiv,*,vol. 1, no. 1, 2019. [*Online] Available from: https://arxiv.org/pdf/1905.01051.pdf [*Accessed 18 February 2021]

[11]   E. Antonio, A. Fajardo and R. Medina, "Tracking Browser Fingerprint using Rule Based Algorithm", *2020 16th IEEE International Colloquium on Signal Processing & Its Applications,* (CSPA) IEEE Langkawi, Malaysia, 28-29 February 2020, pp. 225-229.

[12]   M. Gabryel, K. Grzanek and Y. Hayashi, "Browser fingerprint coding methods increasing the effectiveness of user identification in the web traffic", *Journal of Artificial Intelligence and Soft Computing Research,* vol. 10, no. 4, pp.243-253, 2020.

[13]   H. Wandabwa, F. Mirza, F. and Pears, R., "Multi-interest User Profiling in Short Text Microblogs", *International Conference on Design Science Research in Information Systems and Technology.* Springer: Cham, pp. 154-168, 2020

[14]   H. Zhang, J. Yan and Y. Zhang, "CTR Prediction Models Considering the Dynamics of User Interest", *IEEE Access,* vol. 8, pp.72847-72858, 2020.

[15]   Z. Gharibshah, X. Zhu, A. Hainline and M. Conway, "Deep learning for user interest and response prediction in online display advertising", *Data Science and Engineering,* vol. 5, no. 1, pp.12-26, 2020.

[16]   N.M. Al-Fannah and C. Mitchell, "Too little too late: can we control browser fingerprinting?", *Journal of Intellectual Capital,* vol. 21, no. 2, pp. 165-180, 2020 [http://dx.doi.org/10.1108/JIC-04-2019-0067]

[17]   D. Harborth, S. Pape and K. Rannenberg, "Explaining the technology use behavior of privacy-enhancing technologies: The case of tor and JonDonym", *Proceedings on Privacy Enhancing Technologies,* vol. 2, pp.111-128, 2020.

[18]   M. Namara, D. Wilkinson, K. Caine and B.P. Knijnenburg, "Emotional and practical considerations towards the adoption and abandonment of vpns as a privacy-enhancing technology", *Proceedings on*

Privacy Enhancing Technologies, vol. 1, pp.83-102, 2020.

[19] U. Iqbal, S., Englehardt and Z. Shafiq, "Fingerprinting the Fingerprinters: Learning to Detect Browser Fingerprinting Behaviors", arXiv:2008.04480, 2020. [*Online] Available from https://arxiv.org/pdf/2008.04480.pdf [*Accessed 15 March 2021].

[20] Z. Abi Din, P. Tigas, S.T. King and B. Livshits, "Percival: Making in-browser perceptual ad blocking practical with deep learning", USENIX Annual Technical Conference, 15-17 July 2020, pp. 387-400. [*Online] Available from https://arxiv.org/pdf/1905.07444.pdf [*Accessed 18 February 2021].

[21] I. Castell-Uroz, T. Poissonnier, P. Manneback and P. Barlet-Ros, "URL-based Web Tracking Detection Using Deep Learning", *2020 16th International Conference on Network and Service Management,* (CNSM) IEEE, 2-6 November, pp. 1-5, 2020.

[22] H. Dao and K. Fukuda, "A machine learning approach for detecting CNAME cloaking-based tracking on the Web", arXiv:2009.14330, 2020. [*Online] Available from https://arxiv.org/pdf/2009.14330.pdf [*Accessed 15 March 2021].

[23] H. Wadkar and A. Mishra, A. "Hardening web browser security configuration using machine learning technique", *International Journal of Electronic Business,* vol. 15, no. 3, pp.275-295, 2020..

[24] R.N. Zaeem, S. Anya, A. Issa, J. Nimergood, I. Rogers and K.S. Barber, "PrivacyCheck's Machine Learning to Digest Privacy Policies: Competitor Analysis and Usage Patterns", 2020. [*Online] Available   from https://identity.utexas.edu/sites/default/files/202010/PrivacyCheck%E2%80%99s%20Machine%20Learning%20to%20 Digest%20Privacy%20Policies.pdf [*Accessed 15 March 2021].

[25] R.N. Zaeem, S. Anya, A. Issa, J. Nimergood, I. Rogers, V. Shah, A. Srivastava and K.S. Barber, "PrivacyCheck v2: A Tool that Recaps Privacy Policies for You", 2020. [*Online] Available from https://identity.utexas.edu/sites/default/files/2020-10/PrivacyCheck%20v2%20A%20Tool%20that%20Recaps%20Privacy%20Policies%20for%20You.pdf [*Accessed 15 March 2021]

[26] V.B. Kumar, R. Iyengar, N. Nisal, Y. Feng, H. Habib, P. Story, S. Cherivirala, M. Hagan, L. Cranor, S. Wilson and F. Schaub, "Finding a choice in a haystack: automatic extraction of opt-out statements from privacy policy text", *Proceedings of The Web Conference,* Taipei, Taiwan, 20-24 April 2020, pp. 1943-1954. [*Online] Available from https://par.nsf.gov/servlets/purl/10170230 [*Accessed 15 March 2021]

CHAPTER 10

ARP Spoofing in Launching Man-in-the-Middle Attack

Soon Qi Huan[1] and **Vinesha Selvarajah**[1,*]

[1] *School of Computing, Asia Pacific University of Technology and Innovation, Kuala Lumpur, Malaysia*

Abstract: Man-in-the-Middle (MITM) attack is a typical eavesdropping cyberattack. The attacker can launch a MITM attack whenever the attacker and victims are on the same network. Here is a scenario: A MITM attacker connects to Subway's Wi-Fi and waits for the victim to connect to the Subway Wi-Fi. Eventually, Victim A walks in and connects to Subway's Wi-Fi. Once Victim A gets connected and is on the same network as the attacker, the attacker can launch an attack to intercept the network traffic of Victim A. Therefore, everyone on the same network connection with the attacker can be the target of a MITM attack. In this paper, the MITM attack will be introduced. The attacker can spy on the victim, steal sensitive credentials, disrupt communications, or even corrupt the data through the said attack. To discover how the MITM attack works, this paper explains it based on the ARP Spoofing attack, which exploits the ARP protocol to send out forged ARP responses. ARP Spoofing attack is one of the MITM attacks. This paper emphasises the MITM attack phases, different types of MITM attacks, ARP Spoofing attacks, and how ARP works. The demonstration of steps for launching an ARP Spoofing attack and the tools involved, like Nmap, Arpspoof, and Wireshark, are also included.

Keywords: Arpsoof, ARP Spoofing, Information Security, Man-in-The-Middle, Nmap, Wireshark.

INTRODUCTION

With the development of network technology, the demand for the Internet has become indispensable. Due to that, whoever uses the internet, increases their chance of being a victim of the MITM attack. This chapter is sorted into sections. The first section introduces the MITM attack, including the attack phases and the seven types of MITM attacks. The second section explores the ARP; explains how ARP and the ARP Spoofing attack work. The third section introduces the tools for launching an ARP Spoofing attack involving Nmap, Arpspoof, and Wireshark.

---

* **Corresponding author Vinesha Selvarajah**: School of Computing, Asia Pacific University of Technology and Innovation, Kuala Lumpur, Malaysia; E-mail: tp054609@mail.apu.edu.my

Muhammad Ehsan Rana and Manoj Jayabalan (Eds.)

The fourth section contains the demonstration steps for launching the ARP spoofing attack. The fifth section includes reviewing the MITM attack. Lastly, the sixth section concludes with some countermeasures regarding the MITM attack.

MITM ATTACK

The MITM attack is an unauthorised cyberattack where the unauthorised attacker secretly eavesdrops and intercepts the traffic or communication between two parties by impersonating one of the parties without alerting the victim [1]. During a MITM attack, the attacker will be placed between the user and the web application (Fig. **1**).

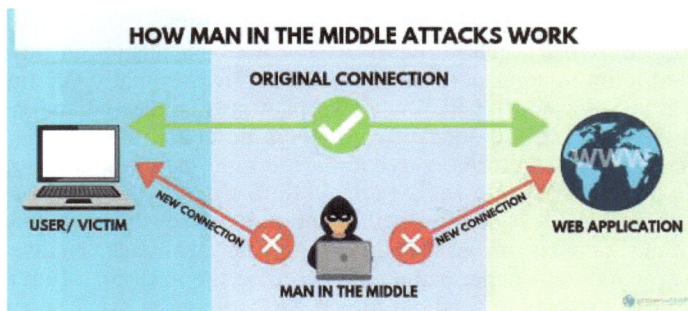

Fig. (1). MITM Attack Concept [2].

The goal of the MITM attack is either observe or manipulate network traffic. The attacker can obtain a lot of information, such as network traffic, login credentials, and other sensitive information, through the attack. In extreme cases, the attacker may alter the communication between two parties to reach specific objectives. After obtaining the data and information, the attacker may use it for their purposes or sell it, usually through the dark web.

MITM Attack Phases

Based on the problem stated above, Hypermarket Stock Monitoring System using IoT Automation can determine the products left on the shelf in real-time. Once the quantity of a product drops to a certain level set earlier, it will automatically notice the hypermarket staff. The team can view the product information, location, and quantity left via the system. The hypermarket can gain several benefits by implementing this stock monitoring system using IoT. Firstly, the products arranged on the market floor will be more organised as the system guides the restocking process. The system can determine which product should get restocked first; hence the on-shelf availability is significantly increased.

Type of MITM Attacks

There are seven types of MITM attacks with different functions, as shown in Table **1**.

Table 1. Seven Types of MITM Attacks and Functions [1 - 3].

MITM Attacks	Functions
IP Spoofing	Attackers imitate the IP address of the application to trick victims into accessing the URL connected to the fake site.
DNS Spoofing	Attackers spoof the DNS by tampering with websites' address records within the DNS server and thus redirect the victims to access the site.
HTTPS Spoofing	Attackers spoof the victims' browsers and pretend it is a secure website by passing forged certificates to the victims' browsers. The victims will see 'HTTPS' in the URL instead of 'HTTP', and the browser will be redirected to an insecure website.
SSL Hijacking	Attackers send phoney authentication keys for the user and web application during a TCP handshake. It appears as a secure site, 'HTTPS', but the attackers monitor the whole session.
Email Hijacking	Attackers spoof the email address and send their instructions to the victim. Attackers usually target the email of financial institutions and banks and then redirect victims to respond or send money to the spoofed email.
Wi-Fi Eavesdropping	Attackers create a fake Wi-Fi access point by setting up a public Wi-Fi connection. Once the victims connect to the Wi-Fi, the attacker can gain access to their network traffic.
Stealing browser cookies	Attackers hijack the victims' browser cookies and gain access to the victim's private information through the victims' browsing history.

ARP

Address Resolution Protocol (ARP) is a protocol that resolves IP addresses to machine Media Access Control (MAC) addresses. It converts 32-bit IPv4 addresses to 48-bit MAC addresses and vice versa.

MITM Attack Phases

Based on the problem stated above, Hypermarket Stock Monitoring System using IoT Automation can determine the products left on the shelf in real-time. Once the quantity of a product drops to a certain level set earlier, it will automatically notice the hypermarket staff. The team can view the product information, location and quantity left via the system. The hypermarket can gain several benefits by implementing this stock monitoring system using IoT. The products arranged on the market floor will be more organised as the system guides the restocking process. The system can determine which product should get restocked first; hence the on-shelf availability is significantly increased.

How ARP Works

When one device wants to communicate with the other, it will first look for the MAC address in the ARP table. If the MAC address cannot be found in the ARP table, ARP Request will be generated and broadcasted to the local network, and all devices will compare this IP address to MAC address until one device in this network matches this IP address [4]. After that, the destination device will send back an ARP Response with its IP and MAC address [4]. Lastly, the address pair will be stored in the ARP table of the destination device, and thus communication takes place.

ARP Spoofing Attack

ARP Spoofing, also known as ARP Poisoning, is a type of MITM attack that carries out attacks on a local network ARP table [5]. This attack occurs on a local network that uses Address Resolution Protocol. Attackers will pretend to be both parties inside a communication by sending forged ARP replies by manipulating the ARP table of the target machine to let the target machine think that it is the actual MAC address (Fig. **2**). Attackers then become the man in the middle. Thus, all network traffic packets are monitored and intercepted without being detected.

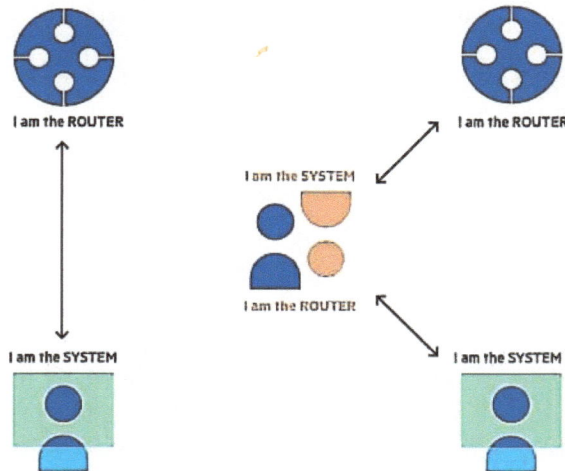

Fig. (2). ARP Spoofing Concept [6].

Once the ARP spoofing attack is launched successfully, attackers can continue to route the traffic as-is to sniff data packets, perform session hijacking by gaining access to the account that the user is currently logged in, alter the communication by injecting malicious files or websites into a workstation or launch a DDoS attack by flooding the target server with traffic, by providing the MAC address of the target server to a large number of IPs [6].

TOOLS FOR ARP SPOOFING ATTACK

Three tools are used to simulate MITM ARP spoofing attacks, including Nmap, Arpspoof, and Wireshark. Initially, Nmap is used to scan for the target machine's IP address. After that, Arpspoof is used to launch an ARP spoofing attack. Lastly, use Wireshark to intercept the target machine's network traffic and data packets.

Nmap

Nmap, short for Network Mapper, is a widely used free network scanning tool. Users can run Nmap in either Command Line Interface (CLI) or Graphical User Interface (GUI), Zenmap. Zenmap is an official GUI for Nmap [7].

Nmap can be used for host discovery, port scanning, version detection, operating system detection, and Scriptable interaction with the target. It identifies all the devices connected to a network using IP packets [8]. Moreover, it provides information on the running services and operating systems. Nmap provides information about every active IP active on LAN connected by the machine, which helps to determine if the IP is being connected by a legitimate service or an outsider [8]. Nmap provides scanning output on the connected network as a whole, including the list of live hosts, open ports, and details of the OS of every connected device [8]. Therefore, Nmap can be used to detect vulnerabilities in a network that may be exploited by the attacker and thus repair the network vulnerabilities.

Arpspoof

Arpspoof is one of the tools from the Dsniff suite toolset. Dsniff is a collection of password sniffing and network traffic analysis tools for network auditing and penetration testing [9]. Different tools are included in the Dsniff toolset collection, as shown in Table **2**.

Table 2. Dsniff Tools [9, 10].

Tools	Functions
	Facilitate interception of network traffic that is usually inaccessible

(Table 2) cont.....

Tools	Functions
arpspoof	Redirect the flow of packets to intercept on a LAN to make them pass through the attacker's machine by forging ARP replies.
dnsspoof	Spoof DNS services on a local network by sending forged replies to pointer queries or DNS addresses.
macof	Flood the traffic of the local network with arbitrary MAC addresses.
	Monitor the network passively to collect data such as e-mail, password, files, *etc.*
dsniff	Sniff passwords from FTP, Telnet, SMTP, HTTP, *etc.*
filesnarf	Sniff saves files from NFS traffic in the current in-progress directory.
mailsnarf	Output email messages sniffer for SMTP and POP traffic.
msgsnarf	Chat messages sniffer for AOL Instant Messenger, IRC, ICQ 2000, MSN Messenger, or Yahoo Messenger chat sessions.
urlsnarf	Sniff HTTP requests in Common Log Format (CLF).
webspy	Display sniffed URLs in Netscape in real-time.
	Carry out monkey-in-the-middle attacks against altered SSH and HTTP/HTTPS sessions
sshmitm	SSH monkey-in-the-middle. Proxy and sniff SSH traffic redirected by dnsspoof, capture SSH password logins, and hijack connected sessions optionally.
webmitm	HTTP / HTTPS monkey-in-the-middle. Proxy and sniff web traffic redirected by dnsspoof, capture most "secure" SSL-encrypted form submissions and webmail logins.
	Interrupt TCP connections
tcpkill	Kill running TCP connections.
tcpnice	Slow down TCP connections.

Wireshark

Wireshark, previously known as Ethereal, is a popular open-source network protocol analyser and packet sniffing tool. Wireshark captures network traffic on the local network in real-time. It then converts the binary traffic and displays it in a human-readable format. The live data can be captured from Ethernet, USB, IEEE 802.11, Bluetooth, Token Ring, *etc* [11]. The captured data can also be stored for offline analysis. Wireshark facilitates users to analyse network traffic in real-time and thus can troubleshoot issues on the network. Common issues that can troubleshoot include latency issues, malicious activity, and dropped packets on the network [12].

Wireshark includes features like filters and colour coding that facilitate users while analysing network traffic and inspecting individual packets [13]. Different filters of Wireshark enable users to inspect specific traffic by filtering the log. This can narrow down the display options and zoom into what users want. Users can apply the filter by simply typing it in the filter box at the top of the window.

The next feature is colour coding. The packets displayed are highlighted in a variety of colours. Different colours are used to help the user identify different types of traffic. The colours of packets are based on the default rules of Wireshark. Users can modify and customise the colouring rules by adding new rules, or removing or changing packet colours' existing rules.

ARP SPOOFING ATTACK DEMONSTRATION STEPS

The setup for this demonstration is as follows. Prepare two VMs using Kali Linux to launch the attack on Windows 10 to act as the victim machine. Next, ensure both VMs are configured to use Network Address Translation (NAT) network connection as it establishes the connection between VMs. NAT enables private IP networks by assigning unregistered IP addresses to VMs to connect to the Internet. VMware will be used to run both VMs.

Check Configuration Status

Open up the terminal in the Linux machine, and change to root user since it is the most privileged and allows users access to all commands and files. Next, type 'ifconfig' to check for the IP configuration of the Kali machine. The IP address of the attacker machine is '192.168.254.131', while the network interface is 'eth0' (Fig. **3**).

Fig. (3). Linux Machine Terminal.

Once that is done, go to the victim machine, open up the command prompt and use the 'ipconfig' command to check for the IP address and default gateway, which is '192.168.254.130' and '192.168.254.2', respectively (Fig. **4**).

Fig. (4). Windows 10 Command Prompt.

In the case that it can go straight to the victim machine, type the 'ipconfig' command to check for the IP address. The attacker can use Nmap scan to obtain the target victim's IP configuration by finding out which host is using the command 'nmap 192.168.254.0/24' to scan the whole network. The results show all the IP addresses and system names of the up-hosts under the same network (Fig. **5**).

Fig. (5). Nmap Command to Search for Up-hosts on the same Network.

Check for the status of the target victim machine. Before ARP poisoning, the victim machine could ping with the default gateway router, and according to the ARP table, the MAC address for the default gateway is '00-50-56-ff-c0-b5' (Fig. **6**).

```
C:\Users\IEUser>ping 192.168.254.2

Pinging 192.168.254.2 with 32 bytes of data:
Reply from 192.168.254.2: bytes=32 time=23ms TTL=128
Reply from 192.168.254.2: bytes=32 time<1ms TTL=128
Reply from 192.168.254.2: bytes=32 time<1ms TTL=128
Reply from 192.168.254.2: bytes=32 time<1ms TTL=128

Ping statistics for 192.168.254.2:
    Packets: Sent = 4, Received = 4, Lost = 0 (0% loss),
Approximate round trip times in milli-seconds:
    Minimum = 0ms, Maximum = 23ms, Average = 5ms

C:\Users\IEUser>arp -a

Interface: 192.168.254.130 --- 0x5
  Internet Address      Physical Address      Type
  192.168.254.2         00-50-56-ff-c0-b5     dynamic
  192.168.254.131       00-0c-29-c2-37-2a     dynamic
  192.168.254.255       ff-ff-ff-ff-ff-ff     static
  224.0.0.22            01-00-5e-00-00-16     static
  224.0.0.251           01-00-5e-00-00-fb     static
  224.0.0.252           01-00-5e-00-00-fc     static
  239.255.255.250       01-00-5e-7f-ff-fa     static
  255.255.255.255       ff-ff-ff-ff-ff-ff     static
```

Fig. (6). Status of Victim Machine before ARP Poisoning.

Launch ARP Spoofing Attack

To connect to the victim network, Arpspoof should be set up using the Arpspoof tool with the command shown in Fig. (**5**). 'eth0' refers to the name of the network interface, '192.168.254.130' is the victim's IP address, followed by '192.168.254.2', the default gateway. This command tells the access point that this machine is the target client (Fig. **7**).

```
root@kali:~# arpspoof -i eth0 -t 192.168.254.130 192.168.254.2
0:c:29:c2:37:2a 0:c:29:3f:46:2a 0806 42: arp reply 192.168.254.2 is-at 0:c:29:c2:37:2a
```

Figure 7. Arpspoof 1.

Run the Arpspoof again to tell the client that this machine is the access point, instead of telling the access point that this machine is the target client. Flip the victim's IP address and the default gateway IP address (Fig. **8**).

```
root@kali:~# arpspoof -i eth0 -t 192.168.254.2 192.168.254.130
0:c:29:c2:37:2a 0:50:56:ff:c0:b5 0806 42: arp reply 192.168.254.130 is-at 0:c:29:c2:37:2a
0:c:29:c2:37:2a 0:50:56:ff:c0:b5 0806 42: arp reply 192.168.254.130 is-at 0:c:29:c2:37:2a
```

Fig. (8). Arpspoof 2.

After the attack is launched, the victim machine cannot ping by default. This is because the victim machine thinks the attacker machine is the default gateway instead of its machine since the MAC address has been poisoned. For the ARP table, the MAC address of the default gateway has been changed from '00-50-- 6-ff-c0-b5'to '00-0c-29-c2-37-2a', the MAC address of the attacker machine. Hence, this means whenever the victim goes to the internet, all the network traffic will first flow through the interface of the attacker machine (Fig. **9**).

```
Pinging 192.168.254.2 with 32 bytes of data:
Request timed out.
Request timed out.
Request timed out.
Request timed out.

Ping statistics for 192.168.254.2:
    Packets: Sent = 4, Received = 0, Lost = 4 (100% loss),

C:\Users\IEUser>arp -a

Interface: 192.168.254.130 --- 0x5
  Internet Address        Physical Address        Type
  192.168.254.2           00-0c-29-c2-37-2a       dynamic
  192.168.254.131         00-0c-29-c2-37-2a       dynamic
  192.168.254.255         ff-ff-ff-ff-ff-ff       static
  224.0.0.22              01-00-5e-00-00-16       static
  224.0.0.251             01-00-5e-00-00-fb       static
  224.0.0.252             01-00-5e-00-00-fc       static
  239.255.255.250         01-00-5e-7f-ff-fa       static
  255.255.255.255         ff-ff-ff-ff-ff-ff       static
```

Fig. (9). Status of Victim Machine after ARP Poisoning.

The attacker then has to enable IP forwarding to let the attacker machine act as the network router. This is because the packets that come from the victim site to flow through the attacker site will not drop on the attacker site but will be forwarded as standard to the client site (Fig. **10**).

```
root@kali:~# sysctl net.ipv4.ip_forward=1
net.ipv4.ip_forward = 1
```

Fig. (10). Enable IP Forwarding.

After enabling IP forwarding, the victim machine can ping with the default gateway again. The victim machine will think of the attacker machine as the access point. Therefore, the victim machine's network traffic will go through the interface of the attacker machine whenever it tries to communicate with the network router, placing the attacker machine in the middle of the connection. This is known as a Man-in-the-Middle attack (Fig. **11**).

```
Pinging 192.168.254.2 with 32 bytes of data:
Reply from 192.168.254.2: bytes=32 time=1ms TTL=127
Reply from 192.168.254.2: bytes=32 time=15ms TTL=127
Reply from 192.168.254.2: bytes=32 time=1ms TTL=127
Reply from 192.168.254.2: bytes=32 time=1ms TTL=127

Ping statistics for 192.168.254.2:
    Packets: Sent = 4, Received = 4, Lost = 0 (0% loss),
Approximate round trip times in milli-seconds:
    Minimum = 1ms, Maximum = 15ms, Average = 4ms
```

Fig. (11). Status of Victim Machine after Enabled IP Forwarding.

Sniff Network Traffic Using Wireshark

Wireshark is launched to sniff the packets. A lot of information can be sniffed through Wireshark, but only two filters will be introduced. Said filters can be used to steal login credentials and intercept the websites visited by the target victim.

The first command filter is 'http.request.method=="POST" '. This allows the attacker to steal the login credentials of the victim's machine (Fig. **12**). However, only login credentials of insecure websites (HTTP websites) can be stolen.

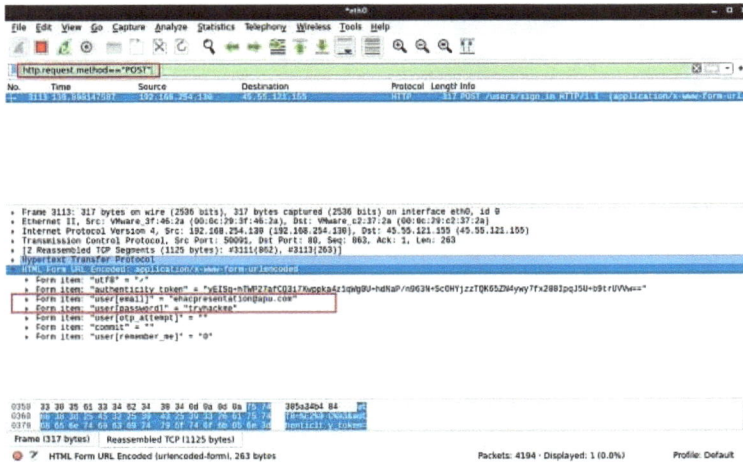

Fig. (12). Wireshark Command 1.

The second filter command is 'ip.addr==192.168.254.130 && http'. The attacker can use this to see the name of the webpage that the victim has visited (Fig. **13**). However, this does not apply to every website.

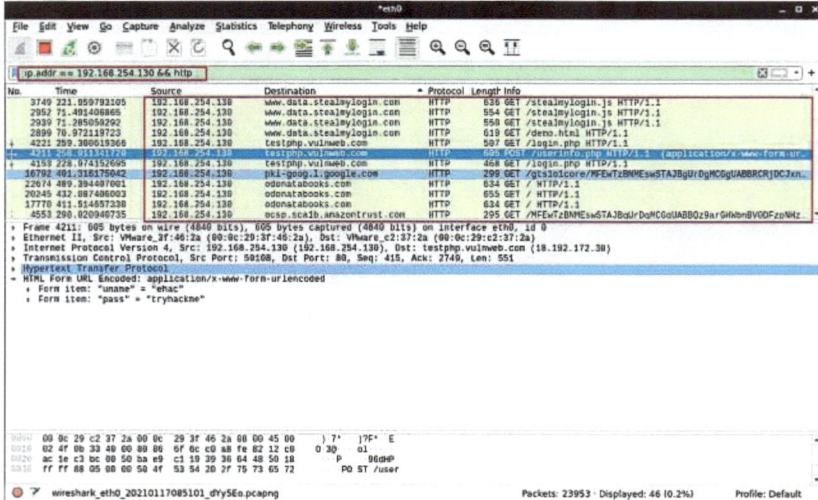

Fig. (13). Wireshark Command 2.

Terminate ARP Spoofing Attack

Lastly, the attacker can terminate the attack by pressing 'Ctrl+Z' to stop the Arpspoof attack (Figs. **14** and **15**).

Fig. (14). Terminate Arpspoof 1.

Fig. (15). Terminate Arpspoof 2.

Disable IP Forwarding by resetting the value to zero by typing the command 'sysctl -w net.ipv4.ip_forward=0' (Fig. **16**).

Fig. (16). Disable IP Forwarding.

REVIEW FOR MITM ATTACK

From the author's perspective, a MITM attack is vicious as attackers can steal users' private credentials and even corrupt the data through it. Furthermore, a MITM attack is a common attack so that anyone can become a victim in an unguarded moment. Attackers can simply invade victims' machines as long as the victims are staying under the same network as the attackers. For example, in the case of public Wi-Fi attacks, a person made an online transaction while connected to public Wi-Fi. The MITM attacker can intercept and steal bank account credentials, including the bank account number and password. This proves that whoever is connected to the Wi-Fi network possesses the potential to become a victim.

Furthermore, a MITM attack is quickly launched and grasped as most MITM attacks do not require a specific device and are easy to learn. In this era of technological advancements, tutorials on various cyberattacks are disseminated on the Internet. Through online learning, anyone can become a hacker and drop a MITM attack effortlessly by referring to said tutorials. Unfavourably, these circumstances lead to rampant cybercrimes.

In addition, a MITM attack is tricky as victims cannot provide corresponding countermeasures in time once the attack occurs. In other cyberattacks such as malware attacks, Denial of Service (DoS) attacks, Distributed Denial of Service (DDoS) attacks, *etc.*, targeted victim machines will have an immediate response regarding the cyberattacks, so instant solutions can be carried out to deal with them. MITM attacks, on the other hand, are challenging to detect as they do not give out any signs during the attack. This allows them to remain unnoticed until the attack is over.

CONCLUSION

All in all, MITM is a dangerous and hidden cyberattack. Even though the MITM attack is difficult to detect, there are countermeasures to prevent it from happening. Avoid connecting to public Wi-Fi networks or hotspots to reduce the chances of sharing networks with attackers. Moreover, always use the 'HTTPS' secure website, avoiding the 'HTTP' insecure website and providing private credentials on the 'HTTP' website. In addition, encrypt your Wi-Fi access point and ensure your router login credentials are strong enough to prevent attackers from being able to force their way into the network. If possible, use Virtual Private Network (VPN) while connected to the network since the attacker cannot decrypt the network traffic in the VPN. Lastly, do not blindly trust email content and avoid clicking suspicious links to prevent email hijacking.

CONSENT FOR PUBLICATION

Not applicable.

CONFLICT OF INTEREST

The authors declare no conflict of interest, financial or otherwise.

ACKNOWLEDGEMENTS

The authors wish to express their sincere appreciation to the Asia Pacific University of Technology and Innovation (APU) for the opportunity to conduct the research.

REFERENCES

[1]   https://www.imperva.com/learn/application-security/man-in-the-middle-attack-mitm/ n.d.

[2]   B. Dobran, *What are Man in the Middle Attacks & How to Prevent MITM Attack with Examples*, 2019.https://phoenixnap.com/blog/man-in-the-middle-attacks-prevention

[3]   K. Chivers, *What is a man-in-the-middle attack?*, 2020.https://us.norton.com/internetsecurity-wif--what-is-a-man-in-the-middle-attack.html

[4]   D. Chhadva, *Man in The Middle Attack (MITM) Part 1 — ARP Spoofing*, 2020.https://levelup.gitconnected.com/man-in-the-middle-attack-part-1-arp-spoofing-6f5b174dec59

[5]   https://www.ionos.com/digitalguide/server/security/arp-spoofing-attacks-from-the-internal-network/

[6]   https://www.imperva.com/learn/application-security/arp-spoofing/ n.d.

[7]   https://nmap.org/book/zenmap.html n.d.

[8]   J. Petters, *How to Use Nmap: Commands and Tutorial Guide*, 2020.https://www.varonis.com/blog/nmap-commands/

[9]   https://www.linuxlinks.com/dsniff/ n.d.

[10]   D. Song, *dsniff*.https://www.monkey.org/~dugsong/dsniff/ n.d.

[11]   https://www.wireshark.org/ n.d.

[12]   J. Porup, *What is Wireshark? What this essential troubleshooting tool does and how to use it*, 2018.https://www.csoonline.com/article/3305805/what-is-wireshark-what-this-esse-tial-troubleshooting-tool-does-and-how-to-use-it.html

[13]   C. Hoffman, *How to Use Wireshark to Capture, Filter and Inspect Packets*, 2017.https://www.howtogeek.com/104278/how-to-use-wireshark-to-ca-ture-filter-and-inspect-packets/

CHAPTER 11

Elderly Monitoring Using the Internet of Things (IoT)

Matthew Tan Xian Long[1,*] and **Intan Farahana Binti Kamsin**[1]

[1] *Asia Pacific University of Technology and Innovation, Kuala Lumpur, Malaysia.*

Abstract: As people get older and their bodies weaken, they become more prone to illnesses and injuries. This paper reviews several research papers that discuss implementing a monitoring system that monitors the elderly. This research aims to improve the healthcare and safety of elderly people alone at home by implementing a monitoring system based on IoT technology in Malaysia. This paper also discusses how stratified sampling methods and surveys can help identify elderly peoples' preferences and improve the monitoring system. The system proposed in this research uses real-time pulse and temperature monitoring, real-time fall detection monitoring, a cloud database, and a mobile application that could help reduce the effort and worry of taking care of the elderly. The findings of this research will help to improve the lives of elderly people that prefer staying in their own homes and will hopefully reduce the effort needed to take care of them. Future system improvements will include blood pressure and respiration rate monitoring, allowing more accurate monitoring of their health.

Keywords: Elderly, Health and Safety, Internet of Things (IoT), Monitoring System.

INTRODUCTION

As people get older, they go through physiological changes. This affects their appearance and causes a decline in their health [1]. Human bodies get weaker as they age, making them more susceptible to health disorders. This can result in them losing their balance while standing or walking, making them more prone to falling and injury. A monitoring system is a system that is designed to monitor the health of elderly people. With the latest IoT technology, it is possible to monitor their health from anywhere in the world if there is a network connection.

---

[*] **Corresponding author Matthew Tan Xian Long**: School of Computing, Asia Pacific University of Technology and Innovation, Kuala Lumpur, Malaysia; E-mail: matthew@staffemail.apu.edu.my

Muhammad Ehsan Rana and Manoj Jayabalan (Eds.)

PROBLEM STATEMENT

The population of elderly people in Malaysia has been increasing over the years. The total population of them has increased from 2.106 million (6.5%) in 2018 to 2.184 million (6.7%) in 2019 [2]. It is projected that by 2030, 15% of Malaysia's population will comprise elderly people above 60 [3]. Due to this, especially for those who live alone at home, it is imperative to develop a monitoring system for them in case of any emergencies.

AIM AND OBJECTIVES

The research aims to improve the healthcare and safety of elderly people alone at home by implementing a monitoring system based on IoT technology in Malaysia.

OBJECTIVES

- To implement an IoT-based monitoring system for elderly people to monitor their health at home.
- To implement a system that detects fire and determines whether the elderly resident has fallen anywhere at home.
- To implement a system that automatically contacts emergency services and close relatives of the elderly resident in case of an emergency.

RESEARCH QUESTIONS

- How IoT-based monitoring systems for elderly people can be implemented to monitor their health at home.
- How the system will detect fire and whether the elderly resident has fallen anywhere at home.
- How the system can automatically contact emergency services and close relatives of the elderly resident in case of emergency.

LITERATURE REVIEW

This section of the research paper reviews past research related to the proposed topic. This is done to gain a better understanding of existing research related to the topic of the proposal. The domains that have been identified and will be reviewed are:

Internet of Things (IoT)

The Internet of Things (IoT) is a network of connected devices such as sensors, network devices, vehicles, *etc.* This network allows these devices to interact and "talk" to each other without human interaction [4]. IoT has allowed a lot of processes, such as sensing, interacting, and communicating between different devices, to be automated. The devices acquire data from sensors and then decide what to do next based on the system's logic [5]. IoT aims to link things together no matter the time, place, device, or person using any ideal network or service [6].

Monitoring System using IoT

According to [7], an IoT monitoring system allows elderly people to be monitored from their homes. The elderly person can wear wearable sensors that monitor vital signs, which allows continuous tracking of the patient's health. A wireless sensor is placed in the elderly person's home to create a wireless sensor network that can transmit real-time data that doctors can access. According to [1], a monitoring sensor that uses IoT, an accelerometer, will be able to detect if an elderly person has fallen by measuring the gravitational acceleration of the accelerometer. The data from the accelerometer will be evaluated and then transferred to an IoT platform to be monitored. Reference [8] stated that an IoT monitoring system consists of sensors that monitor vital signs and detect falls. In the context of this research, this is the definition of a monitoring system.

Elderly in Malaysia

Reference [9] stated that elderly people in Malaysia refer to people who are 60 years old and above. Reference [10] also supports this statement, saying that the elderly in Malaysia are defined as people 60 years and over. Fifteen percent of the population of Malaysia is expected to be 60 or more by the year 2030. Most elderly people prefer staying at home to moving to a care facility. This is because staying home allows them to maintain independence and feel comfortable and secure in a familiar environment.

Elderly Monitoring System at Home Using IoT Technology in Malaysia

An elderly monitoring system at home using IoT Technology in Malaysia means that this system will combine the use of IoT sensors to create a monitoring system to monitor elderly people in Malaysia that stay at home. The elderly person staying alone at home will wear wearable sensors that monitor vital signs, and the data will be acquired and sent to medical professionals and relatives for monitoring.

Similar Systems

This section will compare similar systems primarily focused on IoT elderly monitoring systems.

System 1

System 1, proposed by [11], is a monitoring system that monitors the vital signs of the elderly in real-time, using smartphones and wearable sensors. The sensors will collect the vital data of the elderly and record it in a cloud data centre, which will then be updated in real-time. Medical professionals can access the data at any given time, as shown in Fig. (1).

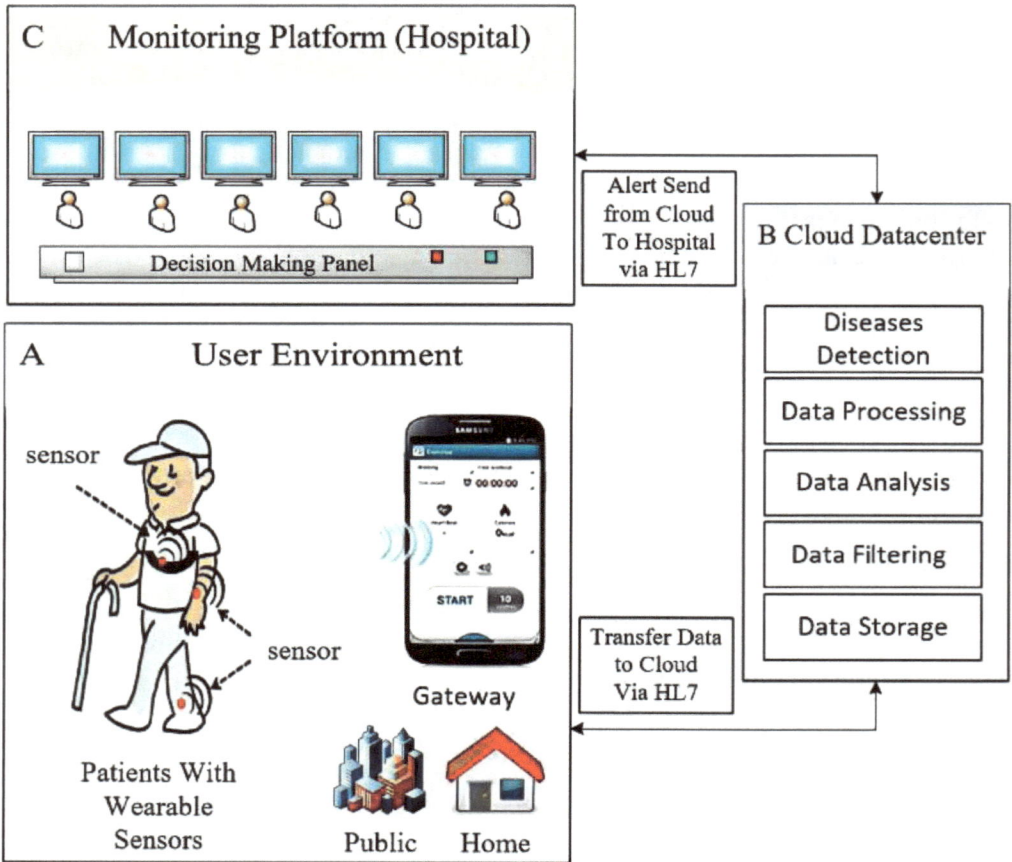

Fig. (1). Diagram of System 1 [11].

System 2

Fig. (2) shows the system diagram of the second system, proposed by [12], which is a monitoring system that detects if an elderly person falls. The system consists of a wearable fall detector, a wireless communication network, an IoT gateway, and cloud services. The wearable device will measure the speed at which the body of the elderly person moves, transmitting the data to the IoT gateway using the wireless network. The IoT gateway will then analyse the data and send alert messages to healthcare professionals if a fall is detected.

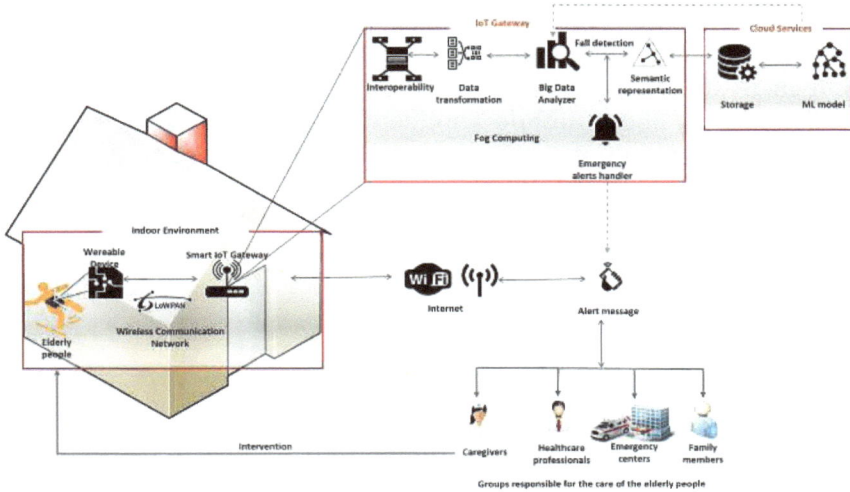

Fig. (2). Diagram of System 2 [12].

System 3

System 3, proposed by [13], is an elderly health monitoring system (Fig. **3**). It consists of wearable sensors, a personal server, a data centre, and an observation station. The sensors will constantly collect vital data from the elderly and send it to the personal server, which will be sent to the data centre. After that, anybody in the monitoring centre with authorisation can access the data. An emergency alert will be sent to ambulances if abnormalities in the elderly person's vitals are detected.

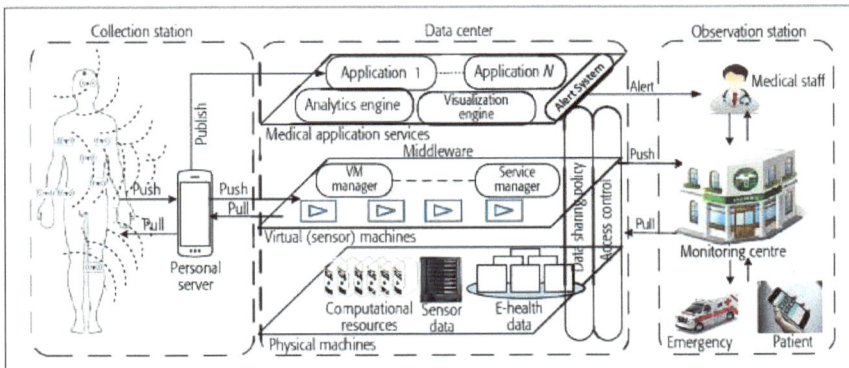

Fig. (3). Diagram of System 3 [13].

Comparison of Similar Systems

Based on Table **1**, it is shown that System 3 has fulfilled most of the criteria. It consists of wearable vital signs sensors, usage of a mobile application, and a database, and it will notify emergency contacts during an emergency. A wearable fall detector in System 2 is not present in System 3. However, System 2 lacks wearable vital sensors and a mobile application. System 1 lacks a wearable fall detector and the feature to notify emergency contacts during an emergency. The proposed system will include all 5 of the criteria.

Table 1. Comparison between Similar Systems.

Criteria/System	S1	S2	S3
Wearable vital signs sensors	/		/
Wearable fall detector		/	
Mobile Application	/		/
Database	/	/	/
Notify emergency contacts during an emergency		/	/

SIGNIFICANCE OF THE RESEARCH

Nowadays, most of the elderly above 60 live alone or at home most of the time. This is because they either have no family or their family is too busy to give them attention and take care of them. This can be dangerous for the elderly, especially if they fall or have a heart attack and there is nobody around to help them or call for help, leaving them helpless for hours or even resulting in death. By implementing an IoT-based monitoring system to monitor the elderly in their homes, family members or medical professionals will be alerted. They can try to reach the elderly as soon as possible. This can decrease the likelihood that the elderly will suffer for extended periods and reduce the likelihood of preventable death.

METHODOLOGY

For this research, 30 elderly people above 60 are the targeted sample. The sampling method that is applied for this research is stratified sampling. The samples are categorised into two different groups, the elderly that stay with their family and the elderly that do not stay with their family. There will be 15 people for each group. This sampling method will help to determine if the effort needed to take care of the elderly can be reduced by using this monitoring system. A survey will be used to collect data for this research. The Survey data collection method is used because surveys are less expensive and easier to perform on a large sample population. The survey will consist of both open-ended and close-ended questions. The open-ended questions will allow the respondents to express their opinions on the system. The close-ended questions are Likert Scale, with answers ranging from Strongly Agree to Strongly Disagree. A statistical analysis will then be performed on the data that was collected. The data will then be used to identify their preferences and improve the monitoring system.

OVERVIEW OF THE SYSTEM

The proposed system mainly consists of a wearable pulse and temperature sensor, a wearable fall detection sensor, a database, and a mobile application to monitor the heart rate and body temperature of the elderly. The elderly person will wear the pulse, temperature, and fall detection sensor while at home. The sensors are connected to the home network. The sensors will acquire data from the elderly in real-time and then transmit the data to the cloud database through the home network. From there, relatives and health professionals with authorisation will be able to monitor the patient's health. If the heart rate and temperature of the elderly go above or below a certain threshold, or if the elderly has fallen, an alert will be sent out to healthcare professionals and relatives of the elderly. Relatives or medical professionals can then choose to call the elderly to determine if there is an emergency. If they do not answer, then this means that there is an emergency, and appropriate action can be taken. Fig. (**4**) represents the overview of the proposed system.

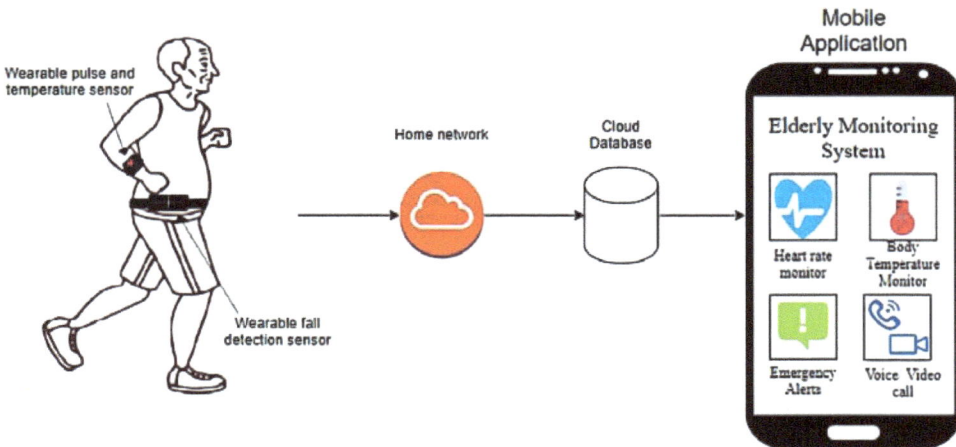

Fig. (4). Overview of the proposed system.

CONCLUSION

This research has proposed a monitoring system that can monitor the health and safety of the elderly in Malaysia when they are alone at home. By monitoring their heart rate and body temperature in real-time, relatives and medical professionals can monitor the elderly's health. They can respond accordingly if there are any abnormalities in the readings. The monitoring system will also be able to send alerts to relatives and medical professionals in the event of an elderly person falling. As a future enhancement, the monitoring system will be enhanced to include blood pressure and respiration rate monitoring.

CONSENT FOR PUBLICATION

Not applicable.

CONFLICT OF INTEREST

The authors declare no conflict of interest, financial or otherwise.

ACKNOWLEDGEMENTS

The authors wish to express sincere appreciation to the Asia Pacific University of Technology and Innovation (APU) for giving them this opportunity to conduct the research.

REFERENCES

[1]   B.J. Cheng, M.M.A. Jamil, R. Ambar, M.H.A. Wahab, and A.A. Ma'radzi, *Elderly Care Monitoring System with IoT Application.* Recent Advances in Intelligent Information Systems and Applied Mathematics, 2020, pp. 525-537.
      [http://dx.doi.org/10.1007/978-3-030-34152-7_40]

[2]   Department of Statistics Malaysia, "Department of Statistics Malaysia Official Portal," www.dosm.gov.my   Jul.   15,   2019.
      https://www.dosm.gov.my/v1/index.php?r=column/cthemeByCat&cat=155&bul_id=aWJZRkJ4UEdK
      cUZpT2tVT090Snpydz09&menu_id=L0pheU43NWJwRWVSZklWdzQ4TlhUUT09A

[3]   T. A. Yusof, "'Malaysia needs to prepare for ageing population,'" NST Online, Dec. 22, 2019.https://www.nst.com.my/news/nation/2019/12/550082/malaysia-needs-prepare-age-ng-population

[4]   M. Thibaud, H. Chi, W. Zhou, and S. Piramuthu, "Internet of Things (IoT) in high-risk Environment, Health and Safety (EHS) industries: A comprehensive review," *Decision Support Systems,* vol. 108, pp. 79–95, Apr. 2018,
      [http://dx.doi.org/10.1016/j.dss.2018.02.005]

[5]   K. Saraubon, K. Anurugsa, and A. Kongsakpaibul, "A Smart System for Elderly Care using IoT and Mobile Technologies," *Proceedings of the 2018 2nd International Conference on Software and e-Business - ICSEB '18,* 2018
      [http://dx.doi.org/10.1145/3301761.3301769]

[6]   https://www.researchgate.net/publication/330425585_Internet_of_Things-
      IOT_Definition_Characteristics_Architecture_Enabling_Technologies_Application_Future_Challenge
      s K. K. Patel, S. M. Patel, P. Scholar, and C. Salazar, "(PDF) Internet of Things-IoT: Definition, Characteristics, Architecture, Enabling Technologies, Application & Future Challenges," *ResearchGate,* May 2016.

[7]   H. Basanta, Y.-P. Huang, and T.-T. Lee, "Intuitive IoT-based H2U healthcare system for elderly people," *2016 IEEE 13th International Conference on Networking, Sensing, and Control (ICNSC),* Apr. 2016
        [http://dx.doi.org/10.1109/ICNSC.2016.7479018]

[8]   B. David Chung Hu, H. Fahmi, L. Yuhao, C. C. Kiong, and A. Harun, "Internet of Things (IOT) Monitoring System for Elderly," *2018 International Conference on Intelligent and Advanced System (ICIAS),* Aug. 2018
        [http://dx.doi.org/10.1109/ICIAS.2018.8540567]

[9]   S. Ariaratnam et al., "Prevalence of obesity and its associated risk factors among the elderly in Malaysia: Findings from The National Health and Morbidity Survey (NHMS) 2015," *PLOS ONE,* vol. 15, no. 9, p. e0238566, Sep. 2020
        [http://dx.doi.org/10.1371/journal.pone.0238566] [PMID: 32915860]

[10]   N. A. Bani et al., "Assessment of Health Status of the Elderly and Pre-elderly at a Malaysia Elderly Care Centre," *International Journal of Integrated Engineering,* vol. 10, no. 7, Nov. 2018
        [http://dx.doi.org/10.30880/ijie.2018.10.07.002]

[11]   M. Al-khafajiy *et al.,* "Remote health monitoring of elderly through wearable sensors," *Multimedia Tools and Applications,* vol. 78, no. 17, pp. 24681–24706, Jan. 2019
        [http://dx.doi.org/10.1007/s11042-018-7134-7]

[12]   D. Yacchirema, J. S. de Puga, C. Palau, and M. Esteve, "Fall detection system for elderly people using IoT and ensemble machine learning algorithm," *Personal and Ubiquitous Computing,* vol. 23, no. 5–6, pp. 801–817, Jan. 2019
        [http://dx.doi.org/10.1007/s00779-018-01196-8]

[13]   J. H. Abawajy and M. M. Hassan, "Federated Internet of Things and Cloud Computing Pervasive Patient Health Monitoring System," *IEEE Communications Magazine,* vol. 55, no. 1, pp. 48–53, Jan. 2017
        [http://dx.doi.org/10.1109/MCOM.2017.1600374CM]

CHAPTER 12

IoT-Based Medical Ecosystem

Wong Wan Jing[1], Nor Azlina Abdul Rahman[1] and **Daniel Mago Vistro[2,*]**

[1] *School of Computing & Technology, Asia Pacific University of Technology and Innovation, Kuala Lumpur, Malaysia*

[2] *Forensic and Cyber Security Research Centre, Asia Pacific University of Technology and Innovation, Kuala Lumpur, Malaysia*

Abstract: The Internet of Things (IoT) is an evolving technology in the emerging digital transformation domain. The healthcare system is also growing, using IoT to improve human life and save more lives. With the assistance of IoT technology, physicians can easily monitor patients' health conditions in real-time. A cardiac pacemaker is a medical device connected to the IoT environment to improve the efficiency of healthcare. However, low-quality IoT design will bring disadvantages, such as cyber-attacks. Every process of building IoT medical devices should evaluate the product before launching it to the market. Manufacturers or hospitals should organise their critical infrastructure orderly to protect confidential data. The data should achieve the confidentiality, integrity, and availability of the CIA triad, which is the foundation of information security. This paper aims to study the vulnerabilities of IoT medical devices, the methods of possible attacks from hackers, and organisational and operational security to address cyber security in the healthcare industry. Moreover, it proposes a framework for the IoT medical ecosystem between the patient and the hospital to improve the existing IoT medical ecosystem.

Keywords: Attack Vectors, Cyberattack, IoT Medical Ecosystem, IoT, Security Framework.

INTRODUCTION

According to ReportLinker [1], the healthcare IoT market is expected to be $534.3 billion by 2025. The technological revolution causes the Internet of Things (IoT) to advance. One of the solutions to create a smart healthcare model is using IoT as the backbone, connecting the countless online connections to become an integrated system running in real-time. Data collection from IoT devices is meaningful insights to healthcare doctors, physicians, and patients because they can more efficiently track the patient's condition. The patient also understands their daily health condition to balance their lifestyle. IoT devices require embedd-

---

* **Corresponding author Daniel Mago Vistro:** Forensic and Cyber Security Research Centre, Asia Pacific University of Technology and Innovation, Kuala Lumpur, Malaysia; Email: daniel.mago@apu.edu.my

Muhammad Ehsan Rana and Manoj Jayabalan (Eds.)

ed software to communicate with hardware and human interaction. Creating IoT applications is convenient as it can read the data coming from devices. Even though IoT healthcare brings many benefits to our lifestyles, many challenges still exist.

The data security and the management of IoT devices are the concern of the healthcare executives and Information Technology (IT) team. For example, a pacemaker is a medical device that connects with the Internet, Bluetooth, and cellular to communicate with other devices and places, such as a home monitoring device and smartphone. IoT medical devices assist doctors or physicians in monitoring patients' heart conditions. The cardiac pacemaker has five years of battery life and implants inside the left of the human chest. The cardiac pacemaker will send the information about the patient's heart to the home monitoring device or smartphone. The monitoring device or smartphone aggregates the data and sends it to the hospital system. The hospital system will show the patient's data by providing an analysis for the doctor or physician to determine and plan the upcoming treatment or expected outcome for the patient. The solution is to prevent the patient from having irregular heartbeats, vascular diseases, cardiac arrhythmias, or heart failure. IoT devices are integrated with many devices to form a systematic management system. However, there is an unnoticed issue regarding security vulnerabilities at the application layer; the IoT device can be compromised by unauthorised access. The impact of the security issue will threaten human lives. Washington [2] mentioned that Muddy Water published the vulnerability of cardiac devices and caused the former St. Jude Medical shares to decrease by more than 8%.

BACKGROUND OF ABBOT AND THE IOT MEDICAL

According to Abbott [1], the global medical device company Abbott Laboratories combined with St. Jude Medical in January 2017. The company is an American multinational medical device in health care and supports 160 countries [3]. The company acquired innovative technology to create better equipment to help people in need and bring advanced technology into the healthcare platform.

Fig. (**1**) shows the IoT medical ecosystem from Abbott. One of the IoT medical products of Abbott is the implantable cardiac device. This pacemaker operates for slow heart rhythms, electric shock for the heart, and pacing to terminate dangerously fast heart rhythms. The cardiac pacemaker is inserted under the skin of the upper chest area. The " leads" wires connected to the pacemaker are put in the heart [4]. This cardiac pacemaker technology saves many patients from slow heartbeat (bradycardia) and fast heartbeat (tachycardia) and coordinates the treatment for heart failure. Radio frequency-enabled (RF) technology applies to a cardiac pacemaker. The pacemaker sends the signal to the transmitter with wireless communication. According to International Organization for Standardization (ISO) [5] indicates that the pacemaker applies 401 to 406 MHz frequency on the electromagnetic compatibility (EMC) standard, ISO 14117:2019 [6]. The transmitter is the home monitor transmitter and receives the RF signals from the cardiac devices. The data is stored in the device for reading. Typically, the transmitter is used at the patient's home. Both IoT medical devices require connecting with the patient's home network to communicate with each other. The network connection needs to be able to reach the Merlin.net Patient Care Network, thus, the patient's data is able to be sent to the physician to monitor and analyse the data. The pacemaker programmer is the external desktop computer used to adjust the cardiac pacemaker, and it is a crucial tool for the doctor. This is because it is essential to download the patient's data stored on the cardiac pacemaker and edit the setting in the pacemaker if necessary. Adjusting the pacemaker programmer can help avoid additional surgery for the patient. The back end of the Merlin.net Patient Care Network (PCN) is the system connected to the web server and the database. Therefore, the physician or doctor can access the server to view the analysis data of the patient. The IoT medical ecosystem server ensures the safety of the patients without the need for additional surgery. This considerably reduces the patients' on-site visits to doctors compared to the past.

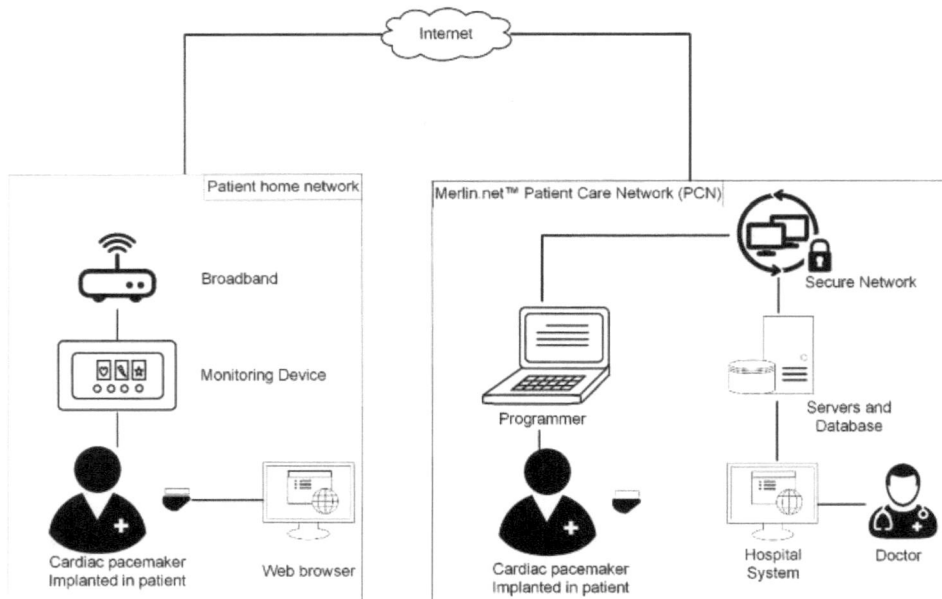

Fig. (1). IoT medical ecosystem from Abbott.

VULNERABILITIES AND IMPACT OF IOT MEDICAL ECOSYSTEM

IoT medical device security leaks are dangerous for the patient's life. One of the vulnerabilities reported is about the Merlin@homeTM transmitter-the monitoring units from former St. Jude had a potential cyberattack. The researcher, Muddy Waters Capital, found cybersecurity flaws when researching medical at MedSec. As mentioned by Spring [7], researcher Muddy Waters found that the Merlin@home device reused the SSH certificate and static username and passwords to gain easy access to the root privilege of the monitoring device equipment. The impact of the vulnerability of the monitoring tools affects thousands of cardiac devices, including CRT-P devices: Accent, Anthem, Accent MRI, Accent ST, Assurity, and Allure. As Hern [8] reported, the vulnerabilities resulted in the recall of 500,000 pacemaker units, and the stock value of former St. Jude Medical had a loss of 2 billion dollars.

According to the United States (U.S.) Food and Drug Administration (FDA) [8], the vulnerabilities existed at the former St. Jude medical devices in 2017. The target audiences are patients with the CRT-P type of cardiac device implanted and the Merlin@home transmitter, caregivers of patients, cardiologists, electrophysiologists, cardiothoracic surgeons, and primary care physicians. The purpose of the FDA is to provide the details to lower the risk of the patient getting hurt due to cyber security flaws. Fortunately, the FDA can take early precautions to protect the patient as there is no report of a patient getting harmed by these vulnerabilities.

Even though Abbott has high network security, it still has another vulnerability: the patient home network. Usually, the home network only has a Wi-Fi router to provide Internet access for the family members. Some Wi-Fi security is old-fashioned, such as wired equivalent privacy (WEP), not Wireless Protected Access (WPA) standard or the second version. Apart from that, the home network's password is easy to guess as things such as the car plate number, phone number, birth date, and family name are used. The weak password can get broken into easily, and the worse part is that the patient's home network never changes the password when the first network is set up. The hacker can use Wi-Fi sniffing and brute force to obtain the home network password to search the IoT medical device. The impact attracts the hacker to perform a man-in-the-middle attack or gain access to the IoT device and destroy it.

The low awareness or training of the employee is the vulnerability of the security chain of the human. Suspicious emails such as bank credit, lottery, job offers and love scams can use trust in relationships to deceive careless employees. Clicking or downloading the malicious attachment could lead to the installation of malware on the desktop or laptop. This behaviour is a social engineering attack used to steal data or enter the internal organisation network. Ransomware is malware installed after the desktop is compromised—the vulnerability results in the data being breached and encrypted by ransomware.

METHODS OF ATTACKS USED IN IOT MEDICAL ECOSYSTEM

Low-security settings in the patient's home network allow attackers to access their network. The hacker can crack the password of the patient's Wi-Fi and Internet Protocol (IP), sniffing to detect the number of devices connected in their home. Fig. (**2**) displays that an attacker may carry out a Man-in-the-middle (MITM) attack to eavesdrop on the network to be involved in conversations between the monitoring tool and the server from Merlin.net. The malicious actor impersonates and gathers information from both sides of the device communication session. When the time is right, the attacker will send the malicious code to the side he or she wants to attack. The attack intercepts traffic flow between patient monitoring devices and the Merlin.net server, sending and receiving information to both sides without anyone recognising it. The risk of the MITM is that the attacker can send false data and insert the data transferred between the patient device and Merlin.net servers.

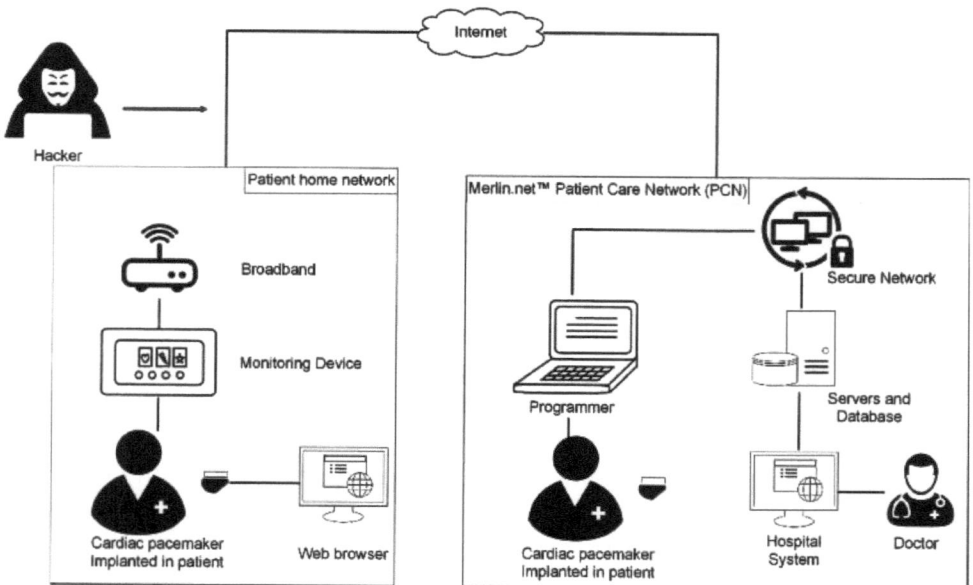

Fig. (2). The man-in-the-middle attack vector to IoT medical ecosystem.

The vulnerabilities first found in the pacemaker devices were the energy depletion attack and the crash attack. Replaying the communication multiple times could crash the cardiac pacemaker, making it unable to recover. This impact results in a broken cardiac pacemaker, and the patient must undergo surgery to replace it. The energy depletion attack drains the cardiac pacemaker to run out of battery quickly and makes it unable to reload. This happens once the attacker modifies the command in the embedded software. Even though wireless communication allows reprogramming to replay the attack, so the pacemaker's battery is drained quickly, hackers do not favour it as it is time-consuming. Zillner [9] mentioned that the attacks required cryptoanalysis and reverse engineering skills. The cardiac pacemaker is likely not the target of the hacker because the distance needs to be close to the devices to detect it. Hackers will use an alternative way to find the new attacker vector; thus, the Merlin@transmitter monitoring tool is probably the hacker's next target. The protocol of the pacemaker is also the same as the transmitter.

Zillner [10] found out that the bootloader from the transmitter is easy to enter by pressing the escape key to trigger the reboot of the device. After the device reboot, it is easy for the hacker to boot into the shell. The insecure hardware interface of the Merlin@home device is easy to debug. Running with the status command of the devices can retrieve information such as the IP address, the kernel cmdline, CPU board ID, and MAC address. Using the "kernel cmdline" from the status information to boot the kernel cmdline with an additional shell argument command ("init=/bin/sh") will allow it to be able to access the root privilege of the device, as shown in Tobias Zillner's presentation, 500.000 Recalled Pacemakers, 2 Billion $ Stock Value Loss. Gaining access to the root shell may allow the device to connect to another. For instance, the transmitter may be able to list the cloud of Merlin.net, static keys, and the IP address. Zillner [11] demonstrated the next action as finding a coding that displayed the list of the File transfer protocol (FTP) and the static password not encrypted. Their findings of the transmitter and the programmer contain insecure source code storage. This vulnerability can extract the data from the device firmware and carry out reverse engineering. The hacker can decide to attack a cardiac pacemaker or Merlin.net. This means that the unauthorised person or attacker can use remote access to the patient's radio frequency-enabled implant device, such as a cardiac pacemaker. The findings of the vulnerability in pacemakers were using hardcoded 24-bit Rivest-Shamir-Adleman (RSA) message authentication code (MAC) [12]. Even though the transmitter uses a hardcoded "Universal key" because Abbott supports 160 countries, this may be the backdoor of the device. In a worst-case scenario, an attacker could use the patient's devices to collect cloud-based information and attack the next location: the manufacturer or the hospital, as shown in Fig. (3).

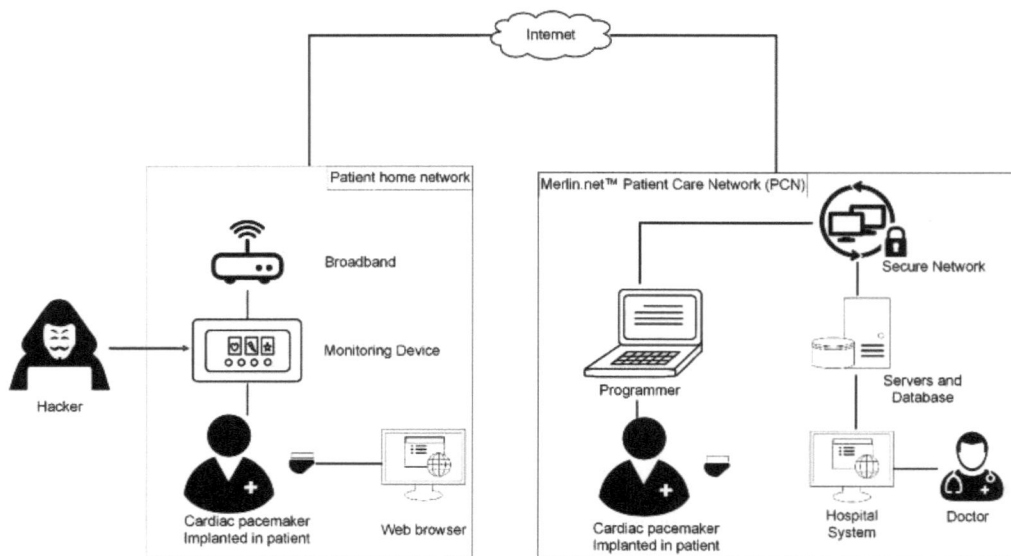

Fig. (3). Unauthorised access attack vector to IoT medical ecosystem.

Fig. (4) shows that the hacker uses the spearing phishing attack on the hospital employee so that they can enter the track. The function of the phishing attack is to gain information such as passwords, account information, and credit card data. The ransomware of the application is attached to the email from which the employee downloads the ransom application. The ransomware encrypts the data and asks for the ransom fee. When the organisation's network is compromised, the hacker attacks the programmer's device to bypass the server or directly attacks the webserver and database. The hacker possibly wants to steal sensitive information from the database and control the data, as it is valuable and worth selling on the black market.

ORGANISATIONAL AND OPERATIONAL SECURITY IOT MEDICAL SYSTEM

The purpose of the organisational and operational system is to provide procedures and policies to guide the employees of organisations and to manage data and security accordingly. Organizational security defines information management and team communication with an appropriate level of security and continuity. The goals of organisational and operational security are evolving the security program successfully.

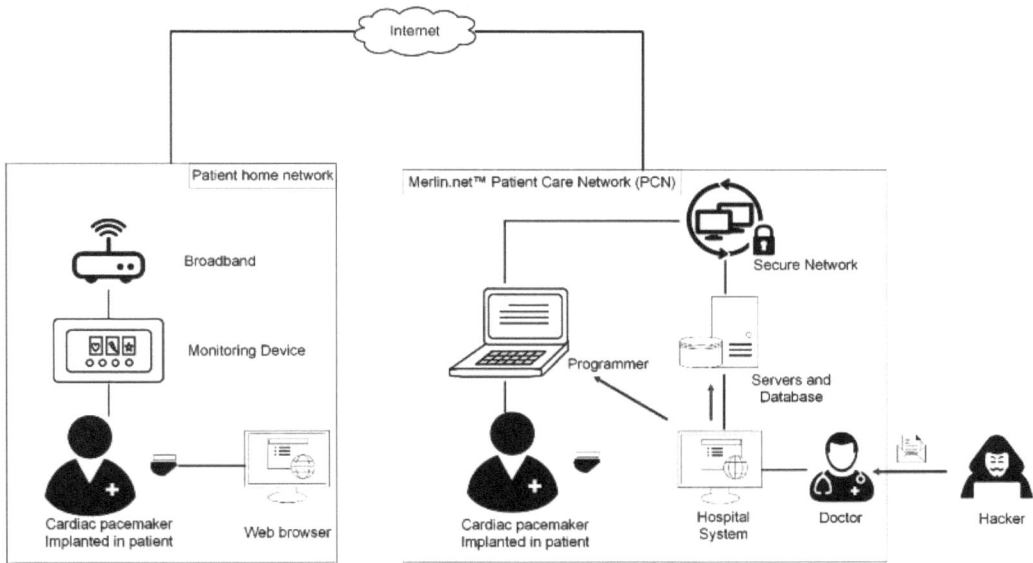

Fig. (4). The phishing attack vector to IoT medical ecosystem.

Risk Management and Vulnerabilities Management

The risks and vulnerabilities of the IoT medical ecosystem are essential to identify the weak points and prevent the threat actor from attacking data security. Vulnerability management is used to ensure compliance and prevent the vulnerability from repeating. Risk management is the process of coordinating the resources impacted by unfortunate events. Risk and vulnerability management should cover and secure human and process data. Salih *et al.* [13] proposed the DEMATEL IoT Risk Assessment Procedure, which distributes three risk parts: secured technology, human privacy, and trustable processes and data. The core process of risk and vulnerability management is to assist the organisation in avoiding vulnerabilities. To prevent an asset inventory, the first process that an organisation should carry out is to identify the number of hardware, the structure of the IT infrastructure, the network structure, and the version of the firmware and software.

The organisation should prepare and create a secure configuration for hardware and software components. The improper configuration of IT assets affects cyber vulnerabilities. The way to manage the configuration is to have a proper checklist ready, templates or images of the system that works for the new deployment of the server, and a secure configuration. The unnecessary parts of the configuration should deactivate in the organisation environment. Patch management is one of the vulnerability management programs, and it requires the vendor to provide and apply the software update to fix the system. For example, the data centre's infrastructure Abbott should verify the patch to update the infrastructure. The patch applies to fix some vulnerabilities in the system. The insecure configuration of the system is one of the tasks in vulnerability management, even if the system is fully patched in hardware and software. A common issue is a server running with default settings, ultimately causing unnecessary services to run. The network elements are also vulnerability management, such as firewalls, routers, network switches, network traffic controls, and internal and external network connectivity. The healthcare organisation needs to configure the network element by essential rules, which can compare to where the malicious traffic from the authorised data flows. The unfollowed rules will lead to a security flaw on the network side, such as unnecessary ports opening in the system, misconfiguring access control in the system, and wrongly applied rules in the firewall. Data theft intrudes into the system when there are unnecessary vulnerabilities in the organisation's network. The server configuration is needed to frequently maintain the IT functions, including printer support, file sharing, database, websites, and organisation domain. The server's default configuration, standard services, and common communication mechanisms run with Windows, Linux, kernel-based Virtual Machine (KVM), or VMware operating system. Organisations should evaluate and reduce the unnecessary configuration from the default settings to minimise the attack risk.

The third process is maintenance detection for vulnerability and awareness. Abbott works with the Chertoff Group to understand the awareness of IoT medical devices on physicians and hospital administrators to know the cyber security risks faced in the hospital environment. The awareness campaign is building a more secure and connected healthcare environment to identify the physicians and hospital administrators towards the perspective on cyber security awareness. Research conducted by [4] and [14] shows that 71% of the physicians and 74% of the hospital administration shared responsibility for cyber security being essential among the stakeholders operating in the healthcare system.

Security Certifications

The organisation should be certified with the Information security standard (ISO/IEC 27001:2005) network such as medical device network former St. Jude Medical certified ISO 27001 and IS 541672- Information Security controls to support the connectivity of the Merlin@home remote monitoring system to communicate with the Merlin.netTM Patient Care Network(PCN). They also have St. Jude Medical Global Information Protection Assurance (GIPA) Department controlling and maintaining this document. The ISO certificate ensures the protection of the CIA on health data by solving the risk of the information lifecycle.

Policies

The organisation should have data policies such as data backups, classification of data, and disposal and destruction policy. Data backup includes data ownership, and the requirement depends on the severity of the backup, restore purpose, retention, and protection requirement. The organisation should ensure the backup is adequate in the proper operating procedures. The organisation contains many data types and needs to classify the integrity and sensitivity level. The organisation should protect the data from being publicly releasable, keep the proprietary company confidential, and be for internal use only. This is to determine the level of protection to arrange for the large data collection organisation. The physicians and the hospital administration should be trained to follow the procedure when dealing with the different data types and authorised access for the valid user. The attacker can use outdated or unnecessary data to gain information. The organisation should have a disposal and destruction policy to manage the old and unnecessary data. Important data should be shredded and not remain in the system if it becomes redundant. The proper way to remove the disk is to delete the data inside the hard disk, overwrite it at least three times, enter random characters, and degauss the storage disk.

Furthermore, human resources policies should control the limitation of the human security chain because the social engineer attack can break it. People management is to track the newcomer and the retired employee to mitigate the employees' retirement or quit the job.

FRAMEWORK ON IMPROVEMENT OF IOT MEDICAL SYSTEM SECURITY

Fig. (**5**) illustrates the overall IoT medical framework from the patient to the organisation. The first is to understand the IoT device vulnerability. The cardiac pacemaker uses RF-enabled to send the signals to the monitoring tool, which is the Merlin@ transmitter. The monitoring tool creates two bootloaders to store the backup bootloader, so the transmitter boot-up mode runs insecurely.

The U.S. Commerce Department's National Institute of Standards and Technology (NIST) is a popular cyber security framework applied to the organisation. The benefit of the NIST framework is enhancing the organisation's critical infrastructure in cyber security. Moreover, the organisation should study the framework to understand how to improve their IT management from the cyber security risks.

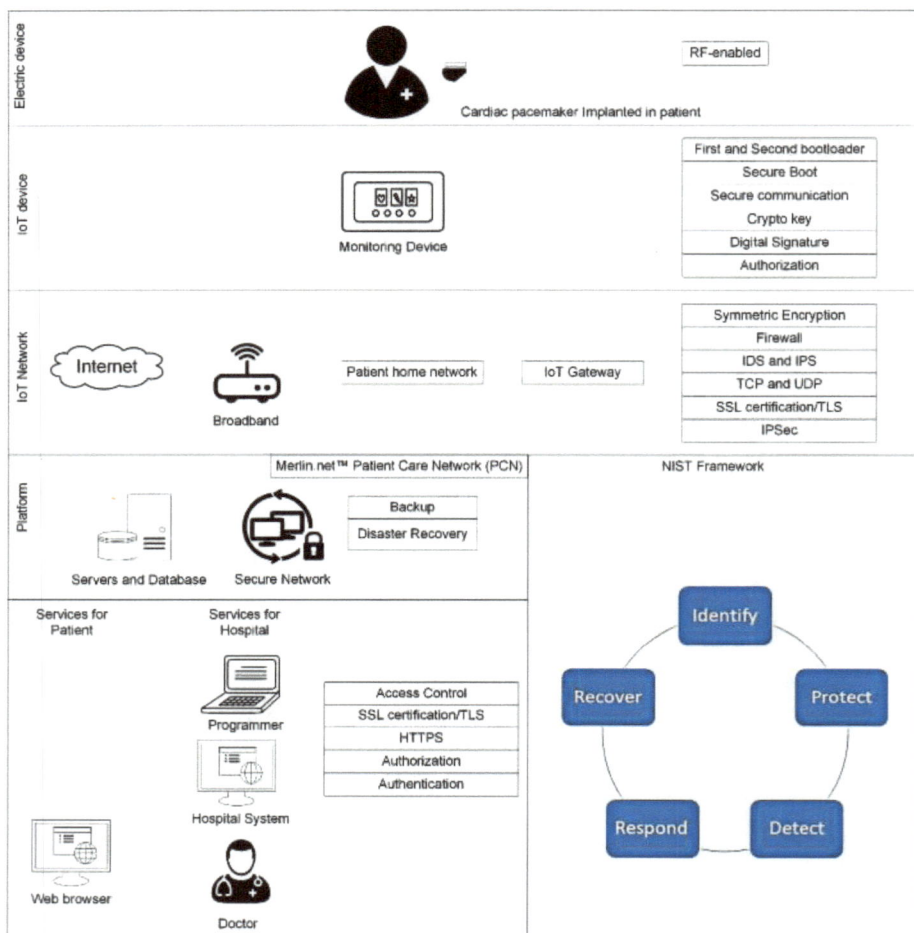

Fig. (5). Overall IoT medical system security framework.

The study [15] described that NIST Cyber security Framework version 1.1 is acceptable to use in the medical environment. The five cores of the NIST functions are identifying, protecting, detecting, responding, and recovering. Identifying is the first function of an organisation to grow the knowledge of the potential risk and the management to reduce the risk of the healthcare. For example, the asset management mentioned that the Organizational and Operational Security IoT medical system tracks the organisation's IT inventory hardware and software.

Next, the protect function is used to sustain cybersecurity events' impact or limitation. The access control, awareness training, data security, information protection and procedures, maintenance and protective technology, followed by the detect function, determines and finds the cyber security events. The automated detection tool uses vulnerability assessment to find the misbehaviour event, detection processes, and continuous security monitoring [16, 17]. After the detect function, the respond function must take action to remove the detected cyber security event. Lastly, the recover function is used to resolve or restore the components or services destroyed by malicious events and recover planning and communication.

CONCLUSION

In this paper, the study concludes that the type of attack vectors is used to find the solution to the source of the risk and vulnerability. The organisational and operational security needs to be well planned to arrange the IoT medical ecosystem systematically. The security framework for the IoT medical ecosystem is the way to mitigate and improve the existing IoT medical system. All the efforts are to prevent the IoT medical ecosystem from zero-day. The design of the security framework includes the IoT medical device from the patient and the organisation's IT security environment management. IoT in the medical field is critical and different from other IoT platforms because a cyberattack can harm human life.

CONSENT FOR PUBLICATION

Not applicable.

CONFLICT OF INTEREST

The authors declare no conflict of interest, financial or otherwise.

ACKNOWLEDGEMENT

This research is supported by the Asia Pacific University of Innovation and Technology.

REFERENCES

[1] Abbott (2017) St. Jude Medical is Now Abbott. [Online]. Available from: https://www.abbott.com/corpnewsroom/strategy-and-strength/st-jude-medical-is-now-abbott.html [Accessed: 21th October 2020].

[2] Abbott (n.d.) Abbott at a glance. [Online]. Available from: https://www.abbott.com/about-abbott/at-a-glance.html [Accessed: 1st November 2020].

[3] Abbott (n.d.) Cybersecurity Coordinated Product Disclosure Program. [Online]. Available from: https://www.abbott.com/policies/cybersecurity/cybersecurity-coordinated-product- disclosure.html [Accessed: 29th October 2020].

[4] Abbott (2018) Cybersecurity in the Connected Hospital. [Online]. Available from: https://www.abbott.com/corpnewsroom/strategy-and-strength/cybersecurity-

in-connected-hospital.html Accessed: 21th October 2020].

[5]　Abbott　(n.d.)　What　is　a　pacemaker?　[Online].　Available　from: https://www.cardiovascular.abbott/int/en/patients/living-wit-
-your-device/arrhythmias/pacemakers.html [Accessed: 29th October 2020].

[6]　BITSENTINEL (n.d.) How often should I perform Penetration Testing? [Online]. Available from: https://bit-sentinel.com/how-often-should-i-perform-penetration-testing
/#:~:text=Penetration%20testing%20should%20be%20performed,be%20exploited%20by%20maliciou
s%20hackers [Accessed: 31st October 2020].

[7]　Debbie,　W.　(2019)　What　is　the　CIA　Triad　?　[Online].　Available　from: https://www.f5.com/labs/articles/education/what-is-the-cia-triad#:~:
text=These%20three%20letters%20stand%20for,objectives%20for%20every%20security%20program
Accessed: 1st November 2020].

[8]　Hern, A. (2017) Hacking risk leads to recall of 500,000 pacemakers due to patient death fears. [Online]. Available from: https://www.theguardian.com/technology/2017/aug/31/hacking-risk-reca-
l-pacemakers-patient-death-fears-fda-firmware-update [Accessed: 29th October 2020].

[9]　(HHS.gov,　n.d.)　Summary　of　the　HIPAA　Security　Rule　[Online].　Available　from: https://www.hhs.gov/hipaa/for-professionals/security/laws-regulations/index.html [Accessed: 29th October 2020].

[10]　International Organization for Standardization (ISO) (n.d.) ISO 14117:2019 (en). [Online]. Available from: https://www.iso.org/obp/ui/#iso:std:iso:14117:ed-2:v1:en [Accessed: 29th October 2020].

[11]　Nkomo, D. and Brown, R., 2019. Hybrid Cyber Security Framework for the Internet of Medical Things. In Blockchain and Clinical Trial (pp. 211-229). Springer, Cham.

[12]　ReportLinker (2019) Internet of Things in Healthcare Market Size, Share & Trends Analysis Report By Component, By Connectivity Technology, By End Use, By Application And Segment Forecasts, 2019 – 2025. [Online]. Available from: https://www.reportlinker.com/p05763769/Internet-of- Things-
in-Healthcare-Market-Size-Share-Trends-Analysis-Report-By-Component-By-　　　　　Connectivity-
Technology-By-End-Use-By-Application-And-Segment-Forecasts.html [Accessed: 29th October 2020].

[13]　Salih, F.I., Bakar, N.A.A., Hassan, N.H., Yahya, F., Kama, N. and Shah, J., 2019. IOT Security Risk

[14]　Management Model for Healthcare Industry. Malaysian Journal of Computer Science, pp.131- 144. Spring, T. (2016) Pacemaker Hacking Fears Rise With Critical Research Report. [Online]. Available from:　https://threatpost.com/pacemaker-hacking-fears-rise-with-critical-research-report/12017　4/ [Accessed: 29th October 2020].

[15]　U.S. Food and Drug Administration (FDA) (2017) Cybersecurity Vulnerabilities Identified in St. Jude Medical's Implantable Cardiac Devices and Merlin@home Transmitter: FDA Safety Communication. [Online].　　　　Available　　　　from:　　　　https://www.fda.gov/medical-devices/safety-
communications/cybersecurity-vulnerabilities-identified-st-jude-medicals-implantable-　[Accessed: 21th July 2015].

[16]　Washington, R. (2016) St. Jude Medical drops after Muddy Water findings of 'negligent product design'. [Online]. Available from: https://www.cnbc.com/2016/08/25/st-jude-medical-drops- after-
muddy-water-findings-of-negligent-product-design.html [Accessed: 29th October 2020].

[17]　Zillner, T. (2019) 500.000 Recalled Pacemakers, 2 Billion $ Stock Value Loss [Online Video]. August 22nd. Available from:https://www.youtube.com/watch?v=s2tgE9az6UE [Accessed: 21st October 2020].

CHAPTER 13

Active Learning-based Mobile Learning System for Students of Asia Pacific University

Hen Kian Jun[1,*] and **Siti Azreena Binti Mubin**[1]

[1] School of Computing, Asia Pacific University of Technology and Innovation, Kuala Lumpur, Malaysia

Abstract: In recent years, mobile technology has become increasingly more available and advanced, especially in education. Mobile learning technology allows individuals to have online distance learning in COVID-19 by transforming traditional Learning from online Learning to mobile Learning. The implementation of mobile Learning in higher education is essential because it allows students and tutors to stay connected and allows students to access online materials for active Learning at any time. Therefore, this research proposes a mobile learning system integrated with active learning practices for Asia Pacific University students in the learning process. This will give students more positive outcomes such as better academic performances and achievements, increased motivation and attention in studies, increased learning satisfaction in students, and training them to be active learners. This research is conducted using the Quantitative method to the selected participations, and the outcome of this research could contribute to the entire education field in promoting active learning practices to improve academic performance and also provide other researchers with an insight into exploring the mobile learning system into higher education.

Keywords: Active Learning, E-Learning, Learning Management Systems, Mobile Learning, Passive Learning.

INTRODUCTION

Active Learning is a form of learning [1] where students are actively involved in the class, thus obtaining opportunities to develop and explore significant aspects of the courses by being one of the active learning group members or individuals [2]. In this digital era, with the growth and availability of technology, many students prefer online Learning and obtaining online resources [3].

---

* **Corresponding author Hen Kian Jun:** School of Computing, Asia Pacific University of Technology & Innovation, Kuala Lumpur, Malaysia. Email: kjhen0929@gmail.com

Muhammad Ehsan Rana and Manoj Jayabalan (Eds.)

A problem with online Learning is that the online resources need to be more accurate, and thus they cannot be fully trusted. Therefore, it will be better if students can use a platform that offers opportunities to communicate and discuss any confusion on tasks, assignments, or homework with tutors and friends. The university is generally considered more stressful compared to high- and primary-schools due to the more competitive environment [4]. Active Learning can lower anxiety in students in the learning process based on how it is implemented [5]. Its limitation is that other practices may lead to greater anxiety than active learning practices, which have not been explored [6]. Moreover, mobile technology can play a beneficial role in promoting academic learning [7]. A study says that the implementation of mobile Learning into Higher Education led to a positive effect on the performances and achievements of students [8]. According to [9], the interactivity of mobile apps can result in more favourable outcomes, as mobile interaction can increase motivation and attention in students. Therefore, it is highly recommended to implement a mobile system integrated with the active learning method into Higher Education [10]. However, the hardware available has limitations as students need to use a high specification of mobile phone to enjoy the benefits of this learning method [10, 11]. According to [10], another limitation is data collection, educational information is chosen as the only one of the centres for the study, but the range of collecting data is comprehensive. Therefore, the rate of accurate data collected could have been higher. Asia Pacific University students are chosen as the target of this research to ensure that students can experience mobile-learning integrated with active Learning. In this paper, a mobile-learning system integrated with the active learning method will be proposed to promote the active learning experience so that all the students can benefit from it. Students can use the system to learn extra knowledge which will not be covered in the course materials, such as streaming the curated videos. However, tutors can make online quizzes for students to assess their knowledge. Integrating these active learning methods into the mobile learning system can increase theoretical knowledge and skill scores from using the system.

The rest of the paper is organised as follows. Section 2 will look into works that have been done along with arguments and limitations similar to the proposed ideas. Section 3 will further explain the need for the study by analysing and studying the problem of passive Learning. Section 4 presents the research's aim and the objectives to achieve the aims. Section 5 simplifies the research paper into individual research questions and answers to the research objectives. Section 6 elaborates on the significance of the research towards the field of the study. Section 7 suggests the most suitable methodology to be carried out in the research. Section 8 provides an overview of the proposed system and illustrates the use case and flowchart diagrams for better understanding. Section 9 concludes the research and raises issues for future research and improvements that could be made.

BACKGROUND

Since the current paper adopts the active learning method in the mobile learning system for Asia Pacific University students, some previous works are briefly reviewed in the Active Learning method and mobile learning.

Active Learning

Active Learning is a form of learning achieved through establishing high engagement between students and tutors rather than keeping a passive learning environment. A previous study by [12] recommended that the learning process should implement the effective learning method concept. According to the findings, it has improved student academic performance, fostered skills development, and increased student satisfaction in the learning process. Its limitation is that the research focuses only on students who use technological equipment to produce skills and knowledge and understand fields to participate in activity lessons [13]. Another study by [5] has stated that students enjoy "doing something" and that a hands-on approach to problem-solving resulted in students understanding better and having reduced anxiety levels. According to the findings, the anxiety level was reduced in students doing group work to solve a problem. Anxiety levels can also be decreased when students who understand the concept explain it to others. Its limitation is focused on the evaluation of situations that are common in active learning courses. Individuals have unique anxiety levels; some consistently have light anxiety levels, whereas others have severe anxiety. Another study by [14] has pointed out that active learning strategies are implemented to promote student engagement, which significantly impacts student learning. According to the findings, implementing active Learning effectively increased students' understanding from 40% to 60% compared to passive learning methods. Its limitation is that the research was done using a poll by the authors, with the involvement of faculty and staff in both the design and teaching of online courses about student engagement [15].

Mobile Learning

Mobile learning is an advanced type of E-learning, which has evolved from distance learning to e-learning, with no time and place limits [16]. Mobile learning enables and improves the ability of learners to access internet information through mobile devices with wireless technology [17]. A previous study by [8] has pointed out that mobile learning can be used in developing a distant-learning system to create extensive communication despite the physical distance. It enables the learner not to have a fixed or predetermined location or use the opportunities offered by mobile technology to learn. Mobile learning can be deemed as a stimulus, and it can generate feedback in educational activities. Mobile learning enables students to freely share and learn exciting topics with friends at any time and place. The limitation of the research is that the data is collected via the documentary method only by using search engines and valid websites [8]. Another study done by [4] has concluded that implementing mobile Learning in higher education positively impacts students in perceiving usefulness, facilitation conditions, self-efficacy, and perceived ease of use factors. Sabah (2016) pointed out that perceived usefulness and perceived ease of use were the main factors influencing the use of mobile Learning. According to the findings, mobile Learning is suitable for academic environments, especially in higher education, because mobile technology meets the requirement in different learning contexts, and no time and location are limited for students. This leads students to have a more straightforward learning process. One limitation of the research is mainly focused on Jordan, while another is that the research could only take some areas of mobile Learning, and user acceptance that is affected by the factors of ordinary constraints needs to be considered [18]. Another study by [19] stated that mobile learning is full of opportunities for students to reduce study restrictions in location, time, and ease of access. Additionally, the advancement of technology has driven learning to improve education levels and positively impact more interactions, especially in unplanned projects and spaces to facilitate a teacher-student approach. The study's limitation is that undergraduate students from a public university in Medellin, Columbia, were selected as the sample [20]. The current paper is different from those related works in proposing a mobile learning system integrated with the active learning method to Asia Pacific University in promoting active Learning. The proposed mobile learning system allows students to have different learning mobile learning experiences, get better theoretical knowledge, score skills in academic performance, and train students to be active learners.

PROBLEM STATEMENT

Education is a combination of both teaching and learning [21, 22]. Passive Learning is a process of learning in which students absorb knowledge and information from tutors or learning environments [20]. Passive Learning is traditional learning [23]. Passive Learning refers to students only listening to tutors without responding or interacting much in the learning process [24]. The general problem is that tutors will have difficulty monitoring students' understanding because they only teach in class while students do the assignment afterwards [25]. This results in the tutors not knowing whether the student has absorbed the knowledge and information. Due to the aforementioned problem, the students might be confused with the topic or not understand it. According to [14], Brooks (2012) claimed that passive learning might be suitable for delivering lectures. Moreover, the study says active learning significantly increased students' satisfaction compared to passive learning [26].

Passive Learning has been studied, and it is found that from an average person's learning style, learners only remember 10% of reading, 20% of hearing, and 30% of seeing [27], which seems like passive learning practice. According to [1], passive learning is a challenge when it comes to evaluation because there are few opportunities to evaluate how well students understand the subject's contents. Passive Learning is a lack of time for questioning, discussion, or even clarification for students; it results in a dull and boring learning process [28].

When students should be given the freedom to work independently while Learning, the learning process is dull and boring. Learning processes should include high engagement between students and tutors to solve and reflect on problems together. Moreover, students should be able to actively work in a group in learning environments because students can remember 90% of what others do [28]. Online Learning is becoming widespread. The design of an online learning environment may use various mechanisms that promote a high level of student engagement, becoming more outstanding in online course delivery [16]. Furthermore, 90% of students chose active learning as a learning preference [20]. In the mobile age, mobile learning is more interactive and instantly delivered, which is a synchronous message, instead of time-delayed ones such as online Learning, which is an asynchronous message [28]. Therefore, a mobile-learnin--based system will be proposed to promote active learning for Asia Pacific University students, preventing students from feeling bored or dull during the learning process, along with providing easily accessible information whenever the students need it [28]. Therefore, students will not be limited to their desks but will move everywhere [27]. A study has shown active learning is more effective than passive learning in improving students' theoretical knowledge and skill scores [13].

AIM AND OBJECTIVES

Based on the issues identified in the problem statement, the main aim of the current research is to propose a mobile-learning system that uses mobile technology for Asia Pacific University students to promote active learning in the learning process. The objectives of the research were: -

1. To investigate effective active learning methods that can be integrated into the proposed mobile-learning system;

2. To conduct a survey of the context of passive learning form;

3. To investigate and produce an evaluation of passive Learning;

4. To propose a suitable mobile-learning system that promotes active Learning;

5. To evaluate the proposed mobile-learning system using appropriate statistical techniques.

RESEARCH QUESTIONS

1. How are mobile-learning systems integrated with active learning methods effectively in the learning process for students?

2. What are the common issues in the context of passive Learning, and how can active learning be used to improve the learning process in the prevention of common issues?

3. How does passive learning not affect students' theoretical knowledge and skill scores in the learning process?

4. What suitable systems need to be developed to improve the learning process?

5. How to evaluate the proposed mobile-learning system?

SIGNIFICANCE OF THE WORK

The current research contributes to improving the learning process of Asia Pacific University students. The proposed system could promote active learning practices by using mobile technology. The study provides insight to other researchers who wish to explore more mobile learning systems that can be integrated with active learning methods into higher or other levels of education. In addition, the proposed system could further solidify the effectiveness and benefits of implementing it into the education system. It could contribute to the entire education field by promoting active learning practices to improve students' academic performance.

METHODOLOGY

The research methodology is illustrated in Fig. (1), which represents the research flow activity diagram.

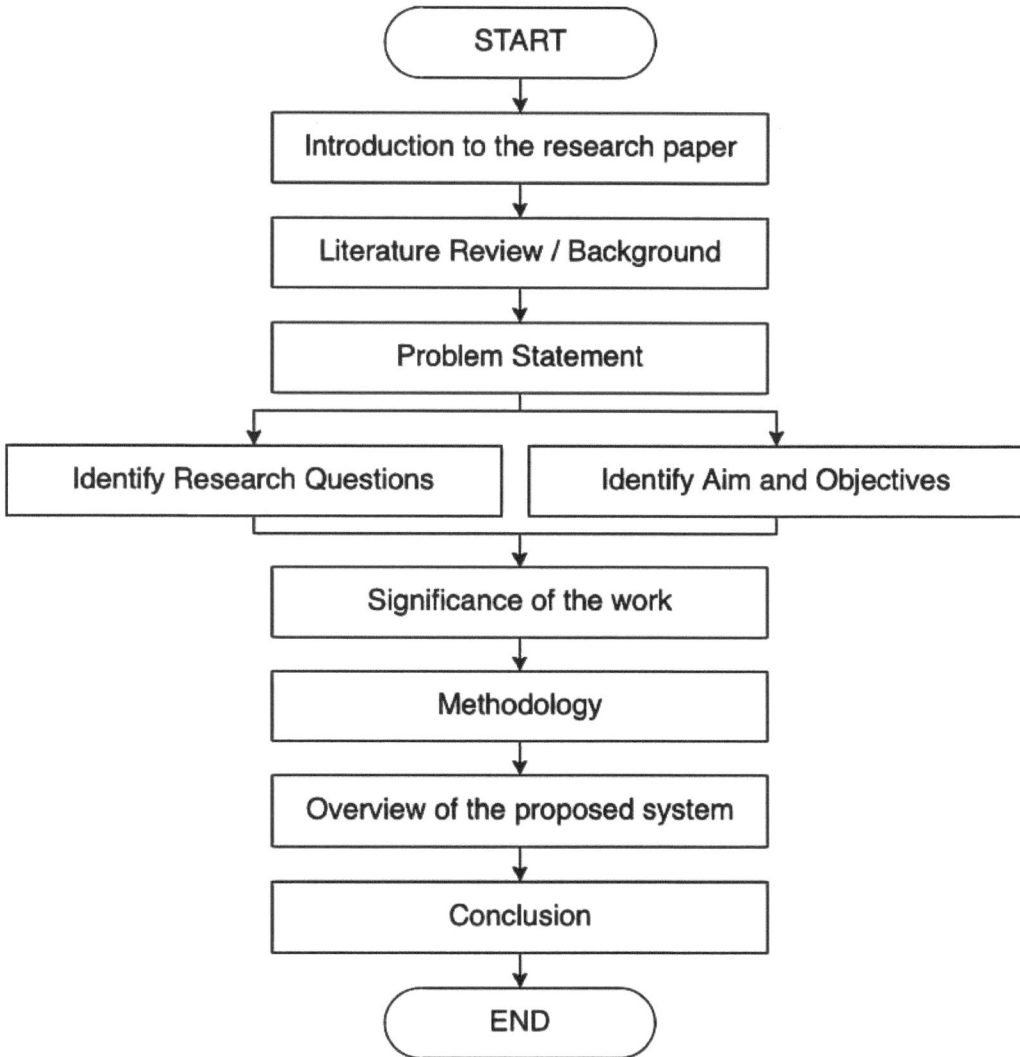

Fig. (1). Research Flow Activities Diagram.

The research is focused on proposing a mobile-learning system for Asia Pacific University students to promote active Learning. To achieve this aim, a well-planned research design and methodology will be conducted to collect appropriate data, analyse the collected data, and infer a conclusion regarding the proposed system to answer the research questions formulated. Quantitative research will be carried out in the current research paper as it manages to send many respondents who meet the criteria. Quantitative research could help to qualify the results, remove ambiguous responses, and promote an instant analysis of the massive data. Besides that, quantitative research can minimise the interference to the responses impacted by biased behaviours [19]. The research respondents are chosen carefully according to the criteria when it undergoes the judgmental sampling process. The collected responses, therefore, will be more relevant to the research and remove the data redundancy. Since the research is about implementing a mobile learning system at the Asia Pacific University to promote active Learning, a minimum of 100 respondents, both students and tutors, are targeted to be the research respondents. To increase relevancy, the targeted students will be chosen from those with at least a 2-year experience in higher education. In contrast, the targeted tutor will be chosen from those with at least a 5-year experience in education fields.

The questionnaire-based survey will be used to collect the responses. The questionnaire will have open-ended and close-ended questions to provide options to increase the accuracy of the responses. A 5-point Likert Scale and multiple-choice questions will be used as the open-ended questions. It will use Google Forms to distribute the questionnaire to the targeted respondents as the survey can quickly be sent to many respondents without any price. Microsoft Excel will analyse the collected responses to support the analysis process. Microsoft Excel provides tools such as constructing the data into diagrams and graphs to visualise the results better. Moreover, a descriptive analysis will be performed to analyse the collected responses as it is an appropriate technique to quantify the collected results. The potential limitation is that the target respondents might ignore or miss out on the sent survey. To overcome the mentioned issue, a gentle reminder will be sent two weeks after to invite the targeted respondents to complete the survey as soon as possible or select another group of targeted respondents who meet the criteria and invite them to participate.

OVERVIEW OF THE PROPOSED SYSTEM

A mobile application integrated with the active learning method will be proposed for the Asia Pacific University students. The mobile application consists of several features, such as creating or commenting on the post, streaming online videos, answering quizzes, providing feedback, etc., to increase interactions and active engagement between tutors and students. Therefore, the main aim is to enhance the user experience and extend daily learning accessibility.

As shown in Fig. (2), the mobile learning application allows both the tutor and students to use the chat service by using a mobile learning system. Everyone can use the private chat or group chat amongst each other, while only students can post a question in the group channel and provide feedback to the tutor. These functionalities allow students to discuss any confusion regarding the topic and increase interactions between the tutor and students. All the data will be stored in the Central Database. Moreover, the tutor can make online notes for students to read, make online quizzes for students to join, upload online videos for students to stream, upload online course materials for students to reference and carry out online discussions with students. These functionalities provide active learning practices to students who tend to do online learning at any time. Practising active learning results in the students having better problem-solving skills, improved 21st-century skills, better knowledge applicability, and an intellectually exciting environment [6]. All the data will be stored in the central database. For the rewards system, data will be retrieved from the central database and sent to the tutor via the proposed system. The tutor will then publish it to the students, leading them to remain competitive by rewarding the top performance in academic results. Therefore, students may use the proposed mobile system to learn more actively to get better academic results and performance. This will help them understand theoretical knowledge and score skills and train them to be active learners using the proposed mobile learning system.

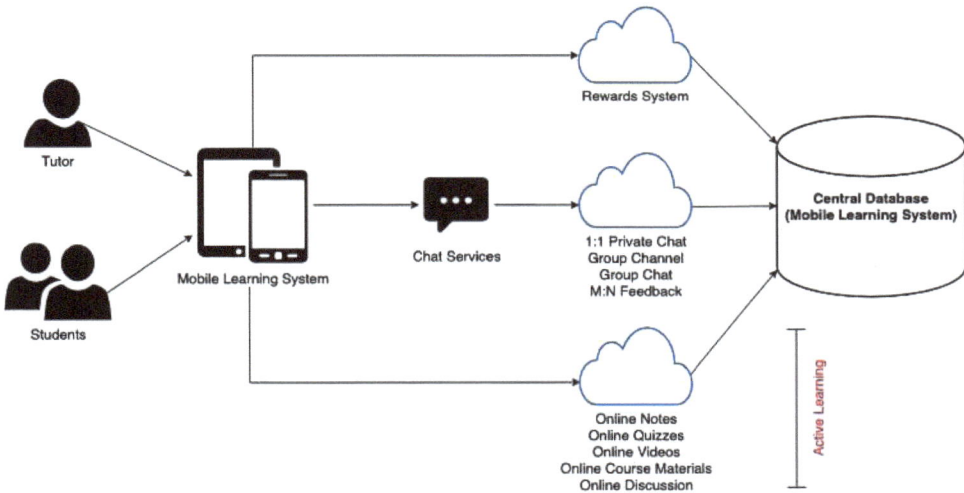

Fig. (2). Overview of the proposed system.

CONCLUSION

Current research revealed the factors that students from Asia Pacific University are concerned about in the mobile learning system. By investigating the overall perceptions of both students and tutors, the mobile learning system is deemed more appropriate to be implemented to promote active learning, given the mobility surrounding it pushes further in gaining theoretical knowledge and skill scores as well as the increase of satisfaction in students. Therefore, a mobile learning system is proposed for Asia Pacific University students to promote active learning in the learning process without time or location restrictions. Future studies need to be conducted to apply the proposed system to other education levels apart from Higher education. This will improve the learning process by using mobile technologies even further.

CONSENT FOR PUBLICATION

Not applicable.

CONFLICT OF INTEREST

The authors declare no conflict of interest, financial or otherwise.

ACKNOWLEDGEMENTS

The authors wish to express sincere appreciation to the Asia Pacific University of Technology and Innovation (APU) for giving them this opportunity to conduct the research.

REFERENCES

[1]   A. Abdelkarim, D. Schween, and T. Ford, "Advantages and Disadvantages of Problem-Based Learning from the Professional Perspective of Medical and Dental Faculty", *EC Dental Science Research Article,* vol. 17, no. 7, pp. 1073-1079, 2018.

[2]   M.A. Alzahrani, "The Learning Experience of International Students in Canada: Progressive Educational Theory and Passive Learning Styles", *Engl. Lang. Teach.,* vol. 11, no. 7, pp. 76-85, 2018.
[http://dx.doi.org/10.5539/elt.v11n7p76]

[3]   J. Boser, S. Scherer, K. Kuchta, S.F.C. Wenzel, and H. Horz, "Empirically Founded Teaching in Psychology – An Example for the Combination of Evidence-based Teaching and the Scholarship of Teaching and Learning", *Psychol. Learn. Teach.,* vol. 16, no. 2, pp. 261-275, 2017.
[http://dx.doi.org/10.1177/1475725716686452]

[4]   A. Chavoshi, and H. Hamidi, "Social, individual, technological and pedagogical factors influencing mobile learning acceptance in higher education: A case from Iran", *Telemat. Inform.,* vol. 38, pp. 133-165, 2019.
[http://dx.doi.org/10.1016/j.tele.2018.09.007]

[5]   K.M. Cooper, V.R. Downing, and S.E. Brownell, "The influence of active learning practices on student anxiety in large-enrollment college science classrooms", *Int. J. STEM Educ.,* vol. 5, no. 1, p. 23, 2018.
[http://dx.doi.org/10.1186/s40594-018-0123-6] [PMID: 30631713]

[6]   L. Dabrowska-Szpakowicz, *Do We Need Active Learning in the Classroom?,* 2018.

[7]   F. Deng, "Literature Review of the Flipped Classroom", *Theory Pract. Lang. Stud.,* vol. 9, no. 10, pp. 1350-1356, 2019.
[http://dx.doi.org/10.17507/tpls.0910.14]

[8]   H. Dokouhaki, and N. Zarifsanaiey, "A Meta-Synthesis Approach to Designing a Conceptual Framework for Mobile Learning in Higher Education", *Interdisciplinary Journal of Virtual Learning in Medical Sciences,* vol. 10, no. 4, pp. 1-13, 2019.

[9]   I. Gómez-Ramirez, A. Valencia-Arias, and L. Duque, "Approach to M-learning Acceptance Among University Students", *Int. Rev. Res. Open Distance Learn.,* vol. 20, no. 3, pp. 142-164, 2019.
[http://dx.doi.org/10.19173/irrodl.v20i4.4061]

[10]   H. Hamidi, and A. Chavoshi, "Analysis of the essential factors for the adoption of mobile learning in higher education: A case study of students of the University of Technology", *Telemat. Inform.,* vol. 35, no. 4, pp. 1053-1070, 2018.
[http://dx.doi.org/10.1016/j.tele.2017.09.016]

[11]   H. Hamidi, and M. Jahanshaheefard, "Essential factors for the application of education information system using mobile learning: A case study of students of the university of technology", *Telemat. Inform.,* vol. 38, pp. 207-224, 2019.
[http://dx.doi.org/10.1016/j.tele.2018.10.002]

[12]   N.F.B. Hassan, S.B. Puteh, and A.B.M. Sanusi, "Elements of Technology Enabled/Enhanced Active Learning (TEAL) to Enhance Quality and Employability of Bachelor's Students,". *MATEC Web of Conferences,* 150(05005), Feb. 2018.

[13]   R. Hu, H. Gao, Y. Ye, Z. Ni, N. Jiang, and X. Jiang, "Effectiveness of flipped classrooms in Chinese baccalaureate nursing education: A meta-analysis of randomized controlled trials", *Int. J. Nurs. Stud.,* vol. 79, pp. 94-103, 2018.
[http://dx.doi.org/10.1016/j.ijnurstu.2017.11.012] [PMID: 29223013]

[14]   J. Hyun, R. Ediger, and D. Lee, "Students' Satisfaction on Their Learning Process in Active Learning and Traditional Classrooms", *Int. J. Teach. Learn. High. Educ.,* vol. 29, no. 1, pp. 108-118, 2017.

[15]   K. Masters, "Edgar Dale's Pyramid of Learning in medical education: Further expansion of the myth", *Med. Educ.,* vol. 54, no. 1, pp. 22-32, 2020.
[http://dx.doi.org/10.1111/medu.13813] [PMID: 31576610]

[16]   A. Khan, O. Egbue, B. Palkie, and J. Madden, "Active Learning: Engaging Students To Maximize Learning In An Online Course", *Electron. J. e-Learn.,* vol. 15, no. 2, pp. 107-115, 2017.

[17]   J.G.M. Kooloos, E.M. Bergman, M.A.G.P. Scheffers, A.N. Schepens-Franke, and M.A.T.M. Vorstenbosch, "The Effect of Passive and Active Education Methods Applied in Repetition Activities on the Retention of Anatomical Knowledge," *Anatomical Sciences Education,* pp. 0-9, July 2019.

[18]   R.E. Mayer, "Contemporary Educational Psychology," *Where is the Learning in mobile technologies for Learning?,* vol 60, 2020.

[19]   S. McLeod, "What's the difference between qualitative and quantitative research?", 30 July, 2019. [Online]. Available: https://www.simplypsychology.org/qualitative-quantitative.html [Accessed: 6th August 2020].

[20]   S.S. Paul, "Active and Passive Learning: A Comparison," GRD Journals- Global Research and Development Journal for Engineering, vol. 2, no. 9, pp. 27-29, Aug. 2017.

[21]   M. Pinto, R. Fernández-Pascual, and F.J.G. Marco, "Self-learning of Information Literacy Competencies in Higher Education: The Perspective of Social Sciences Students," *Self-learning of Information Literacy Competencies in Higher Education,* vol. 80, no. 2, pp. 215 – 237, 2017.

[22]   N. Ragonis, and O. Dagan, *Enhance Active Learning in Higher Education by Using Mobile Learning.,* 2019.
[http://dx.doi.org/10.4018/978-1-5225-8106-2.ch002]

[23]   A. Salajegheh, A. Jahangiri, E. Dolan-Evans, and S. Pakneshan, "A combination of traditional learning and e-learning can be more effective on radiological interpretation skills in medical students: a pre- and post-intervention study", *BMC Med. Educ.,* vol. 16, no. 1, p. 46, 2016.
[http://dx.doi.org/10.1186/s12909-016-0569-5] [PMID: 26842495]

[24]   A. Srinath, "Active Learning Strategies: An illustrative approach to bring out better learning outcomes from Science, Technology, Engineering and Mathematics (STEM) students", *International Journal of*

Emerging Technologies in Learning (iJET), vol. 9, no. 9, pp. 21-25, 2014.
[http://dx.doi.org/10.3991/ijet.v9i9.3979]

[25]   S. Stover, and K. Ziswiler, "Impact of Active Learning Environments on Community of Inquiry", *Int. J. Teach. Learn. High. Educ.,* vol. 29, no. 3, pp. 458-470, 2017.

[26]   K. Wilkinson, and P. Barter, "Do Mobile Learning Devices Enhance Learning In Higher Education Anatomy Classrooms?", *Journal of Pedagogic Development,* vol. 6, no. 1, pp. 14-23, 2016.

[27]   G.K.W. Wong, "A New Wave of Innovation Using Mobile Learning Analytics for Flipped Classroom," *Mobile Learning Design. Lecture Notes in Educational Technology. Springer,* pp. 189-218, Dec. 2016.

[28]   R. Zouhair, B.I.E. Habib, and T. Abderrahim, "A Brief Survey and Comparison of m-Learning and e-Learning", *International Journal of Computer Networks and Communications Security,* vol. 4, no. 4, pp. 89-95, 2016.

CHAPTER 14

Analytics on Airline Customer Satisfaction Factors

Pit Khien Leong[1] and **Rajasvaran Logeswaran**[1,*]

[1] *School of Computing, Asia Pacific University of Technology and Innovation, Kuala Lumpur, Malaysia*

Abstract: Dissatisfaction with the services provided causes customer loss and customer churn in airline companies. Analytics conducted in assessing customer satisfaction in airline companies and their analytical methods are reviewed to identify the analysis's strengths, weaknesses, and gaps. Data analytics on assessing customer satisfaction have been conducted on facilities and services provided, price, service quality, reviews of customers, and flight catering. However, this research indicates that only a few in-depth studies consider flight delays as a critical factor influencing customer satisfaction. A flight is considered delayed if it departs or arrives 15 minutes later than the scheduled time. Therefore, in this research, further analytics can be done on the amount of time-of-flight delay in assessing customer satisfaction.

Keywords: Customer satisfaction, Flight delay, Regression analysis, Sentiment analysis.

INTRODUCTION

There has been noticeable customer loss in airline companies due to the dissatisfaction of customers with the services provided [1]. With the pandemic, many airlines are already facing significant losses, so losing their customer base even further is something airlines cannot afford. Decreasing customer loyalty of airline companies affects the business of the airline companies. Customer satisfaction is essential in determining their profitability and sustainable growth. Airline companies have to refine their services to maintain customer loyalty and their competitiveness among competitors. Studies [2] showed that the cost of gaining a new customer is higher than retaining an existing customer. Therefore, it is essential to improve the satisfaction level of the customers in the airline companies to retain the existing customers. Satisfied customers will promote the airline companies to their friends or relatives, which will differentiate the airline's image from its competitors and increase the chance of attracting new customers.

* **Corresponding author Rajasvaran Logeswaran**: Asia Pacific University of Technology & Innovation, Kuala Lumpur, Malaysia. Email: logeswaran@apu.edu.my

Muhammad Ehsan Rana and Manoj Jayabalan (Eds.)

Therefore, analytics on assessing customer satisfaction are carried out to understand customers' expectations of the services and the facilities provided by the airline companies. It also provides practical insights to airline companies on the critical determinant of customer satisfaction so that they can improve on it to increase their customer satisfaction level.

DATA ANALYTICS ON ASSESSING CUSTOMER SATISFACTION

Many factors influence customer satisfaction in airline companies, including the behaviour of the cabin crew and staff, cleanliness of the aircraft, service quality, and more. Airline companies must pay attention to them because customer satisfaction plays a vital role in developing customer engagement and loyalty [3]. To provide insights to airline companies, analytics have been done on different aspects to assess customer satisfaction, as described below.

Facilities and Services Provided

Most early analytics for assessing customer satisfaction was concerned with the facilities and services provided by the airline companies. The studies conducted by [4] focused on the services used to satisfy the passengers, including pre-flight services, in-flight services, and post-flight services. It showed that in-flight service is the critical determinant of customer satisfaction. The regression analysis has been done on customer relationship management, in-flight services, and cabin environment [5]. Similarly, it also proved that in-flight services significantly affect customer satisfaction. In [6], an analysis was carried out on the facilities provided in the aircraft. It showed that seat comfort, with the highest standardised coefficient of 0.407, is the most dominant factor in customer satisfaction. Therefore, to increase customer satisfaction, airline companies should improve the facilities and the services provided in the aircraft to meet or exceed the expectation of the customers. Customer satisfaction is the appraisal of the customers on the gap between their expectations and experience [7].

Price

In [8], analytics on customer satisfaction in airline companies showed that the price of the flight ticket is a critical factor that affects passenger satisfaction. Recent studies also outlined that price is the most crucial factor influencing customer satisfaction and loyalty to airline companies [9]. It showed that the price variable has the highest estimated values and t-values, as evaluated using the Structural Equation Model (SEM) technique. The flight ticket price is crucial in determining customer satisfaction, especially with the introduction of low-cost carriers, such as AirAsia. If the price is high, the customers will choose other airlines that also provide the same quality of service to them [1].

Besides, price affects customer satisfaction significantly because customers set an expectation of the facilities and services provided by the airline companies based on the price of the flight ticket purchased [10]. Therefore, customers will compare their expectations and experience, rating the airline companies negatively based on the discrepancy between them [11]. When the customers feel that the service does not meet the ticket purchase price, it creates dissatisfaction. Analytics on the price and customer satisfaction helps the airline companies set the price of the flight ticket to be more realistically equivalent to its value, effectively securing customer satisfaction.

Service Quality

Service quality is the ability to meet the needs and requirements of the customers and the extent to which the delivered service matches or exceeds the customers' expectations [12]. In [13], the SERVQUAL model was introduced to measure service quality based on five dimensions: reliability, assurance, tangibles, empathy, and responsiveness. The SERVQUAL model is also known as the RATER model.

According to [14], flight punctuality widely influences customer satisfaction. Airline companies should increase their service quality in terms of reliability by having fewer changes in the flight schedule, increasing customer satisfaction. The study in [6] showed that online flight ticket purchasing affects customer satisfaction the most. Regression analysis was conducted on the service quality in assessing customer satisfaction [15]. The result showed that the customers are most satisfied with the flight ticket reservation system and are least satisfied with the courtesy of the cabin crew. Airline companies must ensure that customers can buy their preferred flight tickets from the online flight booking system and that their personal information is protected. Therefore, the reliability of the service plays a vital role in service quality, which determines the customer satisfaction of airline companies.

In [6], it is mentioned that there is a difference in the need for service quality for the customers of domestic flights and international flights. Service quality in terms of tangibles has to be maintained and improved by the airline companies. Tangibles are the physical facilities, equipment, and personnel [16]. Airline companies must provide in-flight entertainment for long-distance flights so that the customers will not get bored. The traits and quality of the services provided by airline companies affect customer satisfaction and customer loyalty [17]. Airline companies must continuously monitor the service quality and make timely required changes to ensure that high-quality service is provided to satisfy the customers and retain the existing customer base.

Reviews of Customers

In assessing customer satisfaction in airline companies [18], focused on the analytics of customer complaints. Customer complaints can be categorised into controlled complaints and uncontrolled complaints. Controlled complaints are the complaints that can be managed and reduced by the airline companies, such as flight delays, misbehaviour of the staff, fare-related problems, and others; meanwhile, uncontrolled complaints are those related to issues such as technical fault, weather problems, closure of country borders, air space, etc. The result showed that 73.1% of customer dissatisfaction is caused by flight delays [18]. Service delays will cause customers to wait longer and negatively affect their emotional responses [19]. Therefore, airline companies must maintain punctuality on the schedule of the flights as it directly affects customer satisfaction [20].

In recent studies, sentiment analysis was carried out by analysing Twitter data to determine customer satisfaction in airline companies [21]. The reasons behind the satisfaction and dissatisfaction of the customers were analysed through association analysis [22]. Insights gained from the analysis helped the respective airline companies to improve their services and customer experience. Similarly, the study in [23] focused on analytics on customer satisfaction between two airline companies using online customer reviews. A meaningful relationship between the words used was identified using semantic network analysis.

Sentiment analysis must be performed on customer complaints and reviews to assess customer satisfaction. Customers indicate their dissatisfaction by lodging complaints to and against the airline company. Therefore, airline companies can identify the areas for improvement. Customers also express their feelings and experiences on social media platforms. Hence is essential to analyse their reviews as they have already used the services provided and can provide a reliable account of their experience with the airline companies.

Flight Catering

Flight catering is an essential element that influences customer satisfaction, especially in long-distance flights [24]. Studies showed that if customers are not satisfied with the food serving service and food temperature, a negative relationship is shown [25]. In [24], customers were satisfied with the nutritional diet because it exceeded their expectations. It also stated that the higher the quality of the food served in the aircraft, the happier the customers, and the higher the customer satisfaction level. Based on analytics of flight catering in assessing customer satisfaction, airline companies should improve on maintaining the temperature of the food so that the food is hot when served. Airline companies should also conduct training for their cabin crew on food serving. The food menu in the aircraft should be changed at regular intervals so that customers can enjoy new and varied food rather than having the same food again when travelling with the same airline companies. This is especially important for loyal frequent flyers to increase their satisfaction.

ANALYTICAL METHODS USED

Many analytical models, techniques, and tools have been used to assess customer satisfaction. The popular ones are described below.

Regression Analysis

Regression analysis is often conducted when assessing the factors that directly affect customer satisfaction. In [5], regression analysis was conducted based on customer relationship management, in-flight services, and cabin environment to determine the significant factors influencing customer satisfaction. It was also conducted in [6], where results showed that an online flight ticket booking system affects customer satisfaction the most. Multiple regression analysis can be conducted to test whether the hypothesis is accepted or rejected [15]. Therefore, the key factor affecting customer satisfaction in the airline companies can be identified using regression analysis, and the airline companies can take action on the findings.

Random Forest

Random forest is one of the popular analytical methods known to produce highly accurate results when dealing with regression problems [25]. A large number of decision trees is built in the training step. Using the random forest model, an accuracy of 75.5% was achieved, where food serving service and the food temperature were found to be the crucial factors affecting airline customer satisfaction [25]. Studies in [8] achieved an accuracy of 80% on the finding that flight ticket price influences customer satisfaction. This differs from other techniques, such as Extreme Gradient Boosting (XGBoost), which achieved an accuracy of only 67.1% the same [4]. Therefore, the random forest model is the recommended technique for analysing customer satisfaction in airline companies based on its higher accuracy.

Structural Equation Model (SEM)

Studies conducted in [14] stated that the empirical results acquired *via* SEM reveal the relationship between the service quality of airline companies and customer satisfaction. The higher the estimated values and t-values, the higher the factor on customer satisfaction. In [26], using SEM, service quality was found to be the most influential factor in customer satisfaction. SEM can be used when assessing the relationship between latent and observable variables, for example, customer satisfaction, that cannot be measured directly. Therefore, SEM is useful when assessing customer satisfaction by developing and measuring the hypothesis based on measurable factors.

Logistic Regression

Most researchers convert a 5-point Likert scale response into a binary response representing satisfied and dissatisfied when assessing customer satisfaction in airline companies [18]. Binary responses provide a clear distinction on whether the customers are satisfied, so airline companies can improve that criterion to increase the satisfaction level of the customers [21]. Therefore, logistic regression can be used for analytics since there are only two possible outcomes. Predicting customer satisfaction is based on the parameters such as facilities, services, price of the flight ticket, and others.

Other Popular Techniques

When analysing customer reviews and complaints, semantic network analysis is performed to identify a meaningful relationship between the words [23]. CONCOR analysis is also carried out to understand better the content and the specific terms so useful information can be retrieved from the customer reviews and complaints. Studies in [21] showed that Convolutional Neural Network (CNN) provides better accuracy and performance than Support Vector Machine (SVM) and Artificial Neural Networks (ANN). However, a promising result was also achieved using Gaussian Naive Bayes in the studies conducted in [27]. Therefore, various analytic models can be compared to obtain more reliable and accurate results.

STRENGTHS AND WEAKNESSES OF THE ANALYTICS

Existing analytics for assessing customer satisfaction covers most aspects, namely, pre-flight services, in-flight services, post-flight services, and other aspects. Therefore, airline companies can improve in those areas to increase customer satisfaction. The food provided in the aircraft had also been analysed for its temperature affecting customer satisfaction. It is one of the factors usually overlooked by researchers when analysing customer satisfaction. The existing analytics also studied customer reviews from Twitter and social media platforms, where the customers are most likely to express their true feelings towards the airline companies. Analytics were carried out with different models to gain better accuracy and performance.

One of the weaknesses of the existing analytics for assessing airline customer satisfaction is that the sample size of the respondents is small, at around 100-200 people. This sample size should be increased to include more respondents to represent the population of interest with a normal distribution. Small sample sizes may result in wrong predictions and undermine the validity of the findings [28].

The existing analytics for assessing customer satisfaction mainly focused on a single airport or airline company. However, different airline companies provide different facilities and services. Therefore, studies and analytics should be carried out as such, so airline companies have an overview of the factors that will affect customer satisfaction. If the facilities that give the highest customer satisfaction are not provided, airline companies could look into adding new facilities to increase the satisfaction level.

These strengths and limitations of the existing analytics need to be considered when assessing customer satisfaction for future work. More samples should be included in the analyses, including more than one airline. Different analytical models could be explored further to improve the performance and accuracy of the results.

CONCLUSION

This work has reviewed existing work undertaken in terms of analytics on several aspects to assess the customer satisfaction of airline companies. Regression and sentiment analyses are conducted so the airline companies can know the areas they must improve to satisfy the customers. Different studies showed that different main factors influence airline companies' customer satisfaction levels using different models and techniques. Existing analytics are only focused on service quality, where flight delay significantly affects customer satisfaction; however, they do not focus on how customer satisfaction is affected by the amount of time a flight is delayed. Analytics in future work could look into this aspect.

CONSENT FOR PUBLICATION

Not applicable.

CONFLICT OF INTEREST

The authors declare no conflict of interest, financial or otherwise.

ACKNOWLEDGEMENTS

The authors wish to express their sincere appreciation to the Asia Pacific University of Technology and Innovation (APU) for the opportunity to conduct the research.

REFERENCES

[1]   W. Ma, A. Zhang, Y. Zhang and S. Xu, "The growing influence of low-cost carriers in Northeast Asia and its implications for a regional single aviation market", Journal of Air Transport Management, vol. 91, pp. 137-143, 2021. [Online] Available from: https://www.sciencedirect.com/science/article/abs/pii/S0969699720305767

[2]   M.D. Clemes, C. Gan, T.H. Kao and M. Choong, "An empirical analysis of customer satisfaction in international air travel", Innovative Marketing, vol. 4, no. 2, pp. 49-62, 2008. [Online] Available from: https://businessperspectives.org/pdfproxy.php?item_id=2229

[3]   V. Briliana, "Consumer Satisfaction on Airline Passenger Loyalty: Antecedents and Outcomes", *International Journal of Business, Economics and Law,* vol. 16, no. 5, pp. 1-9, 2018. [Online] Available from: http://ijbel.com/wp-content/uploads/2018/07/ijbel16-ISSUE5_201.pdf

[4]   D. Mitra, "Comparative Study between Indian Public and Private (Low Cost) Airlines with respect to their Passenger Service", International Review of Business Research Papers, vol. 6, no. 6, pp. 48-65, 2010. [Online] Available from: https://www.semanticscholar.org/paper/A-Comparative-Stuy-Between-Indian-Public-And-(Low-Mitra/76402cd9c0366f0dbda3a37fbd203fd63195ed93.

[5]   J. Munusamy, S. Chelliah and S. Pandian, "Customer Satisfaction Delivery in Airline Industry in Malaysia: A Case of Low-Cost Carrier", Australian Journal of Basic and Applied Sciences, vol. 5, no. 11, pp. 718-723, 2011. [Online] Available from: https://www.semanticscholar.org/paper/Customer-Satisfaction-Delivery-In-Airline-Industry-Mun-samy-Chelliah/b0445095235d323f830136537b2eb79276414179

[6]   http://www.ccsenet.org/journal/index.php/ass/article/view/48384 I. Sukati, B.K. Tan and Isnurhadi, "Customer Satisfaction Level Provided by Air Asia", Asian Social Science, vol. 11, no. 13, pp. 16-27, 2015. [Online] Available from:

[7]   A. Jahmani, "The Effect of Royal Jordanian Airline Service Quality on Passengers' Satisfaction", *International Journal of Business and Society,* vol. 18, no. 3, pp. 519-530, 2017. [Online] Available from: http://www.ijbs.unimas.my/images/repository/pdf/Vol18-s3-paper7.pdf

[8]   R. Pal, "A Study on Customer Satisfaction in Airlines Industry", Master thesis. India: Unitedworld School of Business, 2014. [Online] Available from: https://www.academia.edu/31799132/RAJAT_PAL_A_STUDY_ON_CUSTOMER_SATISFACTION_IN_AIRLINES_INDUSTRY_

[9]   D.C. Hutagaol and R. Erdiansyah, "The Effect of Service Quality, Price, Customer Satisfaction on Customer Loyalty of AirAsia Customers", *Tarumanagara International Conference on the Applications of Social Sciences and Humanities,* Jakarta, Indonesia, 27–28 June 2019. Amsterdam: Atlantis Press. pp. 356-362, 2019. [Online] Available from: https://www.atlantis-press.com/article/125940621.pdf

[10]   S. Meire, and B. Derudder, "Virtual interlining within the European airport network: An airfare analysis", Journal of Air Transport Management, vol. 94, pp. 111-118, 2021. [Online] Available from: https://www.sciencedirect.com/science/article/abs/pii/S0969699721000569

[11]   D.M.A. Baker, "Service Quality and Customer Satisfaction in the Airline Industry: A Comparison between Legacy Airlines and Low-Cost Airlines", *American Journal of Tourism Research,* vol. 2, no. 1, pp. 67-77, 2013. [Online] Available from: http://worldscholars.org/index.php/ajtr/article/view/0201_1/pdf

[12]   J. Namukasa, "The influence of airline service quality on passenger satisfaction and loyalty: The case of Uganda airline industry", *The TQM Journal,* vol. 25, no. 5, pp. 520-532, 2013. Available from: https://www.emerald.com/insight/content/doi/10.1108/TQM-11-2012-0092/full/html

[13]   A. Parasuraman, V.A. Zeithaml and L.L. Berry, "SERVQUAL: A Multiple-Item Scale for Measuring Consumer Perceptions of Service Quality", Journal of Retailing, vol. 64, no. 1, pp. 12-37, 1988. [Online]   Available   from: https://search.proquest.com/openview/7d007e04d78261295e5524f15bef6837/1?pq-origsite=gscholar%26cbl=41988

[14]   N.M. Suki, "Passenger satisfaction with airline service quality in Malaysia: A structural equation modelling approach", *Research in Transportation Business & Management,* vol. 10, no. 3, pp. 26-32, 2014.   [Online]   Available   from: https://www.sciencedirect.com/science/article/abs/pii/S2210539514000108

[15]   M.A. Hasim, M.F. Shamsudin and M.F. Ishak, "Customer Satisfaction and Purchasing Intention in Airline Service Quality: A Case Study of Malaysia Airlines", *International Journal of Engineering & Technology,* vol. 7, no. 4, pp. 150-153, 2018. [Online] Available from: http://ijbel.com/wp-content/uploads/2018/07/ijbel16-ISSUE5_201.pdf

[16]   M.K.K. Gambo, "Service Quality and Customer Satisfaction among Domestic Air Passengers in Nigeria", *International Journal of Business and Management Studies,* vol. 8, no. 2, pp. 32-49, 2016. [Online] Available from: https://dergipark.org.tr/en/download/article-file/255730

[17]   R.A. Ganiyu, "Perceived Service Quality and Customer Loyalty: The Mediating Effect of Passenger Satisfaction in the Nigerian Airline Industry", *International Journal of Management and Economics,* vol. 52, no. 2, pp. 94-117, 2016. [Online] Available from: https://content.sciendo.com/downloadpdf/journals/ijme/52/1/article-p94.xml

[18]   M. Upadhyaya, "Customer Satisfaction Measurement in Airline Services: An Empirical Study of Need-Gap Analysis", *International Journal of Information, Business and Management,* vol. 19, no. 2, pp. 147-155, 2013. [Online] Available from: https://www.uav.ro/jour/index.php/jebr/article/view/41

[19]   M. Efthymiou, E.T. Njoya, P.L. Lo, A. Papatheodorou and D. Randall, "The Impact of Delays on Customers' Satisfaction: An Empirical Analysis of the British Airways On-Time Performance at Heathrow Airport", *Journal of Aerospace Technology and Management,* vol. 11, no. 1, pp. 1-13, 2019. Available from: https://www.scielo.br/scielo.php?script=sci_arttext&pid=S2175-91462019000100300

[20]   X. Tan, R. Jia, J. Yan, K. Wang and L. Bian, "An Exploratory analysis of flight delay propagation in China", Journal of Air Transport Management, vol. 92, pp. 78-83, 2021. [Online] Available from: https://www.sciencedirect.com/science/article/abs/pii/S0969699721000089

[21]   S. Kumar and M. Zymbler, "A machine learning approach to analyze customer satisfaction from airline tweets", *Journal of Big Data 6,* vol. 62, pp. 1-16, 2019. [Online] Available from: https://journalofbigdata.springeropen.com/articles/10.1186/s40537-019-0224-1

[22]   H. Barakat, R. Yeniterzi and L.M. Domingo, "Applying deep learning models to twitter data to detect airport service quality", *Journal of Air Transport Management,* vol. 91, pp. 102-109, 2021. [Online] Available from: https://www.sciencedirect.com/science/article/abs/pii/S0969699720305846

[23]   A. Shadiyar, H.J. Ban and H.S. Kim, "Extracting Key Drivers of Air Passenger's Experience and Satisfaction through Online Review Analysis", *Sustainability,* vol. 12, no. 9188, pp. 1-20, 2020. [Online] Available from: https://www.mdpi.com/2071-1050/12/21/9188/pdf

[24]   H.M. Moyeenudin, S.J. Parvez, R. Anandan and G. Bindu, "Data Analytics on Gratification of Airline Passenger with their Experience", *International Journal of Recent Technology and Engineering,* vol. 8, no. 5, pp. 1999-2004, 2020. [Online] Available from: https://www.ijrte.org/wp-content/uploads/papers/v8i5/E6000018520.pdf

[25]   A.K. Singh, M. Yoo and R.J. Dalpadatu, "Determinants of Customer Satisfaction at the San Francisco International Airport", *Journal of Tourism & Hospitality,* vol. 8, no. 1, pp. 1-9, 2019. [Online]

Available from: https://www.longdom.org/open-access/determinants-of-customer-satisfaction--t-the-san-francisco-international-ai-port-18136.html#:~:text=In%20this%20study%2C%20three%20types,ratings%2C%20cleanliness%2C%20and%20demographics

[26]   E. Park, Y. Jang, J. Kim, N.J. Jeong, K. Bae and A.P. Pobil, "Determinants of customer satisfaction with airline services: An analysis of customer feedback big data", *Journal of Retailing and Consumer Services,* vol. 51, no. 1, pp. 186-190, 2019. [Online] Available from: https://www.sciencedirect.com/science/article/abs/pii/S0969698919304369

[27]   D.D. Dutta, S. Sharma, S. Natani, N. Khare and B. Singh, "Sentimental Analysis for Airline Twitter data", *IOP Series: Materials Science and Engineering,* vol. 263, no. 4, pp. 23-35, 2017. [Online] Available from: https://iopscience.iop.org/article/10.1088/1757-899X/263/4/042067

[28]   J. Faber and L.M. Fonseca, "How sample size influences research outcomes?", *Dental Press Journal of Orthodontics,* vol. 19, no. 4, pp. 27-29, 2014. [Online] Available from: https://www.ncbi.nlm.nih.gov/pmc/articles/PMC4296634

CHAPTER 15

A Personalized Recommendation System for Academic Events

Henry Khoo Shien Chen[1] and **Shubashini Rathina Velu**[1,*]

[1] *School of Computing, Asia Pacific University of Technology and Innovation, Kuala Lumpur, Malaysia*

Abstract: Academic events are growing in numbers worldwide annually for researchers to discuss their work. The research on recommendation systems in academic domains has high significance for researchers. The classical approach to the recommender system uses content-based and collaborative filtering that tends to produce poor results. The focus of the study is to determine the factors involving the selection of academic events and create a user-based personalised recommender system for academic events. A survey will be conducted to identify the factors affecting the choice of events. The system will filter the results of the events using a matching matrix by conducting a factor analysis and receiving input to find the most relevant academic events from the database. The study's approach evaluates the result based on the pre-processed data and the similarity measures between a similar user (Top-n) and an active user for events with a higher probability of participation. The weighted average of the neighbour's ratings will be generated for the predictions of the events. The study's outcome will prove that the personalised recommendation system is better than the classical approach in finding the most relevant events. The recommendation system can be optimised in domains.

Keywords: Academic Event, Collaborative Filtering, Factor Analysis, Matching Matrix, Recommender System.

INTRODUCTION

The enormous amount of data in the current information system has been increasing rapidly, resulting in enormous options for users. The problem can be solved using a personalised recommendation system to meet customer needs and demands [1, 2]. The recommendation system is considered a subclass of the information filtering system to reduce the issue of information overload on the Internet [3]. The recommender system can create predictions for the ratings of events that have not been voted for to match the user preference [4, 5]. There are

[*] **Corresponding author Shubashini Rathina Velu**: School of Computing, Asia Pacific University of Technology and Innovation, Kuala Lumpur, Malaysia; E-mail: shuba.rv@gmail.com

Muhammad Ehsan Rana and Manoj Jayabalan (Eds.)

three approaches to the design of the recommendation system: collaborative filtering, content-based filtering, and hybrid techniques. The collaborative filtering technique is based on the commonalities of people agreeing in the past, while the content-based filtering is based on similar items that the user has rated. The hybrid system is a combination of both collaborative filtering and content-based filtering. According to Shambour and Lu (2015), popular online companies like Amazon, Netflix, and Last.fm use recommendation systems to service their customers. Netflix provides recommendations based on two filtering techniques: collaborative filtering for previously searched and watched movies of a similar user and content-based filtering for movies with similar characteristics with high ratings.

LITERATURE REVIEW

Academic Events

Academic events are organised for scientific researchers to create opportunities for attendees to share their knowledge and experience in the relevant fields. The academic events are conducted in multiple ways, such as conferences, seminars, workshops, and upskill programs. These events are beneficial for networking [6-8], research collaboration or partnerships [6, 8, 9], job opportunities and career development [6-8], and knowledge transfer [7, 8]. The missed opportunity of going to an unsuitable event will cause time and money wastage. As the students are inexperienced and lack knowledge, they will have trouble selecting the best choice for them according to their current preferences.

The most related tools for academic events are the AllConference, Workshop Finder, and Eventbrite. Functions not found in these tools include user preference and user rating. The user rating is a reliable metric for judging the likes and dislikes of an item [4, 10, 11]. Using linear and ordinal regression, user preference can be converted into a numerical value [11]. These two essential metrics are not found in the tools available for academic events. A recommender system that includes the user rating and contextual information will provide more relevant results for the users. A comparison of the functionality of different tools is provided in Table **1**.

Table 1. Comparison of the functionality of different tools for events.

Function	AllConference	Workshop Finder	Eventbrite
Search by keyword	Yes	No	Yes
User preference	No	No	No
Search by domain	No	Yes	Yes

Function	AllConference	Workshop Finder	Eventbrite
Search by time	Yes	No	No
Search by location	Yes	No	No
User rating	No	No	No
Ranking search result	No	No	Yes
Recommendation for similar event keyword	No	Yes	Yes

Recommender System

The recommender system can solve a vast amount of information by filtering the specific user based on their preference [4, 12]. As the users have different priorities and objectives when choosing academic events, the 2 recommender systems can identify the specific needs and demands of the user. The recommender system can be developed based on a similar user or a list of academic events matching users' context. The recommender system mainly uses three approaches, content-based filtering, collaborative filtering, and hybrid filtering, as shown in Fig. (**1**). The everyday use of recommender systems is found in various sectors like e-commerce, music, hotels, and books [13].

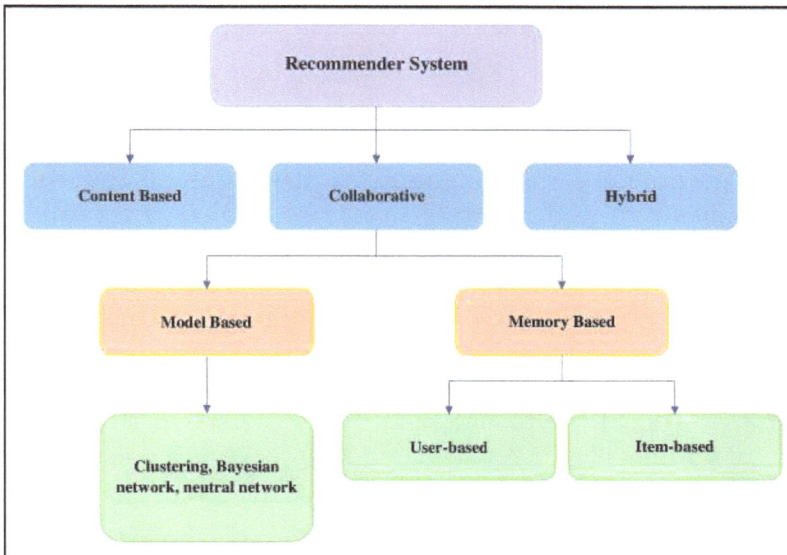

Fig. (1). Different types of recommender systems commonly used.

Content-based filtering is used to make recommendations based on user preferences for product features and characteristics. Collaborative filtering imitates a similar user's request by interest or taste. The disadvantage of using a content-based recommender system is the cold start program [14]. The content-based filtering technique faces the cold start problem when the system has users and items with few ratings or interactions. Collaborative filtering can solve the cold start problem by the history of users, but this technique causes the new thing harder to be recommended. Therefore, a hybrid recommender system combines collaborative and content-based filtering to solve their limitations [2, 3].

Personalised or Contextualize Recommender System

Various domains undertook the development of a recommender system based on the context or personality to improvise its limitation of it [15, 16]. The contextual recommender system is divided into three methods:

1. The first method is pre-filtering or pre-processing the data before computation for recommendations.

2. The second method is post-filtering, where recommendations are produced without context.

3. The last method is contextual modelling, where the recommendations use the user and item data.

PROBLEM STATEMENT

An inexperienced student will have difficulties in selecting the academic events that are most relevant to them [17]. If the wrong educational event is set, the student will waste time and money aligned to the events of the field of study. According to Champiri, Salim, and Shahamiri (2015), the validity of the contextual information needs to be evaluated to build a practical, relevant, and effective recommendation system. The exact user's information, such as purpose, knowledge, experiences, fields of study, and the tasks needed to be done, have to be taken into consideration for the most appropriate selection. The conditions regarding the academic course are the location, accessibility, situation, and time. The classical approach of the recommendation system will not be sufficient to provide the most optimal results for selecting the academic event.

AIMS AND OBJECTIVES

The study's objective is to generate relevant academic events for the students using contextual information for better recommendations and results. The personalised recommendation system will aim to achieve the research objective listed below:

1. To solve the issue of difficulties in choosing academic events.

2. To determine contextual information that affects the choice of academic events.

3. To provide a personalised recommendation system.

4. To evaluate the recommendation system from existing systems.

RESEARCH QUESTIONS

This study's research questions focus on identifying the significance of using a personalised recommendation system for academic events. The research question will be used to address the study's problem statement.

1. How to solve the problem of choosing academic events?

2. What important contextual information affects the choice of academic events?

3. How to develop a personalised recommendation system?

4. How to evaluate the recommendation system from other existing ones?

SIGNIFICANT OF RESEARCH

The study provides better tools for academia or students to find the most relevant events that correspond to their academic studies. The opportunity of selecting a suitable event will have significant benefits, such as gaining new knowledge, networking, and collaboration or partnership with other academia. The personalised recommender system using techniques like collaborative filtering and targeting the users' preferences will generate better and more effective results. This research paper will integrate personalized user data with greater accuracy and relevance for the recommendation results. A user- K Nearest Neighbour (KNN) algorithm will be used for the contextual data to match a similar user.

METHODOLOGY

Introduction

The research methodology chosen for this study is the rapid application development (RAD) methodology. It consists of requirement planning, user designing, construction, and cutover phases. The requirement planning phase will determine the contextual information regarding the academic events. In the user design phase, the representation of the recommender system and the framework of the contextual recommender system is discussed. The construction phase describes the overall system architecture of the recommender system. The cutover phase is a testing phase to find the relevancy with the user.

Requirement Planning Phase

The requirement planning phase is used to identify the contextual information which affects the choice of academic events, as listed in Fig. (**2**). The criteria of the recommender system are cost, location, and time. These factors are important elements when choosing an educational event. Moreover, user preference will be an essential aspect of the relevant information. Some examples of user preferences are the user profile, user behaviour, knowledge, and the purpose of going to the academic event. Other factors include the devices used and the documents provided by the organisers. The data from a survey shows that the four primary contexts are the recommender system's cost, time, location, and schedule [16].

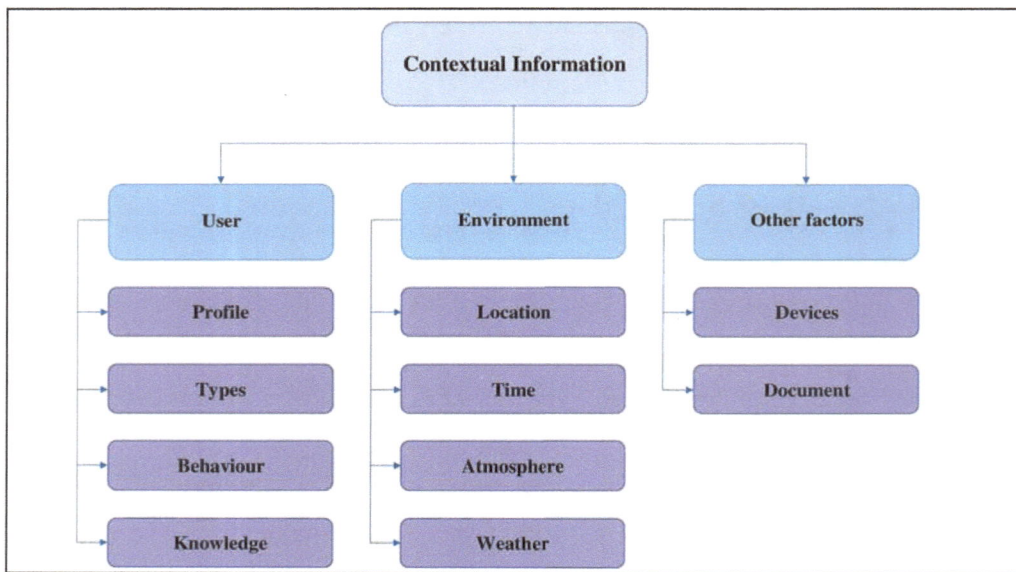

Fig. (2). Contextual hierarchy that affects the choice of academic events.

Data Collection Method

The data is collected using questionnaires and interviews for the target group of university students. A questionnaire is distributed among students who are undergraduates and postgraduates at Asia Pacific University. The questionnaire is focused on the criteria of the selection of academic events by the students, as listed in Table **2**. The questions will develop an understanding of the user preference, their standards of selection, and the other context affecting the choice.

Table 2. The questions that are selected for the questionnaire.

No.	Questions
1	Identifying the user details (The faculty, level of study and the course taken).
2	What are the details of the previously attended events (location, event name and time) and the reason for attending?
3	What are the criteria for the selection of academic events?
4	What are the most important criteria till the least important criteria of the event?

User Design Phase

Table **3** provides a comparison of different types of recommendation systems and their representation in generating ratings. The concept of a recommender system uses the average rating by the users. The classical approach of the representation is the user, item, and the context of the user for the rating. This study is used to evaluate the contextual recommender system that represents many dimensions (Dn), with each dimension representing the user, item, and context of the users. A weighted average is calculated and ranked according to the user preference and contextual information similarity.

Table 3. The representation of different recommender systems.

Different types of recommendation systems	Representation
Recommender system	Rating: User x Item -> Rating
Classical recommender system	Rating: User x Item x Context -> Rating
Contextual recommender system	Rating: D1 x D2….. x Dn -> Rating

The machine learning algorithm used for this study is the K Nearest Neighbour (KNN) algorithm. The KNN algorithm identifies the list of neighbours from the highest to the least based on the user's relevancy. The algorithm uses the Euclidean distance metric for the recommender system. The KNN algorithm is used for the following context, as shown in Table **4** below.

Table 4. The categorisation of the contextual information of the environment.

Context	Categorisation
Context1 (Cost)	Context1a (with cost), Context1b (no cost)
Context2 (Schedule)	Context2a (weekday), Context2b (weekend), Context2c (holiday)
Context3 (Location)	Context3a (within campus), Context3b (outside campus), Context3c (near public transport), Context3d(not near public transport)

Context	Categorisation
Context4 (Time)	Context4a (morning), Context4b (afternoon), Context4c (night)

The basic concept of a recommender system uses two types of entities: users and items, as shown in Fig. (**3**). The recommender system will estimate the rating for the objects that are not rated. The computation power required for this solution is inefficient and expensive to execute. The classical approach, which uses collaborative or content-based filtering, is ineffective if there are new users and the system's quality relies on an extensive historical data-set [18].

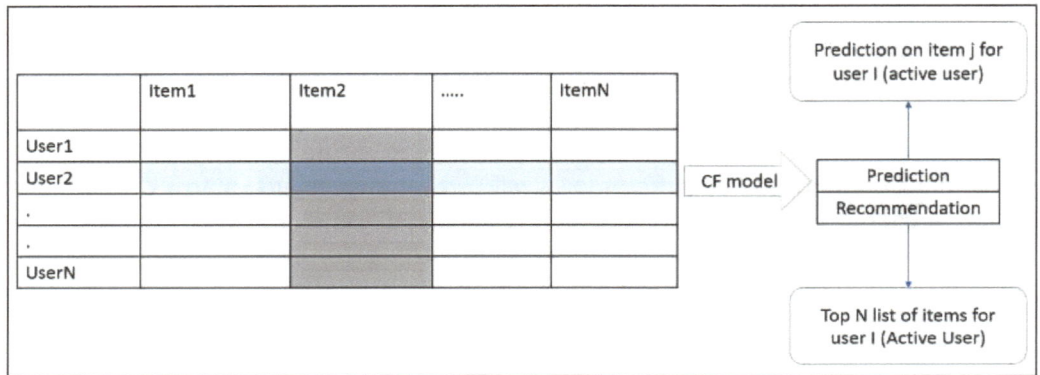

Fig. (3). Entities of items and user are used to estimate the rating.

Construction Phase

As per Fig. (**4**), the contextual recommendation system will receive inputs from the user and the organiser. The event data is pre-filtered by the user's search result using the keywords for the events listed. Another input is the organizer's input, where they can register the event in the system. The recommendation system will provide the most relevant results based on several factors, such as keywords, user preference, similar user's preference, event information, and event rating.

The proposed system is divided into three categories: data collection, pre-processing data, and collaborative filtering, as shown in Fig. (**5**). In the data collection method, the user behaviour and the user rating are extracted from the database. The user input will be combined with the user's contextual information. The process of pre-processing data is data cleaning, generating implicit ratings and integration of data. The collaborative filtering technique is used to predict the missing ratings, ranking of items, and select the top-n items for events. The K Nearest Neighbour (KNN) Algorithm is used for the classification of new events by calculating the similarity of the input with the training model.

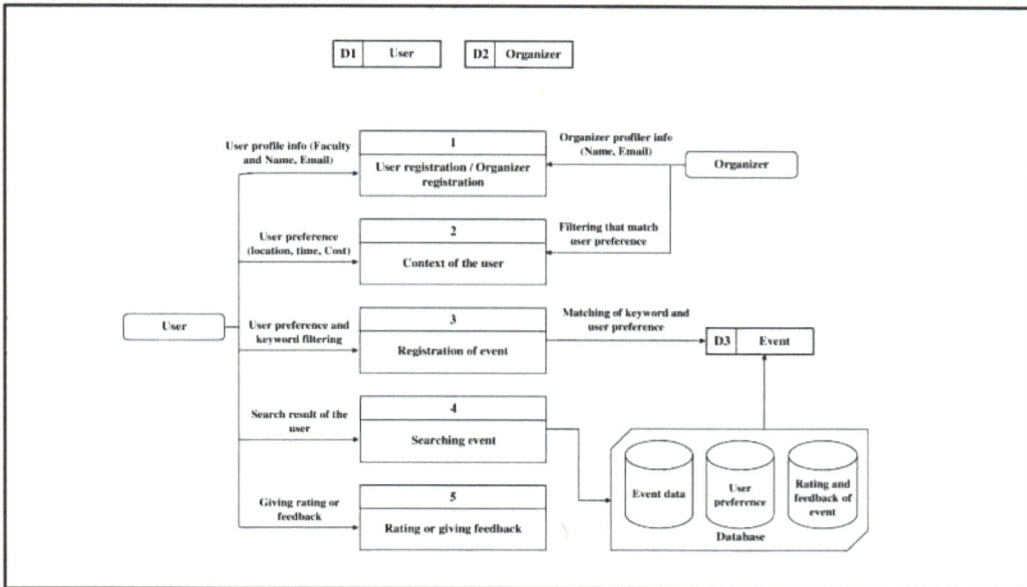

Fig. (4). The framework of the contextual, personalized recommendation system.

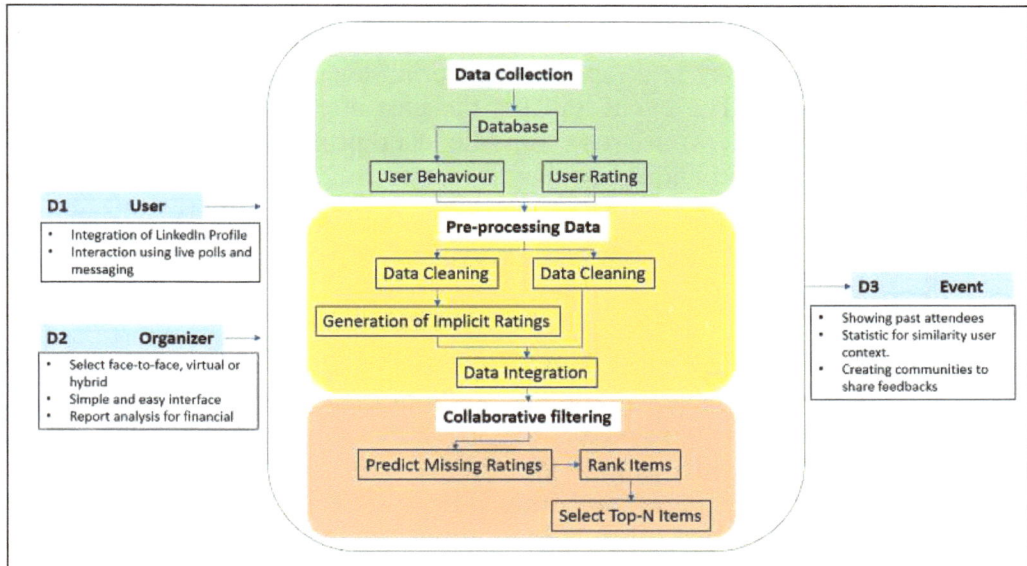

Fig. (5). System Architecture of the proposed system.

Cutover Phase

The cutover phase evaluates the technique, tools developed and the results. The relevancy of the data will measure the accuracy of recommendations based on the academic events that are most suitable according to the user preference. The recall will measure the relevant results in fractions that cannot be retrieved. The tool will be evaluated for its accuracy and the completeness of the academic events in relevancy compared to the classical approach by Eventbrite, Workshop Finder and AllConference.

OVERVIEW OF THE PROPOSED SYSTEM

The proposed system is a personalized recommender system for academic events to help students generate better recommendation results. The contextual information by the user's preferences is academic background, the purpose of attending, and user profile, while the condition for the events considered is the location, cost, and time. The proposed recommender system has higher precision than the classical approach system. The personalized recommender system can generate a better list of events according to the user preference and various contexts of the events.

The proposed recommendation system has several improvements in the user, organizer, and event. The user can link their LinkedIn account for better attendee's user preference data. During the event, users can interact using messaging and live polls. As COVID-19 set some restrictions on the events, the organizer can choose to conduct face-to-face, virtual, or hybrid mode. The system provides a simple and easy interface for registering events and showing financial results using statistics. The event will list the past attendees for reference with statistics that shows the similarity with the user profile. The users can join different communities depending on their interests and preferences to share their personal feedback and discussions. The rating of the academic events will be generated as references for the users when selecting an event.

CONCLUSION

This study proposes a personalized and contextualized recommender system for the selection of academic events. The limitation of this study is that the proposed recommender system only uses the KNN algorithm. Further studies can be conducted based on the different CF algorithms for better results. The proposed system will improvise the current recommender system and better suits the needs of the users using contextual information during data processing. The concept of the proposed system is the user preference that will be mapped for similar user-based in the database. The user-based algorithm, K-nearest neighbour (KNN), and context pre-filtering technique will be implemented when developing the system. All the contextual data will be processed and generate the most suitable events based on user preferences. The main objective of the study has been successfully achieved in developing a personalized recommender system for academic events. This study will help future work on similar topics or domains.

CONSENT FOR PUBLICATION

Not applicable.

CONFLICT OF INTEREST

The authors declare no conflict of interest, financial or otherwise.

ACKNOWLEDGEMENTS

The authors wish to express sincere appreciation to the Asia Pacific University of Technology and Innovation (APU) for giving them this opportunity to conduct the research.

REFERENCES

[1]　M.O. Omisore, and O.W. Samuel, "Personalized recommender system for digital libraries", *Int. J. Web-Based Learn. Teach. Technol.,* vol. 9, no. 1, pp. 18-32, 2014.
[http://dx.doi.org/10.4018/ijwltt.2014010102]

[2]　Y. Guo, M. Wang, and X. Li, "An interactive personalized recommendation system using the hybrid algorithm model", *Symmetry (Basel),* vol. 9, no. 10, p. 216, 2017.
[http://dx.doi.org/10.3390/sym9100216]

[3]　F.O. Isinkaye, Y.O. Folajimi, and B.A. Ojokoh, "Recommendation systems: Principles, methods and evaluation", *Egyptian Informatics Journal,* vol. 16, no. 3, pp. 261-273, 2015.
[http://dx.doi.org/10.1016/j.eij.2015.06.005]

[4]　Q. Shambour, and J. Lu, "An effective recommender system by unifying user and item trust information for B2B applications", *J. Comput. Syst. Sci.,* vol. 81, no. 7, pp. 1110-1126, 2015.
[http://dx.doi.org/10.1016/j.jcss.2014.12.029]

[5]　I. Cantador, I. Fernández-Tobías, and A. Bellogín, "Relating personality types with user preferences in multiple entertainment domains", *CEUR Workshop Proc,* vol. vol. 997, 2013

[6]　S. Oester, J.A. Cigliano, E.J. Hind-Ozan, and E.C.M. Parsons, "Why conferences matter—an illustration from the international marine conservation congress", *Front. Mar. Sci.,* vol. 4, no. AUG, p. 257, 2017.
[http://dx.doi.org/10.3389/fmars.2017.00257]

[7]　G. Roos, J. Oláh, R. Ingle, R. Kobayashi, and M. Feldt, "Online conferences – Towards a new (virtual) reality", *Comput. Theor. Chem.,* vol. 1189, no. August, 2020.112975
[http://dx.doi.org/10.1016/j.comptc.2020.112975]

[8]　C.J. Lortie, "Online conferences for better learning", *Ecol. Evol.,* vol. 10, no. 22, pp. 12442-12449, 2020.
[http://dx.doi.org/10.1002/ece3.6923] [PMID: 33250984]

[9]　S. Chai, and R.B. Freeman, "Temporary colocation and collaborative discovery: Who confers at conferences", *Strateg. Manage. J.,* vol. 40, no. 13, pp. 2138-2164, 2019.
[http://dx.doi.org/10.1002/smj.3062]

[10]　L. Chen, G. Chen, and F. Wang, "Recommender systems based on user reviews: the state of the art", *User Model. User-adapt. Interact.,* vol. 25, no. 2, pp. 99-154, 2015.

[http://dx.doi.org/10.1007/s11257-015-9155-5]

[11]   G. Jawaheer, P. Weller, and P. Kostkova, "Modeling user preferences in recommender systems: A classification framework for explicit and implicit user feedback", *ACM Trans. Interact. Intell. Syst.,* vol. 4, no. 2, pp. 1-26, 2014.
[http://dx.doi.org/10.1145/2512208]

[12]   S. Bansal, and N. Baliyan, "A study of recent recommender system techniques", *Int. J. Knowl. Syst. Sci.,* vol. 10, no. 2, pp. 13-41, 2019.
[http://dx.doi.org/10.4018/IJKSS.2019040102]

[13]   P.J. Gai, and A.K. Klesse, "Making Recommendations More Effective Through Framings: Impacts of User- Versus Item-Based Framings on Recommendation Click-Throughs", *J. Mark.,* vol. 83, no. 6, pp. 61-75, 2019.
[http://dx.doi.org/10.1177/0022242919873901]

[14]   I. Hariyale, and M.M. Raghuwanshi, "Design of recommender system using content based filtering and collaborative filtering technique: A comparative study", *Int. J. Adv. Sci. Technol.,* vol. 29, no. 5, pp. 4852-4865, 2020.

[15]   Z.D. Champiri, S.S.B. Salim, and S.R. Shahamiri, "The Role of Context for Recommendations in Digital Libraries", *Int. J. Soc. Sci. Humanit.,* vol. 5, no. 11, pp. 948-954, 2015.
[http://dx.doi.org/10.7763/IJSSH.2015.V5.585]

[16]   V. Balakrishnan, and H. Arabi, "HyPeRM: A HYBRID PERSONALITY-AWARE RECOMMENDER FOR MOVIE", *Malays. J. Comput. Sci.,* vol. 31, no. 1, pp. 48-62, 2018.
[http://dx.doi.org/10.22452/mjcs.vol31no1.4]

[17]   N. Aliska, and L. Shuib, "Expert Based Recommendation for Academic Event", *International Journal of Information System and Engineering,* vol. 6, no. 2, pp. 45-51, 2018.
[http://dx.doi.org/10.24924/ijise/2018.11/v6.iss2/45.51]

[18]   B. Kumar, and N. Sharma, "Approaches, Issues and Challenges in Recommender Systems: A Systematic Review", *Indian J. Sci. Technol.,* vol. 9, no. 47, 2016.
[http://dx.doi.org/10.17485/ijst/2015/v8i1/94892]

CHAPTER 16

e-Health Web Application with Electronic Medical Records (EMR) and Virtual Appointments

Faridzuan Bin Barakath Rahman[1], **Tanveer Khaleel Shaikh**[1,*] and **Nurul Husna Binti Mohd Saad**[1]

[1] *School of Computing, Asia Pacific University of Technology and Innovation, Kuala Lumpur, Malaysia*

Abstract: Relying on papers to document medical records hinders the United Nations' goal of creating a more sustainable world for future generations. With the excess usage of paper, the world is contributing towards global warming. Medical staff tends to take a long time to pull out a patient's medical record when it can be done in a matter of seconds. Being paperless does not immediately mean it is effective or transparent, as medical providers don't usually share the content of a patient's medical record with the patient itself, let alone a different medical provider. Another issue is the lack of transparency within the healthcare sector. This research focuses on the need for Malaysia to have an e-Health system, preparation and participation towards the e-Health system, and the security of migrating towards the e-Health system.

Keywords: EMR, Healthcare, ICT, Medical Computing, Virtual Appointment.

INTRODUCTION

It is reported that Malaysia is facing a shortage of healthcare workers and providers that has drastically reduced healthcare options for Malaysians over the years [1]. Travelling to appointments on congested roads is also a hassle. TomTom's Traffic Index reveals that drivers in Kuala Lumpur lost seven days and two hours due to traffic in 2019 [2]. Apart from that, there is the issue of overcrowding in hospitals, creating a pressurised situation where it looks like they are inefficient and mismanaged [3]. Malaysia is reported to have a poor track record of transparency in healthcare. An example of this was when a fire erupted in Hospital Sultana Aminah. During the incident, the Ministry of Health could not provide any follow-up information on the cause of damage, loss of records, *etc* [4].

---

* **Corresponding author Tanveer Khaleel Shaikh:** School of Computing, Asia Pacific University of Technology & Innovation, Kuala Lumpur, Malaysia. Email: tanveer.ks@staffemail.apu.edu.my

Muhammad Ehsan Rana and Manoj Jayabalan (Eds.)
All rights reserved-© 2023 Bentham Science Publishers

The current generation lives in an era where information and communication technology (ICT) has become an inevitable force. ICT services and devices have proved to become the present and the future. Be it buying groceries or even a car; you could do all that by browsing through an online platform. Many sectors have matured into accepting that ICT is here to stay and is the tool to move businesses forward. This can be observed by the introduction of Industry 4.0, which focuses on ICT to enhance processes further. The healthcare sector is valued at 11.9 trillion globally [5]. In Malaysia alone, the healthcare sector will be valued at RM127.9 billion by 2027 from RM56.3 billion in 2017 [4]. The healthcare sector is a crucial and lucrative investment option for any country. We have matured in dealing with diseases over time, but diseases have also found ways to adapt and form new variations to challenge us. More research and treatment options are being found, resulting in the masses living longer and being able to deal with more chronic conditions [6]. We have certainly brushed up our capabilities to cure disease, but we still need to improve in keeping track of our medical records, which could be a crucial reference for the future generation. Malaysia's public hospitals and private/public clinics still rely on keeping our medical records in a binder to collect dust; however, this could be changed with the adaptability of EMR. In addition to providing EMR as a preliminary function, the system will also include the capability of running virtual appointments. Due to present challenges such as COVID-19, we are learning to adapt to be present digitally. For example, we rely on virtual communication tools such as Zoom, Google Meet, and Microsoft Teams for several things, such as conducting classes and having meetings. Therefore, it will not be that difficult to use virtual conferencing tools for the healthcare sector.

LITERATURE REVIEW

The literature review looked at the research papers based on the selected domain while investigating similar systems. With the help of published papers, the researchers can gain in-depth knowledge on the selected topics. The medium of collecting data is articles, journals, books, websites, and sources that relate to the domain. It should be done in a professionally documented way, where the research should be able to provide a theoretical base and determine the nature of the study. Apart from acknowledging the work of previous researchers, it can also provide a "landscape overview" for the reader.

Healthcare

The healthcare sector is valued at 11.9 trillion globally [5]. In Malaysia alone, the healthcare sector will be valued at RM127.9 billion by 2027 from RM56.3 billion in 2017 [4]. Medicine has been a lucrative investment for a country to make.

Mediums that may accelerate the growth of the sector are policy, science and technology, regulatory, and social insurance. However, a lack of government coordination and policies will hinder the healthcare sector. The healthcare sector still thrives on being one of the most favoured sectors by analysts and investors [7].

According to a PowerPoint presentation on e-Health by the Ministry of Health, Malaysia is set to become a nation of healthy individuals, focusing primarily on improving the current landscape of the healthcare industry. The current Malaysian healthcare industry is divided into public and private participants. The public is primarily funded by the government, while the private is a profit organisation. The funding sources of the public system are taxes, government funding, individual payments, EPF, and SOSCO. The goal is to provide a wide range of budget services to most domestic and international populations. The private system operates with a fee for the service, where only a segment of the population can afford the service. There are 15 state hospitals, 26 major specialist hospitals, 27 minor specialist hospitals, 10 specialist hospitals, and 66 non-specialist hospitals under Malaysia's public healthcare wing. All this data was gathered through the infographic, as shown in Figs. (**1** and **2**) [8, 9].

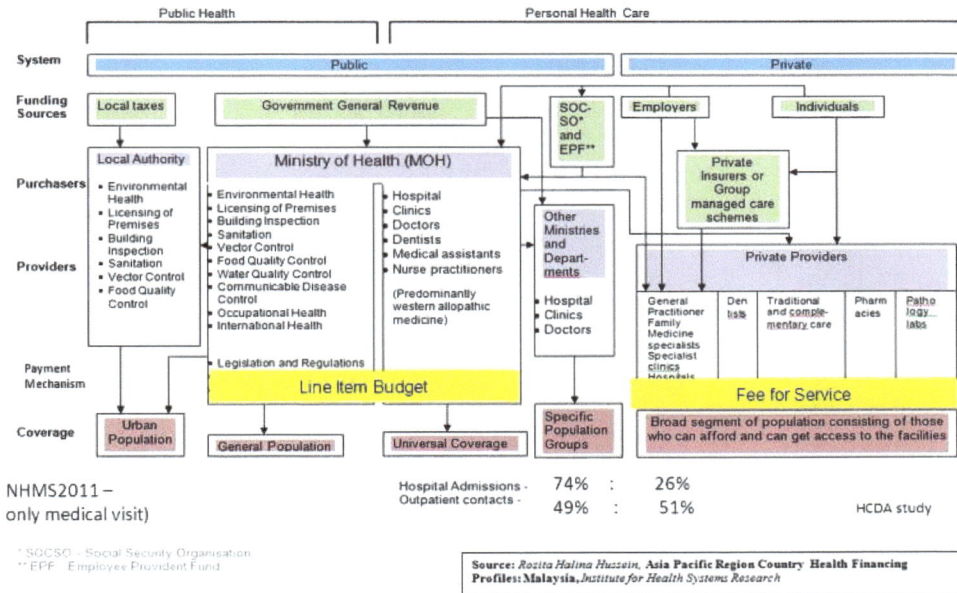

Fig. (1). Malaysia's Current Healthcare System [8].

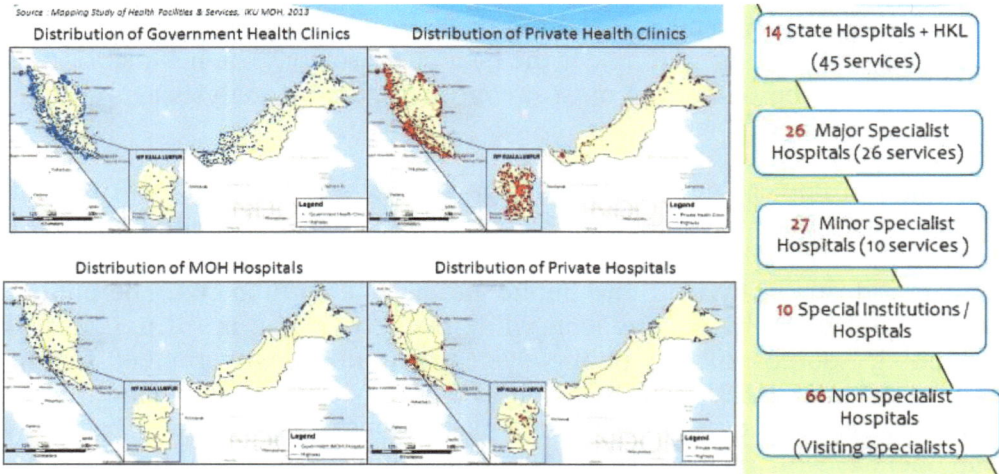

Fig. (2). Distribution and Number of Hospitals [9].

E-Health

The basic definition of e-Health is the support of information and communications technologies (ICT) in health-related fields [10]. Even though e-Health-based apps are emerging, having a unified global or national system is challenging as different players saturate the market [11]. Individually, these systems focus on different areas/fields of health. E-Health solutions are predicted to contribute significantly to a country's sustainable healthcare system [12]. According to Joaquin A. Blaya, e-Health has the potential to improve efficiency, expand treatment delivery, and improve patient outcomes in developing countries. Due to the widespread availability of wireless connections, the communication process has become faster for patients who increased e-health care utilisation [13], thus providing the perfect opportunity for the government to pursue modernisation in the health sector. This sector's importance is meeting the social objectives of quality and standard of healthcare for society and generating economic revenue from exporting health services and medical tourism [13]. This has been proven as the medical tourist arrival to Malaysia in 2018 was 1.2 million, generating around 362 million dollars for the local medical industry [14].

A common downside of adapting to the e-Health systems is age. It can be a complicated and challenging phenomenon for the elderly [15, 16]. With the rise in middle-income and the ageing population in Malaysia, we should expect greater expenditure on healthcare by the Malaysian government to provide more inclusive healthcare. According to [2], Malaysia needs to prepare as they were predicted to have achieved an ageing population by 2030. However, Malaysia is currently not there yet, and the release of the e-Health system would help with the issue in the future. Next will be our network infrastructure. Network availability will be needed across the region as the eHealth industry starts following and adopting new technologies and developments [11]. For any system, the infrastructure is necessary for the smooth delivery of the services, including high-performance servers; networks for every village across the country with high-speed internet connection. This has been investigated by the government, as shown by the implementation of the National Ferberization and Connectivity Plan (NFCP) and the reduction of WIFI prices while increasing its speed across Malaysia.

Security is always a factor that is considered to be paramount in tackling. The e-Health system has the potential to permit the invasion of medical privacy. Thus, the system must satisfy its users regarding privacy, confidentiality, and security. Building a trustworthy eHealth service that will provide security features such as being practised by banks [11]. With technological advancement, the e-Health system can investigate adopting cloud computing and migrating existing healthcare systems towards that [9]. The primary concern is with the aspect of privacy referred to as 'information privacy' – a term that refers to the ability of an individual to exercise control over the data held by others. Additionally, 'health information' is a particularly sensitive subset of personal information, thus justifying the privacy concerns on e-Health systems.

Telehealth

Due to the global pandemic (COVID-19), face-to-face consultation imposes a significant burden on both sides, making telehealth a reliable substitute that is gaining traction among the masses. Telehealth is not new, as the use of remote care has been around since the 1920s, it may be the year with much technological achievement, but a service in Australia called "Royal Flying Doctor" was offering remote care using pedal radios. As concerns over the rising health cost continue to increase, hospitals and governments are looking for a more feasible way to continue providing care. Thus, research was conducted with a sample size of 88 to know the public's perception and acceptance of telehealth. The findings in Fig. (3) show significant positivity towards the solution, with 94% of respondents strongly agreeing and agreeing with telehealth and 6% being neutral about the matter. In conclusion, telehealth is being suggested as an equally effective alternative to physical consultations.

Telehealth is defined as the use of ICT to support clinical healthcare, health-related education, public health, and health administration. Technologies include video conferencing, the internet, store-and-forward imaging, streaming media, and terrestrial and wireless communications". Telehealth has proven to be a valuable tool during pandemics, but a few barriers and hurdles should be ironed out before it continues to thrive. A few barriers to telehealth are information security on patient information, geographic boundaries of medical licenses, and current laws and regulations. Besides that, the benefit of telehealth during pandemics is enormous, such as reducing exposure between the patient and front liners. Patients with mild symptoms can still be at home and not crowded in hospitals. Undoubtedly telehealth will become a significant player in the future of the healthcare sector.

Patient/Caregiver and Provider Perception of Hospice Telehealth

Statement	Strongly Agree (1)	Agree (2)	Somewhat Agree (3)	Neutral (4)	Somewhat Disagree (5)	Disagree (6)	Strongly Disagree (7)	Mean SD
				N (%)				SD
Patient/caregiver perception of telehealth quality and effectiveness								
I could easily talk to the clinician using the telehealth system	32 (38.6)	36 (43.4)	5 (6.0)	7 (8.4)	1 (1.2)	2 (2.4)	—	1.98 1.14
I could hear the clinician clearly using the telehealth system	32 (38.6)	37 (44.6)	7 (8.4)	4 (4.8)	1 (1.2)	2 (2.4)	—	1.93 1.08
I felt I was able to express myself effectively	34 (41.5)	34 (41.5)	6 (7.3)	6 (7.3)	1 (1.2)	1 (1.2)	—	1.89 1.04
Using the telehealth system, I could see the clinician as well as if we met in person	25 (30.9)	33 (40.7)	10 (12.4)	7 (8.6)	1 (1.2)	5 (6.2)	—	2.27 1.35
Provider perception of telehealth quality and effectiveness								
I could easily talk to the patient and/or caregiver using the telehealth system	49 (55.7)	21 (22.9)	7 (8.0)	—	7 (8.0)	2 (2.3)	2 (2.3)	1.97 1.52
I could easily hear the patient and/or caregiver clearly using the telehealth system	48 (54.6)	20 (22.7)	7 (8.0)	1 (1.1)	7 (8.0)	3 (3.4)	2 (2.3)	2.05 1.59
I felt I was able to express myself effectively	51 (58.0)	22 (25.0)	7 (8.0)	1 (1.1)	5 (5.7)	—	2 (2.3)	1.81 1.33
Using the telehealth system, I could see the patient and/or caregiver as well as if we met in person	30 (34.1)	18 (20.4)	21 (23.9)	2 (2.3)	8 (9.1)	7 (7.9)	2 (2.3)	2.65 1.72

Fig. (3). Telehealth Research Findings.

Electronic Medical Record (EMR)

Electronic Medical Record (EMR) has been widely accepted over the past few decades. Its positive impact on patient care and physicians is tremendous, allowing physicians to reduce their workload [6]. Moreover, more than a single doctor is needed for your needs and requires tools such as EMR to facilitate the communication medium between doctors is also widely being accepted [6]. To further prove the point, EMR has been proven to improve patient outcomes and the quality of care, reduce unnecessary investigation and medical errors, and is a fantastic communication and interaction tool used between multiple healthcare providers and patients. Focusing on the data itself brings a more comprehensive look towards data. It provides remote access for doctors and patients while improving the workflow's effectiveness. Donna went further in claiming that EMR can be tweaked into doing a lot more such as "helping to manage prescriptions, improving the scheduling of patient appointments, and being a transaction medium" [6]. EMR should not be shoved away as it may play an essential role in the modern healthcare landscape. Furthermore, it is widely being adopted to replace paper-based systems since EMR is a solution that ensures long-term sustainability with quality, thus having a dampening effect on the healthcare domain [17].

SIMILAR SYSTEMS

Plato

Plato is a healthcare-focused solution provider in Singapore, Hong Kong, and Malaysia. According to TechINAsia, "Plato is Singapore's most popular web-based Clinic Management Software and Electronic Medical Records System (Fig. **4**). It is a beautiful, simple, and easy-to-use product that automates the work of both doctors and staff, letting them focus on what matters: their patients.". Plato originated in Singapore and was developed in the year 2015, their main selling point is to make the admin's work lighter; they strive to make solutions that will reduce admin work drastically. With this focus in mind, they have rolled out a few solutions, Clinic Management, Medical EMR, Third Party Payments, Direct Lab & Radiology Results, PlatoPulse, PlatoPay, and PaltoConnect. Plato focuses on a one-side-channel approach that only targets doctors and clinics. They help them in managing their daily admin and work activities. Plato can be accessed through mobile or web applications [18].

Fig. (4). Plato [18].

BookDoc

A homegrown system out there to the public currently is BookDoc (Fig. **5**). BookDoc has made a firm footing in Malaysia with recognition from the Malaysian Ministry of Health and a strategic partnership between them and FOMENA. According to FOMENA, "BookDoc is an open and neutral platform available on both mobile application and website that allows users to search for healthcare professionals by speciality, locality, and availability". BookDoc's primary focus is to provide online booking for visitations. As they run a very lean and close-focused solution, they can be expanded geographically rapidly. Due to database and usage, they are now trying out new solutions such as BookDoc Activ and BookDoc Marketplace. BookDoc Activ syncs your fitness tracker to keep track of your daily steps. By achieving a certain amount of steps, you will be credible to gain certain rewards, making it more attractive for the users. Moreover, BookDoc Marketplace is a one-stop-shop for Corporate Wellness, Employee Benefits, and Flexibenefits. Launching the app in 2015, it currently has a presence in Malaysia, Singapore, Indonesia, Hong Kong, and Thailand. BookDoc has made their appointment function through google maps and trivago. BookDoc is accessible through mobile or web applications [19].

Fig. (5). BookDoc [19].

Vertikal Systems

The final system is Vertikal Systems (Fig. **6**). Vertikal Systems provides medical software for clinics and hospitals, and their primary goal is to be able to manage the patients and their medical records. Vertikal Systems is based in Timisoara, Romania. Functions provided by Vertikal Systems are Patients Management, Medical Records, Medical Forms, Document Management, Medical Scheduling, Medical Workflows, Medical Billing and Claims, Inventory Management, Wards Management, Nurses Module, Laboratory (LIS), Imaging\Radiology, Pharmacy, Internal Messaging, Health Messaging (HL7), Reporting and Statistics. Vertikal Systems was founded in 2005, and according to the information gathered, it is only present in Romania. According to Vertikal Systems, "Vertikal Systems has all the ingredients for this and is motivated to find innovative ways to fulfill customer needs and to forge the best customer connections". Vertikal System focuses on creating innovative solutions with the help of experienced IT specialists and medics [20].

VERTIKAL
S Y S T E M S

Fig. (6). Vertikal Systems [20].

BUSINESS CASE

Porter's Five Forces

Porter's Five Forces is an effective way to analyse a company or an industry. Five main points will be looked at: new entries, the bargaining power of the consumer, the threat of the substitute product, the amount of bargaining power, and the intensity of the rivalry. This method is used to identify whether the industry is profitable or not and if it is worth investing in the industry. In the case of myHIPPO development processes, we will be carrying out Porter's Five Forces from Malaysia's Healthcare Industry standpoint.

The Threat of New Entrants: High

It can be concluded that there is a high threat in the healthcare industry due to the flexibility of the size of healthcare services. You may open a substantial multitier hospital or even a small-scale general practice; the financial limit depends on you. As the Malaysian government is training and enhancing graduates such as doctors, nurses, and pharmacists every year, there is a cycle of a stockpile of human resources to get your clinic or hospital started. Due to the COVID-19 pandemic, there is significant appreciation towards the frontlines, and the human population is getting more conscious regarding their health. Therefore, it is no surprise that physical and virtual visits to clinics and hospitals are starting to increase. This problem should be addressed, especially since a population of 32 million people is waiting for doctors to serve them, resulting in a high number of new entries in the Malaysian market.

The Bargaining Power of Buyers: Low

Malaysia is a nation of bargainers, be it on the street or in a high-class shopping mall. Nevertheless, healthcare products and services in Malaysia are wired in a way that makes it rather challenging to achieve discounts as the industry is firmly regulated. Buyers or customers demand any price reduction to the product, putting pressure on the healthcare product and services profitability and sustainability in the long run. However, thanks to public healthcare facilities in Malaysia, the population can enjoy a full-body check-up for a minimal fee. It is not limited to a full-body check-up, as the consultation cost for a public clinic or hospital will cost you a minimum of one to five ringgit. The bargaining power of the consumers played no role in the price reduction, and the inference from the government in the healthcare sector as a form of service being offered to their citizens resulted in this. In conclusion, the bargaining power of buyers/customers is low.

The Threat of Substitute Products: Low

It is not likely that there is a product that can substitute healthcare in Malaysian or anywhere else in the world. There are different types of healthcare, but this does not count as a substitute. Anyone entering the industry provides or works to achieve the same goal: to offer the best healthcare option to their patient, possibly curing them. For example, Ayurveda is a type of healthcare, not a substitute for the healthcare industry. If you are sick, you can either go to a doctor or a therapist, but they both fall under the same umbrella: healthcare. Considering the points that fall under the threat of a substitute replacing healthcare, it is evident that it is relatively unlikely to happen.

The Bargaining Power of Suppliers: High

Healthcare has grown widely throughout the Malaysian landscape, and there is a crucial need for a steady supply chain. A chain that is somehow static to avoid any roller-coaster prices. There is a need for considerable investments to formulate medicine, but it takes time to find a stable formula, which is reflected in the price list. This results in clinics and hospitals having limited options and prices for buying from, as there could be only one supplier capable of supplying the medicines, making them agree on prices set by big pharmaceutical companies. On the other hand, there are also instances where there are options to buy medicine from multiple pharmaceutical companies. An example of such a medicine is paracetamol, which can be bought from Panadol or Halbal. A clinic or hospital prefers long-term legal binding contracts, giving the supplier higher bargaining power.

The Intensity of The Competitive Rivalry: Low

Any intense rivalry among the existing industry players can end up harming both sides if they start competing. Even though this may be good for the customer, it will not necessarily benefit the ending financial year for a clinic or hospital. Furthermore, this will affect the dividend pay-out, which simultaneously makes the shareholders unsatisfied if you are a private entity. The possibility of competition between clinics or hospitals is relatively low as there is no platform for this to happen as customers go to the clinic of their choice by preference, location, etc. A rivalry between clinics is unjustifiable or has a very slim chance of happening.

RATIONALE

An e-health web application with an electronic medical record (EMR) and virtual appointments, better known as myHIPPO, will be a standalone web application that allows Malaysians to better facilitate their medical needs via a virtual platform. myHIPPO would be able to deliver medical-related solutions to end-users, focusing on delivering a solution with convenience, transparency, and effectiveness. Additionally, myHIPPO would create a hassle-free environment by reducing the amount of paper used, flushing away the need for a storeroom to store patient medical records. In turn, the storeroom may provide room for another doctor, allowing the clinic to serve more patients and reducing their overall workload. Ultimately increasing profits due to the extra number of patients served. The Electronic Medical Record (EMR) enables healthcare providers to record medical data in a way never achievable before [6], thus opening more possibilities to tap into. Apart from that, the virtual appointment platform enables doctors to gain new sources of revenue while not needing any type of physical presence. It creates an option of borderless environments, as a doctor from Perlis can provide his/her service in Sabah. Thanks to the centralised entity, myHIPPO, medical records are now not only accessible to an individual medical provider. Still, they are available to all medical providers with the patient's approval, thus creating a transparent and effective landscape within the healthcare sector. The two types of benefits the researcher has categorised for the outcome of this web application are tangible and intangible.

CONCLUSION

In-depth research has been conducted with the literature reviews, therefore pinpointing key topics, such as the need for Malaysia to have an e-Health system, preparation and participation towards the e-Health system, and security of migrating towards the e-Health system; this was done to understand the hurdles of why adopting to such healthcare functions is so slow. Moreover, the literature review has helped us gain insight and a clear understanding of the topic. Understanding the need for Malaysia to have an e-Health system, the researcher has made valid points by highlighting the benefits and the losses if we fail. Porter's Five Forces enables the researcher to look at the research from a feasible standpoint and decide whether such a system should be available in the local market. The rationale was provided to gauge the concept of the benefits of an e-health system, thus further concreting the point of such a system.

CONSENT FOR PUBLICATION

Not applicable.

CONFLICT OF INTEREST

The authors declare no conflict of interest, financial or otherwise.

ACKNOWLEDGEMENTS

The authors wish to express sincere appreciation to the Asia Pacific University of Technology and Innovation (APU) for giving them this opportunity to conduct the research.

REFERENCES

[1]   The Star Online. 2020. Urgent Need To Address Shortage Of Medical Officers In Malaysia. [online] Available at: https://www.thestar.com.my/opinion/letters/2020/10/13/urgent-need-to-address-shortage-of-medical-officers-in-malaysia [Accessed 30 November 2020].

[2]   NST Online. 2020. NST Leader: Traffic-Choked In KL | New Straits Times. [online] Available at: https://www.nst.com.my/opinion/leaders/2020/03/573509/nst-leader-traffic-choked-kl [Accessed 28 November 2020].

[3]   Murallitharan, M., 2020. Overcrowding At Government Hospitals. [online] Free Malaysia Today. Available at: https://www.freemalaysiatoday.com/category/opinion/2019/07/24/overcrowding-a--government-hospitals/ [Accessed 30 November 2020].

[4]   Kheng, D., 2020. Malaysia Does Not Have A Good Record Of Transparency. [online] The Star Online. Available at: https://www.thestar.com.my/opinion/columnists/vital-signs/2020/01/15/malaysia-does-not-have-a-good-record-of-transparency [Accessed 21 November 2020].

[5]   WIRE, B., 2020. The $11.9 Trillion Global Healthcare Market: Key Opportunities & Strategies (2014-2022) - Researchandmarkets.Com. [online] Businesswire.com. Available at: https://www.businesswire.com/news/home/20190625005862/en/11.9-Trillion-Global-Healthcare-Market-Key-Opportunities [Accessed 28 May 2020].

[6]   Manca, D., 2020. Do Electronic Medical Records Improve Quality Of Care?: Yes. [online] PubMed Central (PMC). Available at: https://www.ncbi.nlm.nih.gov/pmc/articles/PMC4607324/ [Accessed 30 May 2020].

[7]   User, S., 2020. Technofunc - Overview Of Healthcare Industry. [online] Technofunc.com. Available

at: https://www.technofunc.com/index.php/domain-knowledge/item/overview-of-healthcare-industry [Accessed 1 July 2020].

[8]   [20] "1Care for 1Malaysia: RESTRUCTURING THE MALAYSIAN HEALTH SYSTEM," Gov.my. [Online]. Available: https://hsgm.moh.gov.my/v3/uploads/penerbitan/1Care_for_1Malaysia.pdf [Accessed: 21-Dec-2022]

[9]   A. Bradley, NATIONAL eHEALTH: "Moving Towards Efficient Healthcare." 2017.

[10]   Menachemi, N. and Collum, 2020. Benefits And Drawbacks Of Electronic Health Record Systems. [online]   Available   at: https://www.ncbi.nlm.nih.gov/pmc/articles/PMC3270933/#:~:text=Other%2C%20less%20tangible%20benefits%20have%20been%20associated%20with%20EHR%20use.&text=It%20has%20also%20been%20pointed,controlled%20and%20auditable%20provider%20access [Accessed 29 May 2020].

[11]   Michalas, A. and Dowsley, R., 2015. Towards trusted ehealth services in the cloud. Proceedings of the 8th International Conference on Utility and Cloud Computing, pp.Pages 618–623. Available at: https://dl-acm-org.ezproxy.apiit.edu.my/doi/abs/10.5555/3233397.3233519 [Accessed 28 May 2020].

[12]   Azeez, N. and der Vyver, C., 2020. Security And Privacy Issues In E-Health Cloud-Based System: A Comprehensive   Content   Analysis.   Available   at: https://www.sciencedirect.com/science/article/pii/S1110866517302797 [Accessed 26 May 2020].

[13]   The Edge Markets. 2020. Electronic Medical Record System For All M'sian Hospitals, Clinics To Cost Up   To   RM1.5B,   Says   Minister.   [online]   Available   at: https://www.theedgemarkets.com/article/electronic-medical-record-system-all-msian-hospitals-clinics-cost-rm15b-says-minister [Accessed 29 May 2020].

[14]   Study.com. 2020. [online] Available at: https://study.com/academy/lesson/health-services-definiti-n-types-providers.html [Accessed 3 August 2020].

[15]   A. Blaya, J., S.F. Fraser, H. and Holt, B., 2020. [online] Healthaffairs.org. Available at: https://www.healthaffairs.org/doi/pdf/10.1377/hlthaff.2009.0894 [Accessed 31 May 2020].

[16]   Who.int. 2020. Vision. [online] Available at: https://www.who.int/dg/vision [Accessed 3 July 2020].

[17]   H Weber, J. and Blakley, F., 2020. The Safety Of Electronic Medical Record (EMR) Systems: What Does EMR Safety Mean And How Can We Engineer Safer Systems?. [online] ACM Digital Library. Available at: https://dl-acm-org.ezproxy.apiit.edu.my/doi/abs/10.1145/2047478.2047480 [Accessed 2 June 2020].

[18]   Platomedical.com. 2020. Plato - Clinic Management Software. [online] Available at: https://platomedical.com/ [Accessed 4 July 2020].

[19]   www.bookdoc.com. 2020. Bookdoc. [online] Available at: https://www.bookdoc.com [Accessed 5 July 2020].

[20]   "Easy to use medical software for clinics and hospitals - Vertikal Systems," Vertikalsystems.com. [Online]. Available: http://www.vertikalsystems.com/en/ [Accessed: 21-Dec-2022]

SUBJECT INDEX